Metadrama and the Informer in Shakespeare and Jonson

Metadrama and the Informer in Shakespeare and Jonson

Bill Angus

EDINBURGH
University Press

Edinburgh University Press is one of the leading university presses in the UK. We publish academic books and journals in our selected subject areas across the humanities and social sciences, combining cutting-edge scholarship with high editorial and production values to produce academic works of lasting importance. For more information visit our website: edinburghuniversitypress.com

Edinburgh University Press Ltd
The Tun – Holyrood Road, 12(2f) Jackson's Entry, Edinburgh EH8 8PJ

Typeset in 11/13 Adobe Sabon by
IDSUK (DataConnection) Ltd, and
printed and bound in Great Britain by
CPI Group (UK) Ltd, Croydon CR0 4YY

A CIP record for this book is available from the British Library

ISBN 978 1 4744 1511 8 (hardback)
ISBN 978 1 4744 1512 5 (webready PDF)
ISBN 978 1 4744 1513 2 (epub)

Contents

Acknowledgements

Michelle Houston and all at Edinburgh University Press for their insight and professionalism, Massey University for affording me space and time, Kate Chedgzoy for her sound wisdom and counsel, John Ross for his welcome critical eye, John Drakakis for his comprehensive and weighty reading, all other past readers, including both scourgers and encouragers, Mark Dooley, back in the day, for charting unmarked paths, Amy, Joseph, Stephen, Sonny, Aidan, Elin and Ciara, for their continuing inspiration, and anonymous others for the revisions of body and soul which have accompanied this work.

Suspect Devices – Metadrama and the Narcissism of Small Differences

An Epitaph.
Stay *Reader!* and Piss here, for it is said
Under this Dirt there's an Informer laid.
(John Wilmot, Earl of Rochester, 'Rome Rhym'd to Death', 1683)[1]

It is a curious fact that the elaboration of metadramatic structures in early modern drama coincided with an increasing social awareness of the ubiquity of the informer in the pay of authorities.[2] The extensive employment of informers at the time produced a hazardous environment by no means restricted to those at the centre of political life. There is a heightened consciousness at this time of the dangers of even casual conversation, and Lorna Hutson identifies its 'liability to circulate maliciously, as malevolently construed evidence against the speaker'.[3] Informers came from all social ranks, in search of the potentially substantial remuneration their activities might earn within networks of patronage which took for granted, and in a sense formalised, the collection of information.[4] These widely reviled figures fed the royal administrations and other authorities with information on every aspect of contemporary life, from the content of dramatic performances to the correct pannage of pigs or the activities of smugglers and recusants. Far from being exclusive to the spymasters of the Crown, any person of power and influence might expect a flow of information from such individuals; the Earl of Essex, for instance, employed his own expensive and extensive informing network.[5] In an era often of great need, it seems there were always those potentially at the ready with information for sale.

Thomas Overbury's *Characters* (1611) describes one who is 'Informer-like-dangerous in taking aduantage of any thing done or sayde'; such a person 'makes men as carefull of their speeches and actions as the sight of a known Cut-purse in a throng makes them watchfull ouer their purses and pockets'.[6] Here Overbury indicates the currency of the informer as a pejorative concept, connected with the fear of significantly negative material consequences.[7] Griffin Flood is one such who was prominent enough to merit a short biography, *The life and death of Griffin Flood informer* (1623), which speaks of his 'bad condition, foule speaches, and ill demeanor' and notes his many 'cunning informations of falsehoods'.[8] Flood is even overheard, or imagined, self-consciously issuing his own epitaph: 'Here lyeth Griffin Flood full low in his grave, / Which lived a Rascal and died a Knave.'[9] Francis Lenton describes attitudes to the informer in 1631: 'As hee loues no man, so he is hated of all [. . .] Hee is the scum of Rascality [. . .] All men behold him with indignation.'[10] Joseph Hall's *Cases of Conscience* (1654) concurs with this universal disapprobation that 'every man is loath to be an Informer [. . .] out of the conscience of his owne obnoxiousnesse'.[11] John Stephens's 1615 description of an informer, 'a protected Cheater, *or* a Knave in authoritie, licenced by authoritie', moreover, resounds with indignation at the compromising connection of these hated figures with the authority of those in positions of power.[12]

In differentiating 'informers' from 'spies', it is acknowledged that some were both and that their two nebulous worlds shaded into each other. The chief distinction, in the popular perception, was that spies might carry positive connotations in a way that informers may not. Then, as now, a 'spy' might be perceived as serving the grander interests of legitimate governance, or even the nation, but an 'informer' was always tainted by the implication of betrayal. Among some religious groups, for instance, the Devil was imagined as God's 'informer', but to say he was God's 'spy' would put an altogether different slant on their relationship, and those between God, the Devil and believers.[13] In Thomas Nashe's *Haue with you to Saffron-Walden* (1596) this important distinction is made when a Master Bodley, though happy to be well known as a 'spy' is nevertheless seriously aggrieved that he might be identified with 'the hellish detested *Judas* name of an Intelligencer', or informer.[14] Nashe has ample reason to despise informers in the suspicious circumstances surrounding the death of his friend Christopher Marlowe three years previously.[15]

Being by the nature of the function shadowy figures, these informers rarely emerge to us as named individuals.[16] They are however eminently traceable in their influence on contemporary social discourse, in ballads, sermons, legal statutes and, most significantly, in the structures, characters and plots of an early modern theatre at the height of its cultural flourishing. Concerns over the activities of such perceived parasites abound at this time and the growing awareness of their ubiquity is accompanied by the sense that the authority for whom the informer acts is tainted by the association.[17] In the written texts of the era, this seems to exacerbate the troubled context of post-Reformation authority as a whole.[18] Hutson recognises in the late sixteenth century an increasingly pervasive 'diffusion of judicial rhetoric' throughout society, coming largely through formal classical education, which sets a context in which this perception of the informer might flourish and thus facilitates the discussion of these issues in popular texts.[19] The point at which the drama most clearly reflects these concerns is where it reflects upon its own ontology, in the various devices of metadrama.[20]

Metadrama may be defined simply as drama about drama, either implicit in content or form, or where dramatic codes themselves become 'an explicit object of discourse'.[21] This may involve simple self-reference, role play about role play, plays within plays, or audiences watching audiences. Its related structures of oversight and overhearing now seem so natural to the experience of theatre that one might almost forget to ask why it should be so.[22] The numerous devices of metadrama configure many kinds of interpretative authority, shared and otherwise, that contribute to the production and reception of plays. As, in the late sixteenth century, the drama became more rhetorically complex, so the complexity of the metadrama kept pace, with the play within the play for instance often registering contemporary structures of power, circling around the informer as the avatar of authority.[23]

The very many instances of characters standing aside, hidden, to collect information which might be used to further a dramatic narrative, are too numerous to list, and these often form metadramatic audiences used by authors to shape the response of offstage audiences.[24] The perception of the informer-figure thus seems to permeate both the conditions of early modern dramatic production and the vagaries of its interpretation and reception. Accordingly, the aim of this book is to make the connection between these social phenomena clear and to demonstrate that the structures of informing are fundamentally implicated in the making of metadrama. This offers a new way of conceiving authority and informing in the metadrama of the period, anchored in the material practices of the time. It confirms suspicions in the field that something more than mere artistic experimentation is going on in metadrama, elaborating on broadly understood connections between metadrama and authority, and authority and informing; but, most importantly, it completes the circle with its critical insight into the connections between informers and the authors of metadrama.

To a certain extent the informer and the audience are also conflated in the early modern imagination. A clear example of this, and the metadrama it produces, may be found in John Day's *Isle of Guls* (1606), which constructs an onstage audience in dialogue with its prologue over the content of the play. Day's concerned audience asks, 'Is't anything Criticall? Are Lawyer's fees, and Cittizen's wives laid open in it [. . .] Is there any mans life charactred int?' The prologue denies any such thing and continues in protest:

> If poetic rage
> Strike at abuse, or ope the vaine of sinne
> He is straight informed against for libelling
> [. . .] such is the boundlesse hate
> Of a confused audience. [25]

This metadramatic vignette also hints at the ambiguous position of the author-poet, and the exchange exposes what Robert Weimann calls the 'dialectics of [. . .] interdependence' between audiences and theatrical production, in this case registering the potential presence of the informer.[26] In 1591 John Harington complained that he lived at a time when 'nothing can escape the envious tooth and backbiting tongue of an impure mouth, and wherein every blind corner hath a squint-eyed Zoilus that can look aright upon no man's doings'.[27] The drama reflects this broad perception of a populace in danger of becoming what Jonas Barish termed 'a race of spies and eavesdroppers'.[28] One only needs to think of the impact of Iago, Rosencrantz and Guildenstern, Sejanus, or Webster's Bosola to understand how compelling a character the predatory informer can be onstage, although such a figure offstage is quite another matter. George Chapman's letter of c.1608 regarding the censorship of his *Byron* plays describes directly having been the victim of one who 'plaied the bitter Informer before the french Ambassador', doing so for his own mere 'Politique' advancement, and 'with the Gall of a Wulff'.[29] Such a sense of an audience's potential venality is a constantly recurring theme at the time, and one which may be perceived, for example, in the content of prologues, epilogues and prefaces. The familiarity of this convention should not blind us to its insistent iteration in this period in both performance and print.

Heidi Brayman Hackel argues that the era was a time of 'heightened guardedness' against the 'bad reader', while Lynn S. Meskill describes the 'prophylactic function' of prefaces in defending the work from the 'misreading eye' of the 'malignant, over-curious or envious reader'.[30] Richard Brathwaite offers a not untypical example of this concern in his 1615 preface, imagining and projecting an ideal 'Gentle Reader' who is 'no wri-neck critick, politick informer of States, deprauer of wel intended lines, nor maligner of others labours'.[31] As here, these often contain more than mere pleas for good reception for the sake of reputation; they offer rather a minimum pre-emptive response to the very real risk of imprisonment, and the threat of mutilation, that the incautious author was subject to in the case of an informer's mistaken or malicious interpretation.

The legal basis of this sense of threat may be seen in Elizabeth's 1581 commission of the Master of the Revels, Tilney, to warn any offending player and playmaker that they may be lawfully arrested, and 'remaine without bayle or mayneprise untill such tyme as [. . .] Tylney [. . .] shall thinke [. . .] theire imprisonment to be punnishement sufficient for [their] offences'. That is, potentially indefinitely. She adds, menacingly, that those found not to be 'aydinge supportinge and assistinge' this activity 'will answer to the contrarie at [their] uttermost perills'.[32] The real physical dangers inherent in early modern dramatic authorship have been underplayed at times. Richard Dutton notes the spectrum of scholarly opinions on the level of threat to authors. These depend to an extent on whether or not arbitrary imprisonment and the threat of dismemberment are to be considered 'punishments'. This was a time when, as Jonathan Dollimore notes, dramatists were routinely 'harassed [. . .] for staging plays thought to be seditious'.[33] If sufficiently provoked, Dutton says, 'the authorities and their censors [. . .] reacted with almost paranoid ferocity, threatening death, mutilation or prolonged imprisonment', as Elizabeth's commission to Tilney shows.[34] This present study obviously aligns itself with the cultural materialist critical approach that sees this tendency as expressing what amounts to 'a climate of repression' that has a substantial material effect on the drama.[35] On the other side of the argument, in *Ben Jonson and Envy*, Meskill sets out a good case for the emotional and moral motivations of the activities of the malicious audience-member, but stops short of fully acknowledging their possible material effects. Especially for Jonson, this sense of physical threat was a lived reality and thus, for him, the issue of misinterpretation is not confined to mere concerns over poetic reputation as some critics propose.[36]

As far as we know, none of the principal dramatists of the metropolis were punished by mutilation, their ears or noses cut, but other writers were not so lucky. In 1579 John Stubbs and his publisher, William Page, were imprisoned and had their right hands hacked off for distributing *The Discovery of a Gaping Gulf whereinto England is like to be Swallowed*, which dared to address the question of the Queen's marriage.[37] Dr John Hayward's 1599 *The Life and Reign of King Henry IV*, which was applied to the furore over the Earl of Essex at the time, almost got the author executed.[38] An outstanding case of the punishment of an author is that of William Prynne, imprisoned and ear-cropped in 1633 for his *Histriomastix* and further in 1637 for continuing to write material considered subversive from his prison cell.[39] Prynne complained that punishment of this kind was worse under Charles I than under Mary or Elizabeth, where he estimates there might have been merely 'six months imprisonment in ordinary prisons, and the delinquent might redeem his ears for £200 [. . .] [while] here they are fined £5,000 a piece, to be perpetually imprisoned in the remotest castles [. . .] and to lose their ears without redemption'.[40] Though somewhat untypical, Prynne's case nevertheless indicates the parameters of punishment for authors whose texts are interpreted harshly, especially if they found hundreds of pounds hard to come by.

And the dramatists suffered too. Thomas Kyd, perhaps the most celebrated playwright of his time, died at 35 after being informed upon, arrested and viciously racked over things he had allegedly written. Chapman was informed upon, as mentioned above, and eventually imprisoned for his *Byron* plays, as were his actors.[41] Dutton notes the 1610 case of Sir Edward Dymock who was imprisoned and fined £1,000 for putting on a defamatory play, while his three principal actors were 'pilloried and whipped in Westminster Hall, then taken to Lincolnshire where the punishment was repeated, and fined £300 apiece'.[42] Jonson himself was imprisoned specifically for misdemeanours of writing, undoubtedly at least for *The Isle of Dogs* and *Eastward Ho!* and possibly also for *Sejanus* (aside from being incarcerated for murder and debt) and certainly feared 'defacement', and not just of text or reputation.[43] Not only was he plagued with informers on the inside, but an informer was specifically involved in his arrest for *The Isle of Dogs*, in July 1597. Ian Donaldson describes how, soon after performances of the play began, it was 'an informer's complaint' that found its way to Richard Topcliffe, Elizabeth's chief 'interrogator'; Topcliffe refers to the nameless informer as 'the first man that discovered to me that seditious play called *The Isle of*

Dogs'.[44] Jonson's prison letter to William Herbert, Earl of Pembroke, while incarcerated for writing *Eastward Ho!*, reveals a real desperation in the face of the threat of indefinite imprisonment in the filth of an early modern gaol, and possible dismemberment. 'The Anger of the Kinge is death,' he says, 'and in truth it is little lesse with mee and my frend, for it hath buried us quick.'[45] These are not in themselves trivial punishments, and the instances of other writers suffering worse fates certainly contributed to the paranoia over these matters clearly keenly felt by Jonson and others who served time under such threats. If it is indeed the case that early modern players and playwrights 'were too insignificant for those in power to take all that seriously, except when they were "too insolent"', they clearly were not aware of this at the time.[46] In such an intimidating political milieu, the metaphor of being buried alive aptly describes the deep personal concern which informs Jonson's aspiration to establish a secure social role for the satirist as a Horatian ideal. Jonson's cherished vision of the nature of social merit is thus both energised and problematised by his depictions of a society tainted by the informers who could instigate such vicious proceedings.[47]

This is not to suggest that every author was continually under surveillance, but rather that they perceived a continuum of experience with the extremes of applied informing as inscribed on the writing body. This pressure exerted on authors was felt more broadly also. In the preface to Daniel Featley's *Cygnea Cantio* (1625), the printer Robert Mylbourne complained of an informer who was determined to 'calumniate the writings of my friends living, and to procure them either to be altogether suppressed or to be so gelded and mangled, that the sale of them thereby was very much hindred'.[48] Similarly, the little-read seventeenth-century poet George Daniel described a judging authority, whose censure 'I thought, I'de past / with Applause', who then '(Sprung-gvilty) [. . .] considers, what wee meant / To vse him thus, / [. . .] slips to his State-forme; & Calls his Eyes / To Councell, ere he Doome our Levities'; this authority then with the 'White-Staffe of his Place / [. . .] threatens Poetry, like a Strange Face', 'eyes' in this case being an obvious synecdoche for informers.[49] Though ostensibly sceptical, Meskill herself is drawn to this logic, arguing that Jonson's suspicion of audiences may be attributed not only to 'their immense power to decide the fate of the author's fame' but also their 'frightening power [. . .] to affect the poet's earthly fate'.[50] She admits, for instance, that *Poetaster* depicts poets whose lives may be in danger 'in very real ways' but, finally, resists the material implications of such a portrayal.[51]

For Jonson, driven by his preoccupation with the potentially murderous nature of authorities, the fear of misinterpretation, deliberate or otherwise, generates a drama which articulates these pressures both explicitly, in plots and characters, and implicitly, in its very structures. Shakespeare meanwhile proves a more shadowy player in these interactions, but, whether or not Jonson would agree, in this respect his plays are nevertheless as much 'of' their time as Jonson's own, instancing many dangerous overlookings and overhearings. In differing ways these two exemplary dramatists produce a range of metadramatic devices that work upon the parameters of audiences' perspectives and in doing so register the very suspect structures of hidden watching, eavesdropping and tale-bearing that constitute this pervasive social delinquency.

Throughout the early modern period few informers operated by patent. Although they were potentially subject to legal regulation through the Common Informers Acts of 1575, 1588 and 1623, the vast majority were engaged on an ad hoc basis, casually picking up information which they could use to their own or their patron's material advantage.[52] One notably ubiquitous informer is James Patricke, who, William Cecil writes, 'is everye daye at the privye keies at the water syde'; Cecil's assertion that Patricke 'hath money of me without agreement' is an indication of their ad hoc arrangement.[53] At the other end of the spectrum, T.G. notes that even any aspiring statesman might 'incurre the imputation of an enformer abroad, and at home [. . .] for abroad he must give intelligence of his best friends, and at home flatter his very enemies'.[54] In the drama that represents them therefore, for example, Sejanus and Iago are primarily soldiers, but also function as informers. Bosola is a steward, with informing functions attached. Polonius, Rosencrantz and Guildenstern are courtiers, or aspirants, and, as we find in relation to almost the whole of *Hamlet*'s Danish court, the very occupation of courtier is represented as entailing the function of informer. In Jonson's *Poetaster*, it is Lupus the tribune who plays the informer, telling Caesar of Horace's 'libel'. *Bartholomew Fair*'s Whit is paid to inform the authorities on minor lawbreakers, although his title is 'bawd', also indicating the status of his morality. It is the very extempore nature of this network of irregulars that seems to enhance the sense of their menace, the erratic nature of their work making their presence, and therefore their danger, all the more unpredictable.

Daniel Tuvill's *The Dove and the Serpent* (1614) offers satirical advice for potential informers on the 'procuring of better information' by hanging around in taverns until people's tongues are loosened by drink.[55] Francis Beaumont's *The Woman-Hater* (1606) describes just such a figure: 'This fellow is a kind of an informer, one that lives in Alehouses and Taverns [. . .] he brings me informations, pick'd out of broken words, in men's common talk, which, with his malicious mis-application, he hopes will seem dangerous.'[56] The 'mis-application' of dramatic characters and situations to contemporary figures, was, as Andrew Gurr says, 'a major pleasure of the playgoing game'.[57] Jonson parodies this in *The Magnetic Lady* (1632), which invites two opposing metadramatic interpreters, Damplay and Probee, to censure the play. Damplay enquires about one character, 'whom doth your poet mean now by this – Master Bias? What lord's secretary, doth he purpose to personate [. . .]?' (Chorus 2.1–2). Probee rebukes him: 'It is an insidious question [. . .] Iniquity itself would not have urged it', and insists, 'A play, though it [. . .] present vices in general, flies from all particularities in persons' (Chorus 2.8–11). He adds, 'It is the solemn vice of interpretation that deforms the figure of many a fair scene by drawing it awry' and decries those who 'defame by [. . .] malice of misapplying' and those who therefore 'imperil the innocence and candor of the author by [. . .] calumny' (Chorus 2.27–8, 33–4).[58] The fear of malicious misapplying for financial gain is important to the dynamics of the relationship between the dramatic author and his audience, because it effectively puts a price on any incriminating interpretation. The metadrama that ensues from this both reflects this process and suggests a defensive move against it, its *mise en abyme* often appearing to displace the direct responsibility of the author while facilitating the attempt to manipulate offstage audience responses. This defensive move is, perhaps, partly due to the absence of legal assistance in the event of the author being accused.[59]

Far from offering any refuge from possible accusation, the various legal structures were perceived at the time to be very much in league with the informers they produced and remunerated.[60] In terms of payment, successful informers could earn themselves a very good purse indeed; Walsingham's maxim was 'knowledge is never too dear'.[61] Contemporary legal statutes dictated that the informer should receive a portion of whatever fine was imposed, with the rest going to the Crown; a common share was a third to half of the fine, or value of the goods informed upon, in a so-called *Qui Tam* action of this kind.[62] In 1606 it was established that a merchant found avoiding customs 'shall forfeit his whole Goods; the Ship, shall be [. . .] forfeited [. . .] Two Parts to appertain to his Majesty [. . .] and the third to the Informer', potentially an extremely tidy sum.[63] *Poetaster* offers a literary example of this in Lupus and Tucca's desire to inform on Horace and Maecenas so that they might 'beg of their land'.[64] In 1615 at the Court of the Exchequer alone there were 185 informations on wool illegally sold, with fines totalling a massive £555,000, a significant proportion of which would have lined the purses of informers.[65] But, as we have seen, the business of informing was by no means limited to the field of mercantile transgression; the informer might also make good money in a more aggressively ideological manner. When Kyd was arrested in 1593 over the 'Dutch Church libel', in which threats were made to the Dutch community in a distinctly Marlovian style, he believed himself the victim of an informer, ' "some outcast Ismael" who has "incensed your Lordships to suspect me" '; and this is highly likely given the very substantial 100 crown reward money offered for information, as Charles Nicholl notes.[66] When Seacoal, *Much Ado*'s informer, overhears Hero's slanderer, he sets up a metadramatic scene, saying, 'some treason, masters. / [. . .] stand close' (3.3.103) and at each point in the ensuing transactions on information, money changes hands: from the 'thousand ducats' (3.3.105) Borachio receives for his false testimony and his acknowledgement that now he is arrested he is 'like to prove a goodly commodity, being taken up of these men's bills' (3.3.170–1) to Leonato's simple payment to Dogberry 'for thy pains' (5.1.306).[67] Even in such an otherwise benign episode the financial aspect casts its shadow over the exchanges. In the odious Griffin Flood's case, money is always changing hands. Finding those 'going abroad in Service time' he would 'pick some feeling of money from them', but the mere threat of legal action is enough for a tradesman to be 'brought to composition to be rid of this crafty Informer'.[68] This potential for rich pickings may well have a bearing on the paranoia authors often feel on this issue. Since the informer's point of view typically combines negative construction with the generation of income there is every incentive for them to interpret the content of writings and plays creatively, in ways most unfavourable to the author. As Nicholl says, it 'encourages people to *create* information, to see conspiracy where none exists'.[69] These circumstances go some way to account for the preoccupation with venal watchers and hidden hearers which are coded into the many secret overhearings and tacit observations common to drama of this period.

Curiously and somewhat disturbingly, however, in depicting a social malaise of authority compromised by association with such figures, these metadramatic devices put the author in the position of reproducing the informer's practice in his own, and often discovering thereby a disquieting resemblance. Onstage, the informer uses an empowered position for practical gain; the author often employs this for narrative velocity, but both are exploiting the privileged perspective. Offstage also, the association holds: the author is a paid observer and informer of society, seeking security, preferment and money, through the shaping of discourse, a connection Ben Jonson especially struggled with.[70] In his role-model Horace's defence of satire, as Catherine Keane notes, the classical poet is also keen to deny his own resemblance to 'the opportunistic informers who stalk Rome with notebooks in hand, identifying potential victims'.[71] This connection does not go unnoticed by contemporaries, such as T.G., writing in 1615, who speaks of players' 'artificiall lyes, discoueries of cousenage, scurrilous words' and asserts that 'Players, Poets, and Parasites doe now in a manner ioyne hands [. . .] so that to chast eares they are as odious, as filthy pictures are offensiue to modest eyes'.[72] *Much Ado*'s informer Seacoal, or a relative acting as Sexton, has a writing ability which is deemed crucial to the legal process, the 'pen and inkhorn' of the 'learned writer' Dogberry orders brought to the proceedings (3.5.54, 59). Metadramatic modes are also often informed by such uneasy overtones of connection between the author and an informer who is simultaneously perceived as an empowered observer and portrayed as a fawning lackey to his master. The compulsion to distinguish themselves from informers is far from confined to the subjects of this present study (John Donne is another affected) and this can cause authors to 'protest too much' about the distinction.[73] Hence, for instance, Jonson's desire in *Poetaster* to differentiate the flattering 'fawn' from the nobly satirical 'satyr' and to consolidate his own legitimacy by aggressively representing his fellow poets in the former category, as sycophantic informers.[74] Another example may be found in Day's *Ile of Guls*, where an ex-informer suggests the close connection, explaining, 'Bawdie Informations growing stale, I gaue vp my cloake to a Broker, and crept into credite for a Gowne, and of [. . .] a penurious Informer, I turned Coppie, & became [. . .] a most precise [. . .] expositor'.[75] Asked 'Were you a Reader [. . .]?', he answers, 'And a Writer too [. . .] I could fashion the bodie, of my discourse fit to the eare of my auditorie.'[76] Such opportunistic use of information describes both informer and writer tailoring his discourse to particular audiences, with no regard for an objective truth, purely in order to line his own pockets. Some early modern authors clearly worry that they might be construed as using the same methods of dealing with information as the predatory and fawning informers they, and much of their audience, so reviled. In this case it is understandable they should want to emphasise the differences that exist between these professions. Some of this denial may be perceived in Rochester's 'epitaph' above.

Thomas Nabbs's *Covent Garden* (1638) makes a more dynamic connection between the observant author and the observing informer. There is little doubt that the play's silently observing character Littleword represents Ben Jonson, whose 'constant humour', according to William Winstanley's *Lives of the Most Famous English Poets* (1687) 'was to sit silently in learned company, and suck in (besides wine) their several humours into his observation'.[77] Indeed Jonson admits as much in *Poetaster* where Horace (standing for Jonson) is described as being 'a mere sponge, nothing but humours and observation [. . .] [who sucks] from every society, and when he comes home squeezes himself dry again' (4.3.104–7). *Covent Garden*'s character list designates Littleword 'a reputed Witt'.[78] The text is, however, equivocal about whether he is an author or an informer, and of course we are left assuming that he may be both. In any case Littleword causes havoc in the tavern through the sheer paranoia generated by his sitting in the corner silently making notes, a fear no doubt exacerbated by what Hutson calls the era's 'troubled threshold of commonplace collecting and intelligence-gathering'.[79] The mischievous Dungworth first notes that the vintner 'seems troubled at this Gentleman's table-booke' (4.3.60); he is assured, however, ''Tis his practise of observation. Hee is taking a humour for a Play' (4.3.60). Dungworth's response expresses these connections as well as the general paranoia over reported conversation when he declares, 'That silent Gentleman is an intelligencer [. . .] Hee'l informe against you. Therefore complie with him to prevent it. 'Tis his pollicie to say nothing himselfe, that his observation may be the more, and his owne danger the lesse' (4.3.73–7). Littleword's parallel with Jonson's own habits of keeping his own counsel and taking notes on proceedings as an observer seems to combine aspects of *Bartholomew Fair*'s aptonymic Littlewit, a legal agent who writes the inner play, and Justice Overdo, the self-informing note-taking judge. In *Covent Garden*, however, the character is explicitly a parody of both the secretive author and the authoring informer, and this seems to express disquiet not merely about the exercise of authority over information, but also about the authority which information confers. Echoing Shakespeare's Cleopatra, Essex himself complains of such a person in a letter to Elizabeth of 12 May 1600: 'the prating tavern-haunter speaks of me what he lists; they print me and make me speak to the world, and shortly they will play me upon the stage'.[80] The interpermeable nature of the lives of the rich and famous and the world of drama is evident from the era's deep concern over drama's potential for 'tra-ducing' the powerful, and from the prosecution of Jonson, Chapman and others for just this. The aptitude of the structures of surveil-lance which often underpinned these lives to the milieu of the stage is apparent in many cases included here, though it is often a disturbing interface.[81]

These connections are felt also in relation to the fact that the roles of informer and author have historically overlapped in a far more direct manner. It was by no means unusual for an ambitious author, seeking money or preferment, to be engaged upon an official information-gathering mission or two in the service of the Crown. The nature of Marlowe's 'good service, & [. . .] fathfull dealinge' on behalf of the government is the cause of much speculation in this regard.[82] Nicholl identifies Marlowe firmly as an informer.[83] He certainly associated with known informers, as the infamous Pol-ey's presence at his death affirms.[84] Marlowe is echoed in *Poetas-ter*'s Ovid, and indeed Jonson was another of Poley's victims whilst doing time in the Marshalsea.[85] Other informer-authors may include the influential essayist Michel de Montaigne, George Gascoigne, Thomas Watson, Anthony Munday, John Lyly, Francis and Anthony Bacon, and, many concur, Ben Jonson himself.[86] In 1605 when in prison for *Eastward Ho!* Jonson had petitioned Lord Salisbury for his release and by the November of that year he could be found act-ing as what R. B. Parker describes as Salisbury's 'confidential agent to the chaplain of the Venetian ambassador' in relation to the Gun-powder Plot.[87] There is no evidence of this kind for Shakespeare, though his father John certainly suffered at the hands of informers.[88] Regarding Munday, who seems exemplary in this connection, E. K. Chambers notes that other writers 'jested at his functions as a mes-senger' and refers to Francis Meres's identification of his work 'as a spy and informer [. . .] under the notorious Richard Topcliffe'.[89] In *Palladis Tamia* (1598) Meres employs a careful pun when he refers to '*Anthony Mundye* our best plotter'.[90] Ben Jonson confirms this satire of Munday in *The Case is Altered* (1609), parodying him as Antonio Balladino, pageant poet, 'in print already for the best plotter'.[91] This could also go the other way, however, and Nicholl cites the informer Thomas Drury who was imprisoned for ambiguities in his writing, seeing informers also potentially as frustrated writers.[92] Given these connections we might ask why authors are almost always very nega-tive about informers, especially since early modern legal records may show that informers often underpin justice. The problem for a public figure like an author is simply the popular odium in which these figures are held. A politic distance is obviously necessary in this case, not to mention the psychological imperative to define oneself against an 'other' who in fact shares certain undesirable characteristics.

This association is also suggested by the contemporary semantic landscape. Here an *author* may represent a 'person on whose authority a statement is made [. . .] an informant'.[93] *OED* describes an *informant* meanwhile as 'one who lays an information against a person; an informer'.[94] More generally, an *informant* is also 'that which informs [. . .] or actuates', coming very close to the contemporary concept of the *author*.[95] The term 'informant' is therefore equally applicable to an 'author' or an 'informer' at this time, a fact which may inform the imperative to bestialise and marginalise the position of informer as the author's absolute 'other'.[96] The etymology of the word *author* provides a fascinating possible further connection between the predatory informer and the sense of the author as informant. This relates to the word *augur*, which enters the English language with Chaucer and is closely tied to the sense of divination from the flight of birds.[97] *OED* sees *augur* as deriving from *av-is*, 'bird' and *-gar*, which is connected with *garrire*, 'to talk'. It notes an alternative possible derivation, however, from *augēre* 'to make to grow, originate, promote, increase' (the root of the word *author*).[98] In the absence of a direct derivation, it is nevertheless tempting to see a conceptual continuum between these and *auceps*, which can mean either 'bird-catcher' or 'eavesdropper'.[99] Furthermore, *augēre* is also the root of the verb *to augment*. This should perhaps be no surprise to us since the practice of an augmentative interpretation of events is, after all, common to augur, author and informer. Quentin Skinner notes anxieties over the morality of the arts of rhetoric, from Plato to Hobbes, who laments 'that art of words, by which some men can represent to others, that which is Good, in the likenesse of Evill; and Evill in the likenesse of Good; and augment, or diminish' either.[100] The spymaster Walsingham was very much aware that his informers might bring him 'toyes and matters of their owne invencon'.[101] One of Nashe's complaints against Harvey is that he produces 'ironicall amplifications'.[102] Teate again accords with this view as he describes the informer's propensity for creativity: 'You see then what the informer comes for, which he will either find or make before he go away [. . .] He wrests what he hears to the Preacher's destruction.'[103] The informer as one who 'wrests what he hears' to his own purposes is an unreliable interpreter and this for obvious reasons is a persistent bugbear to the authors and playwrights of the time, offering some incentive for the author of drama to attempt to shape a distinction between himself and these less respectable 'plotters'.

In order to further understand the ways in which authors thought about informers, and thus the conscious antagonism which energised and animated the structures and modes of metadramatic exchange, it will be helpful to study the imagery they employ to describe them. These metaphors and images are almost all focused on the inhumanity or intemperance of the profession. Birds and dogs are exemplary here, birds for their chattering, and dogs for their slavish fawning; both are also notable, along with wolves and foxes, for their inhuman voracity. Audiences in early modern London would have been very familiar with the sound of the barking of the hundred-plus dogs kept for fighting and baiting at places like the Bear Garden in Southwark.[104] This must at times have formed an unwelcome aural backdrop to many productions in the locality, but it also provided a convenient metaphor for the activities of informers. An intelligencer, or informer, Nashe says is, 'a curre, that flatters & fawns upon everie one [. . .] till he may spie an advantage, and pluck oute his throate'.[105] The 1615 edition of Overbury's *New and choice characters* describes the 'Apparatour' (a court summoner commonly conflated with the informer) as 'a cunning hunter, uncouping his intelligencing hounds'.[106] James I/VI himself referred to his head of intelligence Robert Cecil as 'the little beagle that lies by the fire when all the good hounds are daily running on the fields'.[107] *OED* defines a 'beagle' at the time as 'one who makes it his business to scent out or hunt down; a spy or informer'. The imputation of uncontrolled canine appetite here is allied to either a fawning cunning or self-seeking treachery, not limited to a particular echelon of society. In *Essayes and characters* (1615), Stephens notes that 'the base informer [works] upon poore mens fortunes [. . .] His profession affoords practisers both great and small; both buckehounds and harriers: the essence of both is inquisition'.[108] For Jonson especially, canine, lupine and vulpine imagery conveys concerns about the nature of the true poet and the proper authoritative role of the author in relation to the authorities.[109]

Another common metaphor for the informer in early modern writing is that of the perpetually hungry or talkative bird, an image which links the immorality of the uncontrolled appetite described above with a stronger sense of a deliberately predatory overview, and often with the idea that its prey is hopelessly unprotected. This sense of overview is frequently the perspective which metadrama presents as a shared experience between dramatis persona and audience. The later anonymous *Character of an informer* (1675) testifies to the continuity of these tropes throughout the period, and in other forms of writing, describing one who is 'as *eager* after his Prey as a half-starved Cormorant, and cares not that he Ruine half a Nation, to supply his own prodigalities'.[110] When at church, it explains, 'Rich men there skulke down in their Pews when they see him come in, dreading him more than a Partridge does a Hawke.'[111] Overbury also develops this metaphor, 'he is a birde of rapine [. . .] He croakes like a raven [. . .] and so gets a Legacy'.[112] So ancient are these associations that they can be seen in Aristophanes' play *The Birds* (414 BC), in which a character called Sycophant begs, 'I am an accuser [. . .] an informer [. . .] a hatcher of lawsuits [. . .] I have great need of wings to prowl round the cities [. . .] some light, swift hawk or kestrel wings.'[113] Here again, avian imagery relates to the structures of dramatic perception since certain birds are not merely predatory but also represent the privileged viewpoint of author, audience and informer. The above connection with augury may also be noted. This is further complicated by the sense that any over-view is to an extent a view with authority and here again we may encounter the consternation felt in Stephens's description of the informer as a 'Knave in authoritie, licenced by authoritie'.[114] Early modern metadrama negotiates its spaces within these issues of legitimate authority, authorship and the empowered viewpoint.

Authors of metadrama do not merely reflect these political realities passively: they themselves have reason to fear the penalties of encountering a malicious interpreter. Surveillance is never 'without an imminent consequence [. . .] never gratuitous', as George Banu points out.[115] Against a potential informer in the audience, the mechanism of the play-within-the-play may suggest a defensive structure whose fictionally displaced authorship perhaps belies an almost involuntary reaction to the real possibility of accusations of libellous or otherwise damaging representation. In a more concrete sense, metadrama can also work to suggest a number of alternative legitimate viewpoints for an audience in relation to the inner world of the play. So, authors of metadrama play with hierarchies of power in diegetic strata, articulating shifting loci of legitimate interpretation, locating and dislocating perspectives, forming or deforming structures of textual authority, and generating narrative impetus. But also, in the sense that a play is licensed by an authorising body, a play-within-a-play can implicitly lay claim to being a licence-within-a-licence, in both senses of that antithetical term: a liberty-within-a-liberty and an authorised-interlude-within-an-authorised-interlude. As such it can work to loosen the bonds of the authority which licenses the outer play and work as itself a locus of indeterminacy, a constituency of reflection on the proper authority of the author of the outer play. *Hamlet* is a significant example of this in terms of the formal 'play' between the inner- and outer-plays, which reflects on the nature of authority. Here of course, 'The play's the thing / Wherein I'll catch the conscience of the King' (2.2.539-40), and it is through such metadrama that Claudius' audience-reaction is exposed to incriminating interpretation, while the framing device allows that the response of the real offstage audience to the portrayal of regicide might be usefully obscured. In these ways metadrama is operating at the boundaries and possibilities of emergent social structures, modes of thought and perceptions, forming, in Raymond Williams's terms, an 'articulation [. . .] of changes in consciousness'.[116] Metadrama articulates the consciousness of the instability and debasement of any interpretation that is dependent on a mercenary perspective, and simultaneously instances a mode of resistance to this.

One of the defining characteristics of metadrama is that it foregrounds the drama-audience relationship in performance. The focus of this study is on how such an emphasis addresses the content of that relationship itself, rather than simply how it explores the parameters of the art-form. Such self-reflexivity may project the audience into an active and empowered meaning-making role by disordering the boundaries between the onstage and offstage worlds, or it may distance it from such a role through clearly defined framing devices positioning the audience in some subordinate relation to the metadramatic inset. It is within this spectrum that the dramatist is able to play with models of appropriate interpretation and response. The nature of these mechanisms is often related to the ways in which authors handle the perceived potential for moral or financial corruption in their implied audiences.

One metadramatic device offering some defence against such potential for misinterpretation is to endeavour to shape the response of the offstage audience by drawing them into a common experience with an onstage audience whose responses are scripted to reject dangerous misapprehensions, or the mishandling of information.[117] This connection draws on the experience of the early modern audience not of viewing through an invisible 'fourth wall' but taking part in an exchange in which the drama is far more related with its audience on an organic, interpersonal level.[118] For those offstage, the experience of audienceship shared with an onstage audience may create sympathy with certain characters, give an inner narrative greater plausibility, or suggest a community of interpretation, either positive or negative, against which they might measure their own responses. Consciously or not an audience may thus experience one dramatic subjectivity set up in contradistinction to another, one more desirable to the purposes of the author, which the metadrama suggests. The audience may be drawn into sharing these structures via the subtle centripetal motion of concentric metadrama, in which the effect of watching/hearing (with) someone watching/hearing (with) someone watching/hearing someone, and so on, produces 'diegetic gravity', a term which designates the narrative force which pulls the 'viewer' inwards through each successive framing device to the inmost centre of conceptual focus. This pull will be in proportion to the desirability of the viewpoint of the inner audience, or the amount of narrative power it affords. The effect of this on an offstage audience often produces what we might term 'frame-blindness'; as the viewpoint or perspective is drawn through each successive frame, the frame itself becomes less perceptible. This works as a kind of inverted scotoma, where there is an isolated field of imaginary vision and the peripheral areas are diminished.[119] In this mode the audience is acted on by the inner-play as if it were the outer play, and the process often results in the conflation of onstage and offstage audiences. Thus it becomes possible for the author to use his onstage audience to model various reactions to the inner drama and so attempt to shape the response of the offstage audience. This may be merely a momentary experience as a player is overlooked by another hidden from his view, or it may be a protracted experience of being co-audience with an onstage audience of an inner play. In both cases what is engendered is an inward movement which allows the author to play with the audience's perspective in a wider sense, whilst allowing him to remain obscured by the very narratological indirectness of the motion through layers of framing. The precise operations of these mechanisms are of course related to the desirability of the perspective being shared; Iago's, for instance, offers audiences delinquencies which will be explored herein.

At any given metadramatic moment then, the various metadramatic strata in play relate to each other with a hypotactic connection in relationships of causal, spatial, or temporal subordination. The complexities of these relationships also allow the author, if he so wishes, to draw the focus of the narrative away from its most obvious focal point. This can create a disjunction between the scopic pulsion of the spectacle and the diegetic gravity of the narrative which thus distorts the perspective the drama offers. Where audiences do share the perspective of an onstage observer, they may experience metalepsis, a temporary sharing of a common narrative level which allows them to see the two levels together and read them accordingly, each in terms of each other.[120] If there is a disjunction, the author may deny this. Since it is dependent upon the subtlety of this interchange, any control being attempted by the author may, however, if too explicit, produce disorderly results, as described below in the case of audience reaction to Jonson's *Staple of News*.

Furthermore, as the offstage audience of metadrama, the view one is offered may be complicated by the moral perspectives of hidden overlookers or eavesdropping informers. To some extent metadrama is driven by a preoccupation with the haunting presence of these figures and often stages the very structures which may be exploited by informers to wrest meaning from some innocuous situation or piece of information. This is very often used by authors to drive their plots forwards and may or may not produce scopophilic or conceptual hierarchies pleasurable to an audience. W. B. Worthen emphasises that dramatic performance works 'by deploying the text in recognizable genres of behaviour [. . .] [which] determine what the text *can* mean as performance'.[121] These metadramatic structures and narrative devices thus remind us that early modern drama's interactive openness, and acknowledgement of mutual watching, is infused with the alarming possibility that the observer intends harm. Caught up thus in the pleasure and pain of representation, audiences may play many different roles which the metadrama assigns them – informers, members of the Senate, a jury, passers-by, a rioting mob, even a 'play-audience'. Whether or not they resist these metadramatic interpellations, the very acts of critical interpretation they introduce suggest involvement in the production of meaning, and thus an empowered subjectivity which may not always be comfortable for the author.[122] As moral choices between the perspectives of various types of characters are often involved in these processes, this can be very revealing of the imperatives and desires of both the author and the audience.

These structures of perspective have been understood in various ways. One practical model has been outlined in Weimann's designations of *locus* and *platea*, *locus* being the inmost symbolic place of action, a scaffold or throne-dais, for example, and *platea* being the most interactive area closest to the audience, where a 'flexible relationship between the play world and the real world' may be established.[123] These may allow us to locate the power-source of the metadramatic oversight/overhearing, which either comes from the *platea* and is thus offered to the audience as shared experience, or from the *locus*, with the *platea* as focus, offering another kind of empowered perspective. However, as Weimann notes, these conventions are changing throughout the period and transmuting into something more complex and interchangeable, energised, I would argue, by an increased perception of the relative empowerment of the drama and of the authorities of oversight. Since *locus* and *platea* may differ with staging, their interrelation is relatively unquantifiable in comparison to the more clearly unequal positions of the hidden watcher/hearer and their unaware subjects. Weimann often works with levels of illusion as determinants of nuances of authority. Hence for him the interplay between *platea* and *locus* 'accommodates action that is both nonillusionistic and near the audience [. . .] and a more illusionistic, localized action [. . .] in a discovery space, scaffold, tent, or other *loci*'.[124] Spatially, this marks out the onstage interplay of authority but its conceptualisation of the offstage audience's reception of the subtly differing modes of metadramatic self-reference is somewhat lacking in specificity. In critiquing this formulation Harry Berger Jr suggests that, for asides and soliloquies alike, the audience they speak to is in any case 'a fiction, a virtual audience constituted by the direction and express motivation of address [. . .] thus pre-existing any actual audience'.[125] Berger's critique usefully explores audience-construction, but his view also tends towards the assessment of levels of intensities of 'illusion': 'asides tend [. . .] to be more collaborative and non- or counter-illusionistic, while [. . .] soliloquy tends to be more illusionistic'.[126] In terms of other writing about metadrama, Lionel Abel's pioneering work opposes metatheatre to tragedy, which he suggests is its precursor, arguing that each is bound to its own field: tragedy's parish is the 'world'; metatheatre's is the 'imagination'.[127] This somewhat depoliticised view is in some ways opposed to the view I propound here, which argues that the dirty and tragic 'world' is very much implicated in the imaginative interplays of early modern metadrama.[128] Richard Hornby's useful *Drama, Metadrama and Perception* (1986) explains that for metadrama to work there must be 'sharply distinguishable layers of performance', but does not aim to explore these layers in detail.[129] Peter Milward's interesting assessments plough other furrows, often seeing through to the plays' sources in specifically religious readings.[130] James L. Calderwood's studies of content and form typically posit their symmetries within the playwright's desire to explore 'the truth and value of drama'; this approach undoubtedly has merit but is again lacking in particulars.[131] My own methodology aims not so much to deal with authors' relationship with 'truth' or 'illusion' as to historicise the metadramatic constructions of inner plays, audiences and dramatis personae, and to identify power structures and social forces that inform them and exert pressures on their making, including ideas of authorship, perceptions of authority tainted by association with informers and the fear of misinterpretation.

In considering these macro-level historical issues, it is of course necessary to focus on a close reading of the particular functions of any given instance of metadrama. Here, some outline of theoretical terminology is useful. In terms of simple self-reference it is not often possible to situate metadramatic devices in relation to Weimann's *locus/platea* binary, and often in the subtler fields of metadrama we may only find this within a very localised individual dramatic structure. Otherwise, there are two main mechanisms by which audiences are engaged with drama; the first is a visual mechanism and the second is a narrative device. As above, I have referred to these respectively as 'scopic pulsion' and 'diegetic gravity'. These visual and narrative forms generate a centripetal impetus which can be employed either to shape or to distort configurations of interpretative authority. 'Scopic pulsion' might be described as an irresistible urge to look, and here the term will be used to refer to the ways in which metadrama both encourages and resists that pull of the gaze towards the inmost point of the drama. Jacques Derrida uses the term to describe voyeurism, which sufficiently approximates the structures described here to justify its use.[132] Linda Charnes states that, in terms of the power-relations it embodies, 'the first principle of voyeurism [. . .] is that the observed be caught unawares', which is certainly an important element of the generation of uncertainty, or paranoia, over the nature of an audience in drama of the period.[133] Relating to this, Jacques Lacan's use of the term 'the gaze' describes how the subject is constructed partly in relation to the network of relations formed by the scopic fields of others.[134] For Lacan, any picture that utilises conventional linear perspective acts as a snare for the gaze since it offers the observer a clearly defined psycho-social position from which to view the subject of the work. The dramatic medium offers a less well-defined set of psycho-social positions, often differing with each performance, and metadrama especially offers a shifting set of perspectives which is anything but linear. Nevertheless there are such positions available to the audience of metadrama, and these often relate to the ways that audiences and narratives are interlinked by the author and positioned as subject to the 'gaze' of the observer, either visually or conceptually. Lacan's idea of the gaze was developed from Jean-Paul Sartre's 'look', a mechanism of connection with the Other which must refer, as Sartre says, to the 'permanent possibility of *being seen* by the Other'.[135] For Sartre, however, this is not necessarily only to do with sight; the mechanism works just as well when all we have is 'a rustling of branches or the sound of a footstep followed by silence, or the slight opening of a shutter, or a light movement of a curtain'.[136] This offers a reciprocal model of observation in which the watched and the watcher shape each other's subjectivities and are, in a sense, mutually constitutive.[137]

Metadrama is an obvious instance of the operative power of these ideas within an imaginary framework. One of the functions of metadrama is to subvert the ideological authority of a gaze by foregrounding its 'network of relations' and making these a subject of the dramatic narrative. This allows the author to attempt to exert some kind of authoritative influence over the mechanisms of meaning-making within which the gaze operates. Though he may be in danger of being maliciously constructed (or metaphorically castrated) by 'psycho-social positions' structured around the informer-as-proxy for patriarchal authority, this metadramatic function affords him some potential entry into the symbolic order.[138] Thus a Sartrean model would seem to be the most helpful here, as both the author and the informer are shaped by the subjectivity or objectivity of the other as separate social forces. However, Lacan's view that, 'the gaze of the Other [. . .] [is] nothing other than the subjective division itself, expressed in the field of vision' also articulates the fundamental, and problematic, connection between the occupants of these ostensibly distinct subject-positions.[139] Not wishing to focus entirely on theories of subjectivity and objectivity, this study does not attempt to offer analyses based on the Lacanian or Sartrean gaze, and I mention them here mainly for their value as models of possible subjectivisation shaped by the metadramatic interrelations the author and the informer provide. With its aptitude for grounding these potential subjectivities in very material power-relations, however, early modern metadrama might be exemplary. Anthony B. Dawson notes the 'scopic management' inherent in the theatre of the time and this study aims to explore the effects of early modern authors' metadramatic strategies in pursuit of such management.[140]

Importantly also, any viewpoint, for the dramatic spectator, is almost always also a hearing point and the early modern audience is, as the word suggests, to a significant extent an auditory body. Bruce R. Smith describes early modern theatre as an 'auditory field' within which actors and audiences are situated.[141] Whether an audience goes to 'hear' or to 'see' a play, their engagement with that play is to a significant extent formed in the imagination, and in this sense the Sartrean 'look', which includes this 'auditory field', bears a partly imaginary relation also to the diegetic structures which metadrama affords. Seeing and hearing are both obviously essential to the experiences of going to the theatre and of acting as an informer. For the purposes of this study the visual and the auditory are considered to be subsumed into the imaginary and conceptual relationships these plays instantiate between their onstage and offstage worlds.

The nucleus of these metadramatic practices is an uneasy logic of collective experience between author and informer, actor and agent, paying audience and paid observer. As mentioned, the informer-figure points to the latent menace of the audience, but equally, ever Janus-faced, he also tends to become the author's own shadowy doppel-ganger. For this reason authors are compelled by their similarities to foreground their dissimilarities. This desire is driven by what Freud describes as the 'narcissism of small differences', the process by which one group of individuals seeks to distinguish itself from another very similar group by exaggerating the minor differences which exist between them.[142] Somewhat paradoxically, as Freud points out, the by-product of this exaggeration of minor differences is in fact coher-ence between the parties concerned: establishing difference in this way actually posits cohesion with the other by acknowledging the sameness which is at the root of the necessity to establish such dif-ference. The metadrama of Shakespeare and Jonson is at least partly motivated by this personal and social imperative, and thus their the-atrical self-reflexivity reveals their attitudes not only to theatre but to the question of authority itself, especially insofar as it relates to their own authorship.

Williams has argued that emerging modes of address on the early modern stage amounted to 'developments in social practice [. . .] fundamentally connected with the discovery, *in dramatic form*, of new and altered social relationships, perceptions of self and others'.[143] I describe here some historical practices, 'social relationships', and 'perceptions of self and others' which produce the fears and creative tensions that drive or facilitate much metadramatic activity. Regard-ing the potentially revolutionary undercurrents of the time, Williams argues that it was 'in the deep formal qualities of the dramatic mode itself, and in the specific qualities of these forms, that the real social relationships were specifically disclosed'.[144] I would maintain that the 'deep formal qualities' of metadrama contain the seeds of resistance to a milieu of social authority corrupted by the possession and sale of information. Since the informer is both an agent of authority and a means by which that authority may be deconstructed, the dread of the informer works here as a floating variable in the equations of power between the author, the audience and the early modern authorities. This establishes a point of indeterminacy at the heart of the relationship between the author and the audience which is evolv-ing as a discourse of authority in the period. Resembling Polonius' arras, it obscures and complicates this relationship by interposing a sensibility woven of fear, self-interest and dangerous misinterpretation. Like the author's evil twin, the figure of the informer therefore informs the changing notion of authority at this crucial time in the cultural development of the nation. In an early modernity gripped by a sense of shifting authority, the authoritative voice of many play-texts is almost bound to draw fire (as does that of Jonson) from those whose personal interest lies in the preservation of their own interpretative right. Since the material power of this authority is concerned with the policing of representations of real situations and people, the conventional metadramatic apologetic here becomes an absolute necessity. But a further inscription of resistance to this indeterminate authority is to be found in the metadramatic structures and forms which explore its mutable and compromised nature.

Though informed by all previous writing on metadrama, this book adopts a strategy that is distinct from earlier readings, aiming to identify the formative ideas, conceptual structures and social forces that define these plays, reflecting on the operation of these pressures in the work of the two most prominent dramatists of the age. The reading of these social pressures has involved collating a mass of compelling if sometimes circumstantial evidence, and, like crime-scene DNA, fingerprints and witness accounts, such evidence relies upon the kinds of inferences I have drawn here. A reasonable accumulation of circumstantial evidence, however, allows us to corroborate one inference over another, and thus to assert it as a fact. Having no wish to be credulous over a supposed Foucauldian vision of the era, I have become increasingly convinced that authors' perception of the threat posed by informers is more significant than recent scholarship has credited. Such a perception may be partly due to contemporary authorial histrionics, but then perception is everything, and in this case the documentary facts tally with the weight of evidence offered by dramatic representation.

The seven modes of metadrama[145]

Metadrama may be defined as a dramatic mode which, either overtly or covertly, comments or reflects upon its own dramatic nature. As of 2016, *OED* has no entry for this but lists *metafiction* as 'fiction in which the author self-consciously alludes to the artificiality or literariness of a work by parodying or departing from novelistic conventions (esp. naturalism) and narrative techniques'. Metadrama's dynamic structures act upon an audience and suggest collective responses of various kinds; these constructions take many forms and I have formulated them into seven modes:

1. Self-reference (simple to complex)*
2. Frame narrative† – open
3. Frame narrative‡ – closed
4. Onstage audience of inner play
5. Onstage audience as representation of audience
6. Offstage audience foregrounded as such
7. Offstage audience constructed as other body

1. Self-reference – simple to complex

This refers only to specific forms of self-reference, since, in a sense, all of the following modes are obliquely self-referential. An example of this is in Francis Beaumont's *The Knight of the Burning Pestle* where the onstage audience are a constant reminder of both the dramatic nature of the exchange and the interpretative power of the real audience. This type of metadrama always reflects a reciprocal performativity in which the experience of reality is just as much a subject of comment as the drama which reflects it. Self-reference can be as simple as a mention of the author's name and as complex as a web of self-consciously theatrical allusions. There are many examples of this not covered in this book, and of these I would like to mention three. In William Stevenson's *Gammer Gurton's Needle* (1575) the character Diccon protests, 'I wold not for an hundred pound, this matter shuld be knowen, / That I am auctour of this tale, or haue abrode it blowen / Did ye not sweare ye wold be ruled, before the tale I tolde' (2.2). Diccon's anxiety about being held responsible for being the subversive 'auctour' of the tale is an example of metadramatic self-reference, as is the idea that someone might make a play of the material it presents:

> Here is a matter worthy glosynge
> Of Gammer Gurtons nedle losynge
> And a foule peece of warke,
> A man I thyncke myght make a playe
> And nede no worde to this they saye. (2.2)

---

* This includes intertextual and real-life reference which Hornby breaks down further into the categories 'citation, allegory, parody and adaptation'. I hold these to be both an aspect of mode 6 and an oblique form of complex self-reference.

† Can be on any scale from role-playing within the role to the full-blown play within the play.

‡ Ditto.

The vice character Ambidexter in Thomas Preston's *Cambises* (1569) addresses the audience self-referentially on a number of occasions, explaining his dubious actions –

> My name is Ambidexter. I signify one
> That with both hands finely can play [. . .]
> For while I mean with a souldier to be,
> Then give I a leap to Sisamnes the judge, –
> I dare avouch you shall his destruction see.[146]

Ambidexter is the personification of double-dealing and moral equivocation, but as an integral part of the motive force of the narrative, his voice nevertheless speaks with a curious and uncanny authority. He is co-author of the action as well as part of its cause; the play's theocentric narrative is centred on a fundamentally authoritative structure with which Ambidexter is complicit. He is also a character in his own right, speaking directly to the King: 'if it please your grace, O king, I heard him say, / For your death unto the God[s] day and night he did pray'.[147] Thus, shifting in and out of abstraction, Ambidexter slides effortlessly from one mode to another – he is a metadramatic metamorph, playing roles of audience, author and informer to the King. His is a role which gives a constant cast of self-referential metadrama to the play.

Shakespeare's *Anthony and Cleopatra* (1623) has Cleopatra lamenting her future representation in a way that would have resonance for any audience:

> the quick comedians
> Extemporally will stage us, and present
> Our Alexandrian revels; Antony
> Shall be brought drunken forth, and I shall see
> Some squeaking Cleopatra boy my greatness
> I' the posture of a whore. (5.2.214–21)

Such self-referentiality speaks of the inevitability and inherent ambiguity of dramatic representation. All of the plays we deal with here are more or less continuously self-referential.

2. Frame narrative – open

Open-ended frame narratives are often fairly loose structures that tend to invite the interpretation of the offstage audience. This is the case in Shakespeare's *Taming of the Shrew* (c.1590–4) in which

Christopher Sly simply disappears from the equation in the first Act after having been chastised by one of his attendants, 'My Lord you nod, you do not mind the play' (1.1.533). This gives the audience no sense of the closure of the narrative and leaves them with an ongoing sense of the performative in which no guidance is offered to their interpretation of the text.

Richard Edwards's *Damon and Pithias* (1564) contains an apologetic prologue, but no epilogue, in place of which are simple songs to Queen Elizabeth, expressing hope that she will have friends like Damon and Pithias. This leaves the audience with their own interpretations of the play in relation to the prologue's agenda and the ensuing characterisations of viewpoints, venal and otherwise. The eventual disappearance of Jonson's onstage audience in *The Staple of News* (1625) makes it also an open-ended frame narrative. The accessibility that this gives the offstage audience to the interpretation of the play backfires on Jonson in this case as his written response clearly demonstrates.[148] A frame narrative may of course be open at the beginning and closed at the end; depending on the content of the play, this will tend to close off the interpretative engagement of the audience.

3. Frame narrative – closed

This mode depends upon a clearer distinction between the outer and inner metadramatic frames in use. It often needs an explicit onstage audience in order to facilitate this clarity, as in Beaumont's *Knight of the Burning Pestle* (1607), where there is a recognisable onstage audience to the play as a whole. The result of this is to parody, or otherwise represent, the interpretative power of the audience. From their privileged position on the stage, the onstage audience is able to interject, interfere with the course of the narrative and shape the fates of the characters. This mode allows the author to frame the outer or inner narrative with propositions or suggestions as to the possible consequences of various interpretations. This is also found in the anonymous Elizabethan text *The Taming of a Shrew* (1594) in which Slie follows the pattern of the drunk in Edwards's *The Waking Mans Dreame* (1570), though in this case there is no anxiety about the resumption of the character's original role. He simply shrugs off the mantle of nobility and sees the episode as a lesson in taming a 'shrew'. The puppet show in *Bartholomew Fair* (1614) is also a frame narrative of this mode, though the narrative in that case provides no diegetic gravity and little scopic pulsion, leaving the focus firmly on the onstage audience.

One other application of this is the magic 'glass' convention as found, for instance, in Robert Greene's *Friar Bacon and Friar Bungay* (1594). In this case there is an inner drama which is the subject of the view of some of the characters, and the information from this is used to drive the narrative. Another convention relating to the frame narrative is the use of a masque in order to cover the activity of a threatening participant, as in Kyd's *Spanish Tragedy* (c.1582–92). In John Ford's *'Tis Pity She's a Whore* (1629) a masque provides an entry for Hippolyta who tries to poison Soranzo, her ex-lover, but is deceived and poisons herself (4.1.36–7). This creates potential connections between the offstage audience and the audience of the masque. In Thomas Middleton's *Women Beware Women* (c.1622), there is a metadramatic chess game reflecting the action above but not commenting on its significance.[149] In Philip Massinger's *A New Way to Pay Old Debts* (1625), Wellborn creates a whole aristocratic metadrama set up in order to defeat the meritocratic Vices Marall and Overreach and reinstate Wellborn in his rightful position (cf 2.2.32). In many of these cases the audience is in a position to know more than the characters about the structures in which they exist and by which they are defined. This dramatic irony is also potentially empowering to the offstage audience as it emphasises the dependence of the drama upon their interpretation. Closed frame narratives, however, can also include the use of both a prologue and epilogue to form apologetic barricades against unruly interpretations.

The effects of frame narratives depend on the level of open-endedness:

Interpretative consequences
Closed narratives may have dramatic consequences based on the interpretations of characters in the onstage audience. This may be used as an instructive for the offstage audience.

Allegorical dramatic consequences
The frame narrative, either closed or open, may provide an allegory for an element of the 'outer' narrative. The extent to which the frame narrative provides its own *gestalt* or closure may determine the level of integration between the two in terms of its importance to the workings of plot.

Actual dramatic consequences
In the case of an entirely open-ended frame narrative, the plots may become mixed and the sense of reality generated by the drama of the

outer frame is disrupted at the point that the 'inner' drama fails to close. This may result in a heightened sense of *theatrum mundi* in the outer narrative, and for those watching in the onstage and offstage audiences.

Audiences
Where there are onstage audiences, any frame narrative provides the possibility of interpretations of the audience response. This may be used as an allegory for the suggested response of the offstage audience. Actual consequences here take us into the realm of the material results of interpretation in a world fraught with danger for authors, especially authors dealing with contemporary social realities.

4. Onstage audience of inner play

This mode usually relates to closed frame narratives, such as the masque in Kyd's *Spanish Tragedy*, where the primary focus is on the inner play, or masque, itself and the audience is largely incidental as an interpretative force. This may apply also, however, on occasions where the closure of a framed narrative is ambiguous, for instance where one character continues on in the outer play, as does Caesar after killing Paris in Massinger's *The Roman Actor*.[150] This mode may shift into the following mode, depending on the extent to which the metadrama enables the reaction of the onstage audience to the inner narrative to be used by the author as a model either positive or negative, for the manipulation of the offstage audience.

5. Onstage audience as representation of audience

As mentioned above, Beaumont's *The Knight of the Burning Pestle* exemplifies this mode in which a primary focus of the metadrama is the onstage audience, rather than the inner drama. The offstage audience is thus overtly represented to itself and the subject held up for their interpretation is interpretation itself. This can be for narrative reasons as in *Hamlet* or for attempts at comedic self-reference as *Bartholomew Fair*'s puppet-show audience which provide an insulting parody of contemporary spectators. Offstage audience reaction to this is of course always unpredictable, but its use nevertheless can indicate a desire or need to attempt at least to manage the spectrum of possible reactions. Offering thus the very interpretative power of the audience for their own interpretation obviously has defensive value for the author, since it situates an audience within their own objectifying gaze. This process is only objectifying inasmuch as the audience accepts the representation offered, and the extent to which the representation shapes the response of the audience will depend largely upon the audience's sympathy with the characters. Beaumont's pushy citizens are certainly less objectionable than Jonson's onstage audience of gossips in *Staple of News*, which are an insulting parodic representation of the real audience. In this case their lack of intervention in the narrative gives the whole play the cast of an innerplay. As noted above their dissolution towards the end of the play is an equivocal move which does not pay off for Jonson. Another example of this is described in Chapter 2 here with *Every Man Out*'s choric 'Grex'.

6. Offstage audience foregrounded as such

This can be a defensive mechanism, as in Ben Jonson's elaborate induction to *Bartholomew Fair* or in the case of *Poetaster*, explored herein, where the character of the audience is called into question and the author offers choices between imitating either an audience which weeps for the misfortunes of men, or one which copies the lupine informer. In *The Knight of the Burning Pestle*, the offstage audience is appealed to in this mode in order to control their own mode 5 representation which is out of control (3.1.305–8). At this stage the offstage audience are very much aware, however, that the onstage audience are actors and that therefore they have no control over them. This has the effect of asserting the author's overall command of this representation. Onstage audiences may also rarely be foregrounded as such, but it is hard to imagine how this would not also work as a representation of the offstage audience.

7. Offstage audience constructed as other body

Often this other body is one or another kind of informer and again this mode may be used to highlight the dangers inherent in misinterpretation. In *The Roman Actor*, in the scene where Paris is on trial within the Senate, however, there is an instance where the offstage audience are watched by Caesar's soldiers for their reaction to an onstage torture-scene as if they too were potential traitors in the plot (3.2.48–50). In Middleton and Dekker's *The Roaring Girl* the audience are constructed at one point as a tapestry (1.2.14–30ff.). Again onstage audiences may also rarely be constructed in this way, but in any case this would be a version of mode 4.

The identification of these modes in the plays I am working with has been far from a simple task, since the character of early modern metadramatic production is one which shifts fluently from one mode to another, and often employs more than one mode at any given time in an overdetermination of dramatic strata. Although it would have become overly repetitive to enumerate the multiple modes in play at any given time, it seemed nevertheless appropriate to explain their operation, and I have done so in the hope that the taxonomy and the narrative might prove mutually complementary.

Notes

1. John Wilmot, *Rome Rhym'd to Death* (1683) <http://gateway.proquest .com/openurl?ctx_ver=Z39.88-2003&res_id=xri:eebo&rft_ id=xri:eebo:citation:12255983> (last accessed 2 November 2015).
2. Fischer and Greiner note that metadrama often emerges as 'an agency of action and reflection in the context of cultural conflict', citing 'the proliferation of the play within the play in the Volkstheater movement [. . .] where it was used to [. . .] subvert the idea of theatre as the property and domain of the ruling classes'. See Gerhard Fischer and Bernhard Greiner (eds), *The Play within the Play: The Performance of Meta-Theatre and Self-Reflection* (New York: Rodopi, 2007), p. xv. Note also Walsingham's personal subvention from the Crown for paying informers went from £750 in 1582 to £2,000 in 1585 and continued thus for some time, see Charles Nicholl, *The Reckoning* (London: Vintage, 1992), p. 125.
3. Lorna Hutson, 'Civility and Virility in Ben Jonson', *Representations*, Vol. 78, No. 1 (Spring 2002), pp. 1–27, 15.
4. Nicholl sketches the structure of such a system, describing an informer having secret recourse to Walsingham through the office of his second cousin Thomas, Marlowe's patron; see Nicholl, pp. 140, 265; Daphne Du Maurier, *Golden Lads: A Study of Anthony Bacon, Francis and Their Friends* (London: Gollancz, 1975).
5. Neale notes that in pursuit of this Essex's chamber was constantly 'full of suitors and sycophants'; see J. E. Neale, *Queen Elizabeth I* (London: Jonathan Cape, 1958), pp. 332–3. Nicholas Skeres, a notorious informer present at Marlowe's death, was one of these: Essex was his 'Lord and Master' according to evidence given in Star Chamber. See Nicholl, pp. 33–4.
6. Thomas Overbury, *Sir Thomas Ouerburie his wife with new elegies vpon his (now knowne) vntimely death* (1611), <http://gateway. proquest.com/openurl?ctx_ver=Z39.88-2003&res_id=xri:eebo&rft_ id=xri:eebo:citation:20234643> (last accessed 2 December 2015).

7. This perception is current also until at least 1682: see George Whitehead, *Judgment fixed upon the accuser of our brethren* (London: Andrew Sowle, 1682), <http://gateway.proquest.com/openurl?ctx_ver=Z39.88-2003& res_id=xri:eebo&rft_id=xri:eebo:citation:14582034> (last accessed 7 November 2015).

8. Anon., *The life and death of Griffin Flood informer Whose cunning courses, churlish manners, and troublesome informations, molested a number of plaine dealing people in this city of London. Wherein is also declared the murther of Iohn Chipperford Vinter, for twich fact the said Griffin Flood was pressed to death the 18. day of Ianuary last past* (London: [G. Eld] for I.T., 1623), <http://gateway.proquest.com/openurl?ctx_ ver=Z39.88-2003&res_id=xri:eebo&rft_id=xri:eebo:image:17716:10> (last accessed 16 February 2016), p. 1.

9. Ibid. p. 16.

10. Francis Lenton, *Characterismi: or, Lentons leasures* (London: I[ohn] B[eale] for Roger Michell, 1631), <http://gateway.proquest.com/openurl?ctx_ ver=Z39.88-2003&res_id=xri:eebo&rft_id=xri:eebo:image:9918:68> (last accessed 13 November 2015).

11. Joseph Hall, *Cases of conscience practically resolved* (1654), <http:// gateway.proquest.com/openurl?ctx_ver=Z39.88-2003&res_id= xri:eebo&rft_id=xri:eebo:citation:11415099> (last accessed 2 November 2015).

12. John Stephens, *Essayes and characters* (1615), <http://gateway.pro-quest.com/openurl?ctx_ver=Z39.88-2003&res_id=xri:eebo&rft_ id=xri:eebo:citation:99853040> (last accessed 10 October 2015).

13. George Fox, the dissenter and founder of the Religious Society of Friends, the Quakers, writes, 'He that is an Informer, is a Persecutor, and Spoiler, and a Destroyer; and the DEVIL is the Head of all Inform-ers'; see George Fox, *The devil was and is the old informer against the righteous* (London: Iohn Bringhurst, 1682), n.p. <http://gateway. proquest.com/openurl?ctx_ver=Z39.88-2003&res_id=xri:eebo&rft_ id=xri:eebo:citation:11327409> (last accessed 16 October 2015). Hutson mentions the writing demon Tutivillus whose own function it was, from around 1215 to 1530, to record the sins of believers; see Lorna Hutson, *The Invention of Suspicion: Law and Mimesis in Shakespeare and Renaissance Drama* (Oxford: Oxford University Press, 2007), pp. 22–30.

14. Thomas Nashe, *Haue with you to Saffron-Walden. Or, Gabriell Har-ueys hunt is up* (London: Iohn Danter, 1596), p. 106, <http://gateway. proquest.com/openurl?ctx_ver=Z39.88-2003&res_id=xri:eebo&rft_ id=xri:eebo:citation:99845702> (last accessed 23 November 2015).

15. See Nicholl, pp. 61–9.

16. There are exceptions (Griffin Flood, Richard Baines, Nicholas Skeres, Robert Poley, for instance; see note 8 here and Nicholl, pp. 32, 36, 54), but perception of this is also contemporary: 'No-body telleth strange newes, inuenteth lyes, disperceth libels, setteth friendes at varience,

and abuseth many millions: for when a priuie search is made for the authors, no-body is found to auoch the actions.' T.G., *The rich cabinet furnished with varietie of excellent discriptions, exquisite charracters, witty discourses, and delightfull histories, deuine and morrall* (London: I[ohn] B[eale] for Roger Iackson, 1616), p. 99.

17. As Banu says, whether or not a surveillance device may be reliable, 'it denounces, in a roundabout way, the motivations and identities of those who are putting it in place' ['il dénonce [. . .] de manière détournée, les motivations et les identités de ceux qui le mettent en place']; my translation. Georges Banu, *La Scène Surveillée* (Paris: Actes Sud, 2006), p. 79.

18. See G. R. Evans, *Problems of Authority in the Reformation Debates* (Cambridge: Cambridge University Press, 1992), pp. 37–8, 81–2. Also Robert Weimann, *Authority and Representation in Early Modern Discourse* (Baltimore: Johns Hopkins University Press, 1996), pp. 35–7.

19. Hutson, *The Invention of Suspicion*, pp. 7, 122, 127. She sees this as the basis for perceptions of depth in dramatis personae in Shakespeare and other late sixteenth-century writers.

20. See Joel Hurstfield (ed.), *The Reformation Crisis* (London: E. Arnold, 1961), p. 1. See also Appendix 2 of B. Angus, '"A hawk from a handsaw": Early Modern Metadrama and the Staging of the Informer', PhD thesis, University of Newcastle upon Tyne, 2006, for more information.

21. Francois Laroque, *The Show Within: Dramatic and Other Insets* (Montpellier: Publications de Université Paul-Valery, 1990), p. 42.

22. I use the term 'oversight' to mean 'seeing from a privileged position', with resonances of the related idea of supervision, not in its other sense of missing seeing something.

23. Hutson notes that at this time plays made 'greater use, in particular, of narration to convey (often misleading) accounts of unstaged events'; see *The Invention of Suspicion*, p. 106.

24. The term 'offstage' is borrowed from theatrical terminology to denote the house audience in its relation to those onstage.

25. John Day, *Isle of Guls* (London: Iohn Hodgets, 1606), n.p., <http://gateway. proquest.com/openurl?ctx_ver=Z39.88-2003&res_id=xri:eebo&rft_ id=xri:eebo:citation:99840846> (last accessed 2 November 2015).

26. See Robert Weimann, *Shakespeare and the Popular Tradition in the Theater*, ed. Robert Schwarz (Baltimore: Johns Hopkins University Press, 1987), p. xii.

27. John Harington, 'A Preface, or Rather a Briefe Apologie of Poetrie', *Orlando Furioso in English Heroical Verse* (London: 1591), sig. ii.

28. Ben Jonson, *Sejanus*, ed. Jonas Barish (New Haven, CT and London: Yale University Press, 1965), p. 16. For more evidence of the climate of fear and the gathering of intelligence in this era see the 1590 letter of Sir John Smythe to Lord Burghley in Curtis C. Breight, *Surveillance, Militarism and Drama in the Elizabethan Era* (Basingstoke: Macmillan, 1996), p. 265, n. 2.

29. George Chapman, *The Conspiracy and Tragedy of Byron*, ed. John Margeson (Manchester: Manchester University Press, 1988), p. 25.

30. Heidi Brayman Hackel, *Reading Material in Early Modern England: Print, Gender and Literacy* (Cambridge: Cambridge University Press, 2005), p. 124. Lynn S. Meskill, *Ben Jonson and Envy* (Cambridge: Cambridge University Press, 2009), pp. 79, 66.

31. Richard Brathwaite, *A strappado for the Diuell Epigrams and satyres alluding to the time, with diuers measures of no lesse delight* (1615), <http://gateway.proquest.com/openurl?ctx_ver=Z39.88-2003&res_id=xri:eebo&rft_id=xri:eebo:image:6650:4> (last accessed 19 October 2015).

32. Janet Clare, *"Art made tongue-tied by authority": Elizabethan and Jacobean Dramatic Censorship* (Manchester: Manchester University Press, 1999), p. 33.

33. Jonathan Dollimore, *Radical Tragedy: Religion, Ideology and Power in the Drama of Shakespeare and His Contemporaries* (Brighton: The Harvester Press, 1984), p. 24.

34. Richard Dutton, *Mastering the Revels* (Houndmills: Macmillan, 1991), p. 126.

35. Ibid. p. 8.

36. For example, Meskill, p. 86.

37. Dutton, *Mastering the Revels*, p. 59.

38. Ibid. pp. 119–22.

39. See Ethyn Williams Kirby, *William Prynne: A Study in Puritanism* (Cambridge, MA: Harvard University Press, 1931).

40. John Rushworth, *Historical Collections*, Vol. II (London: 1706), p. 293.

41. See Chapter 5.

42. Dutton, *Mastering the Revels*, pp. 193, 186.

43. Meskill, p. 80ff.

44. Ian Donaldson, *Ben Jonson, A Life* (Oxford: Oxford University Press, 2011), pp. 111–12, 114, 146.

45. Donaldson, p. 211.

46. Richard Dutton, *Licensing, Censorship and Authorship in Early Modern England* (Houndmills: Macmillan, 2000), p. 14.

47. See Donaldson, p. 71.

48. Daniel Featley, *Cygnea Cantio* (1625), <http://gateway.proquest.com/openurl?ctx_ver=Z39.88-2003&res_id=xri:eebo&rft_id=xri:eebo:citation:99855853> (last accessed 2 November 2015).

49. George Daniel, 'Idyllia: The Distemper', 'Idyll iii' (1646), *The poems of George Daniel, esq. of Beswick, Yorkshire (1616–1657)*, Vol. IV (Printed for private circulation, 1878), p. 229.

50. Meskill, p. 95.

51. Ibid. p. 101.

52. Maurice W. Beresford, 'The Common Informer, the Penal Statutes and Economic Regulation', *Economic History Review*, Vol. X (1958),

pp. 221–37, 232–3. See also G. R. Elton, *Policy and Police: The Enforcement of the Reformation in the Age of Thomas Cromwell* (Cambridge: Cambridge University Press, 1972). Nicholl calls them a 'shifting legion of freelancers', see p. 130.

53. Breight, p. 109. See also pp. 102ff., 105, 273, n. 13; 276, n. 22.

54. T.G., p. 133.

55. Daniel Tuvill, *The Dove and the Serpent* (London: 1614), p. 43.

56. Francis Beaumont, *The Woman-Hater*, in Fredson Bowers (ed.), *The Dramatic Works in the Beaumont and Fletcher Canon*, Vol. 1 (Cambridge: Cambridge University Press, 1966), pp. 168–9 (1.3.173–4, 178–80).

57. Andrew Gurr, 'Who is Lovewit? What is He?', in Richard Allen Cave, Elizabeth Schafer, Brian Woolland (eds), *Ben Jonson and Theatre: Performance, Practice, and Theory* (London: Routledge, 1999), p. 12.

58. Ben Jonson, *The Magnetic Lady*, ed. Helen Ostovich, in David Bevington, Martin Butler, Ian Donaldson (eds), *The Cambridge Edition of the Works of Ben Jonson*, Vol. 6 (Cambridge: Cambridge University Press, 2012).

59. See David Roberts, 'The Play within the Play and the Closure of Representation', in Fischer and Greiner (eds), p. 39.

60. Robert Greene describes a 'M. Informer, you that looke like a ciuile Citizen, or some handsome pettie fogger of the law' whom he says has 'as much slie knauerie in [his] side pouch [. . .] as woulde breede the confusion of forty honest men'. See Robert Greene, *A quip for an vpstart courtier* (London: Iohn Wolfe, 1592), <http://gateway.proquest.com/openurl?ctx_ver=Z39.88-2003&res_id=xri:eebo&rft_id=xri:eebo:citation:99841591> (last accessed 21 November 2015).

61. Nicholl, p. 125. Banu also points this out: 'surveillance, as everyone knows, is not free [. . .] it involves financial benefits'. ['la surveillance, chacun le sait, n'est pas gratuite [. . .] elle implique des retombées financiéres']; my translation; Banu, p. 55.

62. Beresford, p. 225.

63. *House of Commons Journal*, Vol. 1 [21 November 1606] (1802), *British History Online*, p. 170, <http://www.british-history.ac.uk> (last accessed 16 November 2015).

64. See Ben Jonson, *Poetaster*, ed. Tom Cain (Manchester: Manchester University Press, 1995) (5.3.48). Unless otherwise stated, all references to *Poetaster* are drawn from this edition.

65. Beresford, p. 230. See also pp. 223–4.

66. Nicholl, pp. 47–50.

67. William Shakespeare, *Much Ado about Nothing*, ed. Claire McEachern (London: Arden, 2006). Critics since Hazlitt have noted Dogberry's 'misprisions of meaning' (his substituting 'dissembly' for 'assembly' [4.2.1] for instance), and this is a further trait of the misusers of information; see p. 120.

68. Anon., *The life and death of Griffin Flood informer*, pp. 2–3.
69. Nicholl, p. 135.
70. Meskill points out that Jonson takes care to differentiate himself from the malicious interpreter in his prefatory poem to the Shakespeare First Folio; see Meskill, pp. 36–9ff.
71. Catherine Keane, *Figuring Genre in Roman Satire* (Oxford: Oxford University Press, 2006), p. 79.
72. T.G., pp. 116–17.
73. For John Donne's concern to distinguish his own role from those of the 'fondling motley humorist' and the informer, see Joshua Scodel, '"None's Slave": Some Versions of Liberty in Donne's Satires 1 and 4', *English Literary History*, Vol. 72, No. 2 (Summer, 2005), pp. 363–85, 371–2ff.
74. See Jonson, *Poetaster* (4.7.9–10).
75. Day, n.p.
76. Ibid. n.p.
77. William Winstanley, *Lives of the Most Famous English Poets* (Samuel Manship: 1687), p. 124.
78. Thomas Nabbs, *Covent-Garden* (London: R. Oulton, 1639), <http://gateway.proquest.com/openurl?ctx_ver=Z39.88-2003&res_id=xri:eebo&rft_id=xri:eebo:citation:99848292> (last accessed 12 December 2015).
79. Hutson, 'Civility', p. 14.
80. Cited in Jonson, *Poetaster*, p. 41.
81. For further discussion of the fit between metadrama and surveillance in European theatre, see Banu.
82. Public Records Office, *Privy Council Registers*, PC2/14/381 [29 June 1587].
83. Nicholl, pp. 111, 121ff. See also John Michael Archer, *Sovereignty and Intelligence: Spying and Court Culture in the English Renaissance* (Stanford: Stanford University Press, 1993), pp. 69, 92ff.
84. Skeres, sometime Essex's informer, was also there. Marlowe was arrested in September 1589 following a brawl in which Thomas Watson killed one William Bradley; Watson was both poet and informer; see Nicholl, pp. 30, 209ff.
85. See Donaldson, pp. 112, 114; Jonson, *Poetaster*, p. 19.
86. See Helen Ostovich (ed.), *Ben Jonson, Four Comedies* (London: Longman, 1997), p. 12; Archer, p. 26; David Riggs, *The World of Christopher Marlowe* (London: Faber and Faber, 2004), p. 155; R. Warwick Bond, *The Complete Works of John Lyly*, Vol. 1 (Oxford: Clarendon Press, 1902), p. 14; Du Maurier, pp. 60, 64, 71, 97–8. Also Father Thomas Wright – very possibly the converter of Jonson to Catholicism at Newgate in 1598 – was himself a 'loyalist informer', see Donaldson, p. 139.
87. Ben Jonson, *Volpone, or The Fox*, ed. R. B. Parker (Manchester: Manchester University Press, 1999), p. 9. Unless otherwise noted all references herein are to this text.

88. Michael Wood, *In Search of Shakespeare* (London: BBC Books, 2003), p. 69.

89. E. K. Chambers, *The Elizabethan Stage*, Vol. 3 (Oxford: Clarendon, 1923), p. 445.

90. Francis Meres, 'Poetrie; Poets; and A Comparatiue discourse of our English Poets, with the Greeke, Latine, and Italian Poets', in *Palladis Tamia Wits Treasury* (London: P. Short, 1598), <http://gateway. proquest.com/openurl?ctx_ver=Z39.88-2003&res_id=xri:eebo&rft_ id=xri:eebo:citation:99845635> (last accessed 13 December 2015).

91. Ben Jonson, *The Case is Altered* (London: Nicholas Okes, 1609), <http://gateway.proquest.com/openurl?ctx_ver=Z39.88-2003&res_ id=xri:eebo&rft_id=xri:eebo:citation:99844834> (last accessed 18 November 2015).

92. Nicholl, pp. 376–80, 382.

93. To be precise, *OED* gives the dates involved for instances of this usage as 1384 and 1784.

94. *OED* lists 1783 as the earliest occurrence, however, *The Character of an informer* (1675) confirms the synonymous nature of *informer* and *informant* as current over a century earlier. See Anon., *The Character of an informer wherein his mischeivous nature, and leud practises are detected* (London: T.P., 1675), p. 4, <http://gateway. proquest.com/openurl?ctx_ver=Z39.88-2003&res_id=xri:eebo&rft_ id=xri:eebo:citation:15564016> (last accessed 14 December 2015). Fox's 1683 reference, noted above, is more specific where he explains, 'the DEVIL is the Head of all Informers'.

95. Joseph Glanvill uses it in this way in 1661: 'the matter can be actuated at once but by a single Informant'. See Joseph Glanvill, *The Vanity of Dogmatising* [1661] (Hildesheim: Georg Olms Verlag, 1970), pp. xvi, 153.

96. Though principally attuned to later times, E. P. Thompson's observations hold true here: that popular attitudes towards crime have at times amounted to a tacit code in which some crimes were 'actively condoned by whole communities – coining, poaching, the evasion of taxes', and that although several crimes were prohibited by both codes, 'only the most hardened criminal was held in as much popular odium as the informer'. See E. P. Thompson, *The Making of the English Working Class* (London: Penguin, 1968), pp. 64–6.

97. Circa 1374.

98. See *OED*: 'a. L. *augur*, earlier *auger*; perh. f. *av-is* bird + -*gar*, connected with *garrire* to talk, *garrulus* talkative, and Skr. *gar* to shout, call, show, make known; but Fick would derive it from *augēre* to increase, promote'.

99. Seán Burke (ed.), *Authorship from Plato to the Postmodern* (Edinburgh: Edinburgh University Press, 1995), p. xviii.

100. Quentin Skinner, *Forensic Shakespeare* (Oxford: Oxford University Press, 2015), pp. 251–2.

101. John Bakeless, *The Tragicall History of Christopher Marlowe* (Cambridge, MA: Harvard University Press, 1942), p. 160.

102. Thomas Nashe, *Haue with you to Saffron-Walden. Or, Gabriell Harueys hunt is up*, in R. B. McKerrow (ed.), *The Works of Thomas Nashe*, Vol. III (Oxford: Basil Blackwell, 1958), p. 122.

103. Faithful Teate, *The uncharitable informer charitably informed, that sycophancy is a sin, pernicious to all, but most of all to himself* (Dublin: William Bladen, 1660), p. 52, <http://gateway. proquest.com/openurl?ctx_ver=Z39.88-2003&res_id=xri:eebo&rft_ id=xri:eebo:citation:99868810> (last accessed 12 November 2015).

104. See extract from Lupold von Wedel, *Journey through England and Scotland* [1584–5], trans. Gottfried von Bulow, in Russ McDonald (ed.), *The Bedford Companion to Shakespeare* (Boston: Bedford Books, 1996), pp. 226–7.

105. Though also, he concedes, 'a necessarie member in a State to bee usde to cut off vnnecessarie members'. See Nashe, *Saffron-Walden*, p. 106, <http://gateway.proquest.com/openurl?ctx_ver=Z39.88-2003&res_ id=xri:eebo&rft_id=xri:eebo:citation:99845702> (last accessed 12 November 2015).

106. Sir Thomas Overbury, *New and choice characters* (1615), n.p. <http:// gateway.proquest.com/openurl?ctx_ver=Z39.88-2003&res_id=xri: eebo&rft_id=xri:eebo:image:25104:55> (last accessed 9 December 2015).

107. S. J. Houston, *James I* (London and New York: Longman, 1995), p. 27.

108. Stephens, *Essayes and characters*, n.p.

109. For wolf imagery for malicious and envious informers in Jonson, Spenser and Sidney, see Ben Jonson, *Poetaster*, p. 43.

110. Anon., *The Character of an informer*, p. 4.

111. Ibid. p. 5.

112. Overbury, *New and choice characters*, n.p.

113. Aristophanes, *The Birds*, lines 1422–55, <http://perseus.uchicago. edu/perseus-cgi/citequery3.pl?dbname=GreekTexts&getid=1&query =Ar.%20Av.%201410> (last accessed 15 November 2015).

114. Stephens, *Essayes and characters*, n.p.

115. ['Il n'y à pas de surveillance sans l'imminence d'une conséquence. Elle n'est jamais gratuite']; my translation. Banu, p. 21.

116. Raymond Williams, *Culture* (Glasgow: Collins, 1981), p. 142.

117. Meskill speaks of such scripting as a protective 'imported "objection"' in pursuit of a poetic sanctuary: Meskill, pp. 112ff., 124.

118. For insight into these and related issues, see Linda Charnes, *Notorious Identity: Materializing the Subject in Shakespeare* (Cambridge, MA and London: Harvard University Press, 1993), p. 128ff; and Anne Higgins, 'Streets and Markets', in John D. Cox and David Scott Kastan (eds), *A New History of Early English Drama* (New York: Columbia University Press, 1997), p. 92ff.

119. This relates to Lacan's concept of *méconnaissance*. Alan Sheridan, translator of Lacan's *Four Fundamental Concepts of Psycho-Analysis*, put this as 'failure to recognize' or 'misconstruction'. See Alan Sheridan, 'Translator's Note', in Jacques Lacan, *Écrits: A Selection* (New York: Norton, 1977), p. xi. Lacan himself aligned it with *scotoma* (a blind spot) in his description of the *mirror stage*. See 'The Mirror Stage as Formative of the Function of the I', in Lacan, *Écrits*, pp. 93–100.

120. See William Nelles, *Frameworks: Narrative Levels and Embedded Narrative* (New York: Lang, 1997), p. 155.

121. W. B. Worthen, *Shakespeare and the Force of Modern Performance* (Cambridge: Cambridge University Press, 2003), p. 12.

122. Ben Jonson is particularly exercised with this and evidence of its persistence may be found in the prologue to Shackerley Marmion's *A Fine Companion* (1633).

123. Weimann, *Shakespeare and the Popular Tradition*, p. 80ff.

124. Ibid. p. 212.

125. Harry Berger Jr, 'The Prince's Dog: Falstaff and the Perils of Speech-Prefixity', *Shakespeare Quarterly*, Vol. 49, No.1 (Spring, 1998), pp. 40–73, 49.

126. Ibid. p. 50.

127. Lionel Abel, *Tragedy and Metatheatre: Essays on Dramatic Form* (New York: Holmes and Meier, 2003), see p. 10ff.

128. Ibid.

129. Richard Hornby, *Drama, Metadrama and Perception* (London: Associated University Presses, 1986), p. 35.

130. See Peter Milward, S.J., *Shakespeare's Meta-Drama: Othello and King Lear* (Tokyo: Renaissance Institute, 2003).

131. James L. Calderwood, *Shakespearean Metadrama: The Argument of the Play in Titus Andronicus, Love's Labour's Lost, Romeo and Juliet, A Midsummer Night's Dream, and Richard II* (Minneapolis: University of Minnesota Press, 1971), p. 53.

132. Jacques Derrida, *Memoirs of the Blind: The Self-Portrait and Other Ruins*, trans. Pascale-Anne Brault and Michael Naas (Chicago: University of Chicago Press, 1993), p. 68.

133. Charnes, p. 129.

134. Jacques Lacan, *The Seminar, Book XI, The Four Fundamental Concepts of Psychoanalysis*, trans. Alan Sheridan (New York: Norton, 1981), pp. 72–3ff.

135. Jean-Paul Sartre, *Being and Nothingness: An Essay on Phenomenological Ontology*, trans. Hazel E. Barnes (London: Methuen, 1958), p. 256.

136. Ibid. p. 257.

137. Lacan, however, refuses the 'fundamental connection' with the Other that this implies, and instead 'conceives of an antinomic relation between the gaze and the eye: the eye which looks is that of the subject, while the gaze is on the side of the object and there is no coincidence

between the two'; see Dylan Evans, *Dictionary of Lacanian Psycho-analysis* (Hove and New York: Brunner-Routledge, 2003), p. 72.

138. For Lacan, the gaze precedes the eye and 'is presented to us in the form of a strange contingency [. . .] as the thrust of our experience namely, the lack that constitutes castration anxiety'. See Lacan, pp. 72–3.

139. Dylan Evans, p. 72.

140. Anthony B. Dawson and Paul Yachnin, *The Culture of Playgoing in Shakespeare's England* (Cambridge: Cambridge University Press, 2001), pp. 101–5. Yachnin also identifies a 'visual field' in this context, p. 82.

141. Cited in Wes Folkerth, *The Sound of Shakespeare* (London: Routledge, 2002), p. 78. See Bruce R. Smith, *The Acoustic World of Early Modern England: Attending to the O-Factor* (Chicago: University of Chicago Press, 1999).

142. Sigmund Freud, *Civilization and its Discontents*, trans. J. Riviere (London: Hogarth Press, 1930), p. 90.

143. Williams, p. 142.

144. Ibid. p. 158.

145. Hornby notes five types:
    1. The play within the play
    2. The ceremony within the play
    3. Role-playing within the role
    4. Literary and real-life reference
    5. Self-reference

    Of these I have incorporated types 3 and 4 into my taxonomy, since 3 is an interesting variation of 1, and 4 is a subtle sub-category of 5. Types 1 and 5 are the most obvious from a performance point of view; the distinction between 1 and 2 I hold too fine to be useful for this study. See Hornby, p. 32.

146. Thomas Preston, *Cambises, King of Percia*, in J. Q. Adams (ed.), *Chief Pre-Shakespearean Drama* (Cambridge, MA: Riverside Press, 1924), pp. 150–1, 154–6.

147. Preston, pp. 676–7.

148. A more modern version of this is to be found in Bertholdt Brecht, *Caucasian Chalk Circle* (London: Methuen, 1963).

149. See also (4.2.159) and (5.2.50).

150. See Bill Angus, 'The Roman Actor, Metadrama, Authority, and the Audience', *Studies in English Literature 1500–1900*, Vol. 50, No. 2 (Spring 2010), pp. 445–64.

Chapter 1

Hamlet's 'lawful espials': Metadrama, Tainted Authority and the Ubiquitous Informer

One like the vnfrequented Theater
Walkes in darke silence, and vast solitude,
Suited to those blacke fancies which intrude,
Vpon possession of his troubled breast
[. . .] he is a malecontent:
A Papist? no, nor yet a Protestant,
But a discarded intelligencer.

(Edward Guilpin, *Skialetheia*, 1598)[1]

Like Elsinore's power structures, *Hamlet*'s metadramatic devices are entirely suffused with the figure of the informer, the plotter and the tale-bearer. Claudius, Polonius, Gertrude, Ophelia, Rosencrantz and Guildenstern, Horatio and Hamlet himself are examples. Even old Hamlet carries the mark of these diseased structures of authority; as Derrida has said, the ghost is 'third party and witness' to his own murder.[2] He is the disembodied informer to his own theatrical homicide. The duplicitous atmosphere which this informing generates is so integral to the movement of the play's narrative that it becomes if not quite invisible then transparent: a facilitation. It is also so much the very air that Denmark breathes that it generates a way of seeing whose vicious nature is obscured by its own corruption, and whose 'espials' are both assertively 'lawful' and ubiquitous (F: 3.1.32).[3] Here, informing functions as a tragic social *hamartia* which the play projects from the personal experience of its protagonist onto the world of the whole court, and beyond this onto the authority-structures of Elizabethan England. The 'something rotten' in the state of Denmark is not merely the King, its most visible manifestation, but more so it is the corruption of the moral authority of the Danish state itself, perpetrated by murderous ambition and manifested in its reliance on structures of informing. It is not Claudius' delegitimising crime that finally brings down the Danish court, but the very mechanisms of his maintenance of power, excessively exercised via poison, poisonous words and poisoned swords. Conversely, however, Hamlet's own supposed *hamartia*, traditionally his vacillation and consequent procrastination, arises in fact from a reluctance to submit to the role offered in the system of murderous surveillance that surrounds him. Hamlet's refusal to assimilate, however, does not preclude him replicating some of the offending authority structures in his desire to write his own legitimate part, and he thus extends the continuum of onstage informers, plotters and tale-bearers, to include the onstage author. In doing so, he locates in himself the conjunction between informing and metadrama. Noting, with Weimann, his debt to 'the *platea* tradition of the Vice',[4] Hamlet takes the self-consciousness of that tradition to a much more complex level, becoming, as Richard Fly says, 'the first stage figure with an acute awareness of what it means to be staged'.[5] This metadramatic self-awareness extends throughout the play, and is often correlated with structures of interpretative authority which have been poisoned by informing. The effect is to subvert such 'sterile' authority at an ideological level, but also to offer that very subversion to the offstage audience's critique, with mortal warnings attached.[6]

The potential for theatre audiences to include informers, as the introduction outlines, is of interest in this case, and equally of significance is the audience's competence to understand theatrical cues and devices. The boundaries between the early modern theatre and its audience were porous. At the margins of the well-known acting companies, and in audiences it is safe to assume, were numbers of those who had been, or would like to have been, company-members themselves. Stephen Gosson's *Schoole of Abuse* (1579) alludes to some such hangers-on, decrying 'the pryde of [players'] [. . .] shadowes (I meane those hangebyes whome they soccour with stipend)', those who cause players to be 'il talked of abroade'.[7] What exactly these 'hangebyes' might do for their 'stipend' (which, Gosson tells us, may stand at six shillings a week) is not obvious, but there is more than a hint of patronage detectable in this description of the relationship between these 'shadowes' and their 'il talked of' patrons. The exact cause of their 'pryde' is not made clear, though its effect in terms of outward appearances is noted: 'the very hyerlings of some of our Players [. . .] iet vnder Gentlemens noses in sutes of silke, exercising themselues too prating on the stage, and common scoffing when they come abrode'.[8] Greene's *Groats-worth of witte* (1592) describes 'an Arch-plaimaking-poet' who had 'his boy [. . .] beside retainers in sundry other places'.[9] Greene continues,

> His companie were lightly the lewdest person in the land, apt for pilferie, periurie, forgerie, or any villany [. . .] by these he learnd the legerdemaines of nips, foystes, connicatchers, crosbyters, lifts, high Lawyers, and all the rabble of that vncleane generation of vipers: and pithily could he paint out their whole courses of craft.[10]

Not only could he thus 'paint out their whole courses of craft' in his plays but significantly for present purposes, this reflects on his own character: 'So cunning he was in all craftes, as nothing rested in him almost but craftines.'[11] The author is very much a part of the dubious world he depicts. Even in this hyperbole, the picture of a thriving, boisterous, chaotic and morally dubious theatrical scene, based in and around the theatre environs, is compelling, and its self-awareness helps us to understand, for instance, Jonson's readiness to present such a heavily metadramatic play as *Poetaster*. The constant allusions made to the processes of drama and the dangers of venal interpretation in many plays only make sense if a significant element of the audience has experience in this area also. Furthermore, Greene's parallel between 'nips, foystes, connicatchers, crosbyters, lifts' (deceivers all), and 'high Lawyers', as the poet's companions, is illuminating: linking them together as an 'uncleane generation of vipers' suggests the areas of common practice between the author, the legal authorities and illegitimate self-interest outlined previously.

Exploring such self-interest, Harold Jenkins recalls the argument that audiences may have contained note-takers attempting to copy the substance of the performance, possibly later utilising the memories of cast-off actors to reconstruct the play in order to sell it on.[12] Though such 'memorial reconstruction' is now disputed, Thomas Dekker's *Gul's Horne-booke* (1609) seems to hint towards something akin to this, describing how 'your groundling and gallery-commoner buys his sport by the penny, and, like a haggler, is glad to utter it again by retailing'.[13] *OED* defines contemporaneous senses of 'retailing' as both 're-telling' and 're-selling' and thus Dekker's parodic audience seems to be involved in financially-motivated gathering and distribution of information. In this case, his assertion that, 'Your gallant, your courtier, and your captain had wont to be the soundest paymasters [. . .] are still the surest chapmen and [. . .] deal upon this comical freight by the gross' suggests at least a dig at the general commodification of the patronage system and its reliance on informers.[14]

This perception of the audience as both theatrically aware and disposed to the retailing of information is seen in *Hamlet*'s metadramatic core, my starting point in showing the ways in which metadrama links structures of authority with a dominant culture of informing. This begins with the entry of Rosencrantz and Guildenstern and the revelation of their status as both actors and informers, living in the 'secret parts of Fortune', with allusion to the Fortune Theatre, as 'her privates' (2.2.229–30).[15] The bawdy cast of this exchange serves as a distraction from the subtle heightening of the metadramatic tone of the play that occurs at this point. Hamlet responds, 'In the secret parts of Fortune? O, most true – she is a strumpet. What news?' (2.2.230–1) and Rosencrantz's response, in the same jovial register, 'None, my lord, but the world's grown honest' (2.2.232–3), is a humorous attempt to change the topic and deflect Hamlet from thinking any further about the 'secret parts' that he and Guildenstern are there to play. Hamlet, refusing to be distracted from his desire to find out why these two old school friends have suddenly become interested in his mental state, plays on the connection this seemingly simple metadramatic self-reference makes between informing and acting as he insists, 'You were sent for, and there is a kind of confession in your looks, which your modesties have not craft enough to colour' (2.2.244–6). With some determination, he gets them to admit, partially at least, to these roles, telling Rosencrantz and Guildenstern his thoughts (but not his purpose) so that their 'secrecy to the King and Queen moult no feather' (2.2.260–1). The bird-related imagery here may not be accidental, recalling abundant contemporary metaphors for predatory informers, as these old friends-turned-'legal espials', act their 'secret parts' upon Claudius' instigation.

The King's suspicion that Hamlet knows something which has the potential to disturb the equilibrium of his state and his personal safety necessitates appropriate action, and this requires information. Far from being an egregious need, this is fundamental to the operation of power; 'all political authority may be defined by its wide-eyed gaze, eager for intelligence', as Banu has noted.[16] The information Claudius so badly needs, however, is that to which the audience is already privy, and there must be a moment of recognition here that this is a very desirable position to occupy. To possess information which a patron, or government, would pay handsomely for is both a fantasy of wealth and influence of the age and a reality for some.

This may provide some sympathy, in an early modern audience, for Rosencrantz and Guildenstern, even though they are aware that these actor-informers plot to betray their old friend. Their services are certainly not rendered gratis, though both Rosencrantz and Guildenstern suggest that they might have been, had Claudius and Gertrude put their 'dread pleasures more into command / Than to entreaty' (2.2.28–9). As informers, they have in fact been assured that they will 'receive such thanks / As fits a king's remembrance' (2.2.25–6) and, given the potentially vast sums informers could make from their trade at this time, any other incentivising response from these royals would have seemed implausible. Also, when Rosencrantz and Guildenstern are asked by Claudius to watch Hamlet, in order to, 'draw him on to pleasures and to gather [. . .] / Whether aught to us unknown afflicts him thus / That opened lies within our remedy' (2.2.15, 16–18), the original audience may imagine exactly what Claudius' idea of a 'remedy' for Hamlet's affliction might be, the understated language used merely adding to its sinister nature. When Guildenstern prays, 'Heavens make [. . .] our practices / Pleasant and helpful to him' (2.2.38–9), the early modern audience should catch the contemporaneous senses of 'stratagems', 'treachery', 'wiles' and 'deceits' that the seemingly innocuous term 'practices' also carried.[17] The audience will be further aware that their initial report back to Claudius and Gertrude is somewhat augmented, in accord with common depictions of informing at the time, though the informers do confess that they do not find Hamlet 'forward to be sounded' (3.1.7). When he hears of the arrival of the players and Hamlet's intention to have a play presented, the King again instructs Rosencrantz and Guildenstern to act as agents provocateurs, to 'give him a further edge / And drive his purpose into these delights' (3.1.26–7) and they are thus given royal authority to shape the circumstances of a metadrama of Hamlet's design upon which they will later be asked to report. The audience are positioned throughout by the play's metadrama to be critically aware of these equivocations and anomalies, and are thus afforded a growing vision of the compromised nature of Denmark's structures of authority, whose mechanisms they might equally recognise closer to home.

Though not quite as well-informed as the audience, Hamlet's suspicion that the two have been set to inform upon him means that their exchanges continually explore connections between acting, informing and the nature of authority. As he establishes the superiority of his perspective over those of the informers, Hamlet also establishes his own moral authority over that of the compromised system, and by metadramatic self-reference makes this plain for the audience both to see and share in. The dynamics of Hamlet's authority may be seen in the transition from the deflective 'confession' which he makes to Rosencrantz and Guildenstern, through the authorial 'what a piece of work is a man' speech, and into his directorship of the players. These, Rosencrantz and Guildenstern have overtaken on the road, or 'coted [. . .] on the way' (2.2.283), as we are told. Again the associated imagery is significant here; Jenkins glosses 'coted' as a metaphor from coursing, 'in which one dog is said to cote, or run ahead of, another'.[18] This canine imagery would appear to an early modern audience as part of a familiar metaphorical set of signifiers depicting informers as simultaneously voracious and fawning, and here it is applied equally to the players and to Rosencrantz and Guildenstern, obviously reflecting negatively upon them. In contrast, when Hamlet later praises Horatio he is careful to distinguish these praises from fawning, 'where thrift may follow' (3.2.58), 'thrift' meaning 'profit', demonstrating his moral superiority over those driven by greed or ambition.

Although tainted by these associations, the players seem delightful to Hamlet as he fantasises a theatrical ideal offering both a contrast to his own inaction and a rebuke to the duplicity of the characters he is addressing. In this highly metadramatic context, Rosencrantz mentions that the visiting players are out of favour in the city because of 'an eyrie of children, little eyases' (F: 2.2.337), baby hawks or falcons, who 'are now the fashion' (F: 2.2.339).[19] These child actors are here characterised as birds of prey crying out 'on the top of question' (F: 2.2.338) that is, as Jenkins has it 'with the maximum of contention.'[20] However one dates this contentious passage, it is nevertheless a directly metadramatic reference to other concurrent drama, and is concerned with the representation of authority, poetic or otherwise.[21] The allusion to these issues may be intended to link debates over poetic authority with the venality of informers like Rosencrantz and Guildenstern.[22] The 'eyases'' aggressive predatory behaviour is also something in which the wider community surrounding the theatres is implicated, as Rosencrantz informs us, 'the nation holds it no sin to tar them to controversy' (F: 2.2.350–1). In Shakespeare's usage, to 'tar' is to incite dogs to fight.[23] Reference to 'the nation' here creates an indirect metadramatic mode in which the audience are foregrounded yet displaced, generating a potential critical distance between the present audience and those perceived as 'the nation'; a subtle audience-construction which allows for a gentle self-critique. Whatever social disruption 'the late innovation' of

F: 2.2.331 connects these child actors to, their characterisation as 'little eyases' places them within a field of imagery which links acting with predation.[24] This is seen again where Hamlet asks Rosencrantz and Guildenstern 'why do you go about to recover the wind of me, as if you would drive me into a toil?' (3.2.338–9), accusing them explicitly of predatory manoeuvres against him, with imagery again drawn from hawking. In Hamlet's mind the response to this news is to associate the children's behaviour with the shifting nature of authority: 'It is not strange, for my uncle is King of Denmark, and those that would make mouths at him while my father lived give twenty, forty, an hundred ducats apiece for his picture in little' (F: 2.2.359–62). An authority which is so transient cannot be one that derives its legitimacy from a stable source, and thus Hamlet's imagined ideal offers an unflattering contrast with the real nature of authority in Denmark, which is based on treachery and predation and which the offstage audience should increasingly perceive.

Hamlet's metadrama also addresses the fact of authority as exercised in the theatre, and that the fear of misrepresentation between authors and audiences at the time cut both ways.[25] This echoes in Hamlet's warning to Polonius about the players: 'let them be well used, for they are the abstracts and brief chronicles of the time. After your death you were better have a bad epitaph than their ill report while you lived' (F: 2.2.519–22). There is some irony in Hamlet requesting this of Polonius, since just as Claudius has set Rosencrantz and Guildenstern to report upon Hamlet so also Polonius has commanded Reynaldo 'to make inquire' (2.1.3ff.) of Laertes, giving him detailed instructions in the Machiavellian subtleties of information-gathering, including lying about his conduct in order to find out the truth of his actions, and remaining incognito (2.1.1–72). Defamatory representation is also implied in the avian metonymy of the metadramatic statement that 'many wearing rapiers are afraid of goose-quills and dare scarce come thither' (F: 2.2.341–2). Two derogatory usages of this term are both attributable to Nashe, firstly in *The vnfortunate traueller* (1594) where he refers to 'goosequil braccahadocheos'[26] and secondly in *Summers last will and testament* (1600): 'Bowles, cards and dice, you are the true liberal sciences, Ile ne're be Goose-quil, gentlemen, while I liue.'[27] Relating an author's dangerous tool of expression to the goose makes an uncomfortable fit, but a fit all the same, with Jonson's, and many others', metaphors of informers as talkative or predatory birds: parrots, canaries, magpies, lapwings, rooks, ravens and hawks.[28] Both Hamlet, in author-director mode, and the players are included in this avian imagery when he suggests

that together they should go 'to't like French falconers – fly at anything we see' (F: 2.2.429). Since, in the prevailing climate of informing, authors and actors had to be extremely careful of what or whom
they might be perceived to 'fly at', this expresses the reckless nature
of Hamlet's madness.[29] It also expresses the potential for similarity
in the roles of author and informer which the audience will shortly
witness in the metadrama of the inner-play.

It is when the players arrive that Hamlet, alluding to outward
'show', declares famously that he knows 'a hawk from a handsaw'
(F: 2.2.377), and this relates to a later usage where he is instruct-
ing the players in the art of acting and gives them a piece of advice
whose source is Quintilian: 'do not saw the air too much with your
hand, thus' (3.2.4–5).[30] This reflects a general concern Shakespeare
has with bad actors.[31] This is then employed as wordplay in punning
on the typical contemporary prey of royal hawking, the heron, or
'hernshaw'.[32] To know a 'hawk from a handsaw' is therefore both
to know an informer from his prey and to know an informer from a
mere bad player, and it is thus significant that this statement is made
to Rosencrantz and Guildenstern, who are both informers and defective actors, in the presence of the players he later instructs. Hamlet,
it seems, wants us (and possibly them) to know that when the wind
blows in the right direction he still has the discernment to detect
the serious political motivations behind mere outward show.[33] This
is clearly an appealing perspective to offer to an audience who are
considering their own response to the various perspectives afforded
on all of this, ranging from that of the resistant victim of informing
to those of accessories to the whole predatory business.

Other imagery used of informers here plays on the eye and ear.
Literal violence against the ear is significant most obviously in that
the old Hamlet is killed by a 'leperous distilment' being administered
'in the porches of [his] ears' (1.5.63–4), but this is also an apt analogy for a negative use of heard, or overheard, information.[34] For
instance, when Polonius, the King's chief informer and proxy, arrives
just after the actors, Hamlet says to Rosencrantz and Guildenstern, 'Hark you, Guildenstern, and you too – at each ear a hearer'
(2.2.318–19) such 'hearers' would then include each of Polonius,
Rosencrantz and Guildenstern. This alludes both to their common
office as informers and to the ubiquity of informing at even the very
highest levels. When Horatio admits his own 'truant disposition',
Hamlet is quick to ask him not to 'do my ear that violence / To
make it truster of your own report / Against yourself (1.2.169–72).
Graham Holderness relates the ear-administered poison to the 'false

reports' with which Rumour wishes to stuff the ears of the audience in *2 Henry IV*, though he identifies Hamlet's concern with 'forged process' as a reference to 'historical reconstruction' rather than the everyday lived reality of life under a tainted authority.[35] Lady Macbeth is just such a poisonous informing authority as she asks the vacillating Macbeth to come, 'That I may pour my spirits in thine ear, / And chastise with the valour of my tongue / All that impedes thee' (1.5.25–8).[36] The ghost of old Hamlet himself also claims that 'the whole ear of Denmark / Is by a forged process of my death / Rankly abused' (1.5.35–7), and the correction of this reported misinformation forms the imperative for much of the narrative of the play; with the exception of Claudius, this casts the rest of the characters, whether informers or not, as receivers of false information. The source of this false information is of course Claudius.

Sight is also used in *Hamlet* as a vehicle to describe authority, surveillance and the presence of the informer, a 'frequent metonymy for the royal presence', as Jenkins says.[37] Elizabeth's 'penetrating sight in discovering every man's ends and drifts', as Francis Bacon termed it, significantly involved the proxy vision of informers.[38] At the beginning of the play, Claudius orders Hamlet to remain 'in the cheer and comfort of our eye' (1.2.116). For obvious practical reasons this metonymy extends beyond the physical scope of the King's eyesight; the implication being that he has 'eyes' everywhere, one of which is the 'politic' watcher Polonius. When Polonius denies to the King looking at Ophelia and Hamlet's relationship 'with idle sight' (F: 2.2.135), he implies the 'sight' that he has applied to it is active and purposeful, as that of a good statesman and informer should be. Ophelia's description of Hamlet as 'the observed of all observers' (3.1.156) contains a much richer store of meanings than modern usage allows. *OED* notes contemporary usages of the term 'observer' to include not only an adherent of 'a law, religion, custom, ritual, method' and a 'person who watches or takes notice; a spectator';[39] a further use denotes a 'person who watches for and interprets omens',[40] giving the concept of observing the vatic quality of an authority fundamentally interpretative in nature. Daniel's interpretative authority who 'Calls his Eyes / To Councell [. . .] [and] / threatens Poetry, like a Strange Face' applies this surveillance to authors.[41] This imagery of ear, eye and authority reflects authors' understandable preoccupation with the reception of their own works, and as Meskill says of Jonson's attentive approach to this, 'Vigilance, like envy, is bound up in obsessive looking.'[42]

In a society so wedded to informing, such an ambiguous figure as Hamlet is bound to be kept under observation, and he is the subject of surveillance not only by Claudius, Polonius, Ophelia, and Rosencrantz and Guildenstern, but also by old Hamlet. He is watched from both sides of the grave, from both within and without his 'madness' – which is acting – because of both his threatened action and his inaction; that is, because of the direct threat he poses and of the direct threat he fails to pose. Trapped between these accusing audiences, he is damned if he does and damned if he doesn't. Like a ghost himself, Hamlet is made impotent by the tension between the agendas of these hidden watchers and is stuck in a liminality between an inassimilable past and an incommensurable future. All he has between these two states is 'Words, words, words' (2.2.189) with which to forge (in both senses) an identity of sufficient conviction to facilitate the required action. But, in a world of informing, words are the problem, and in his two main soliloquies these words turn to self-accusation, in both cases resulting in a comparison with those who can 'act': Fortinbras in the 'real world' of the play; and the player in the 'fictional world' of the inner-play.

As the narrative moves on, Claudius and Polonius form an onstage audience for the inner drama of Hamlet and Ophelia's private conversation, using Ophelia as bait. Claudius explains this to Gertrude: 'Her father and myself – lawful espials – / Will so bestow ourselves that, seeing unseen, / We may of their encounter frankly judge' (3.1.32–4). It is worth noticing that the words 'lawful espials' are absent in Q2; this may be merely a reflection of their metrical redundancy, but there is a case for suggesting that the very omission of the justifying phrase may be intended to make a point about the kind of authority that relies so much on the power of the hidden accuser, 'seeing, unseen' (3.1.32). Subsequently, as the audience is watching Hamlet's 'To be, or not to be' speech, his conversation with Ophelia (3.1.56–160), and her speech following his exit, they share the perspectives of both Polonius and the Claudius, who are audience-members too, though ulterior, and thus menacing. So, being in the audience at that point is to be watching (with) Claudius and Polonius watching Hamlet and Ophelia within a structure which ends, classically, with the stage direction '*King and Polonius step forward from behind the Arras*'. Such metadramatic foregrounding of the informer-in-the-audience makes plain the corruption of legitimate authority, especially since one of the 'informers' is the King himself. The ubiquity of this problem is shown in Hamlet's rawly confessional exchange with Ophelia, where he almost informs upon himself, declaring,

I could accuse me of such things that it were better my mother had not borne me. I am very proud, revengeful, ambitious, with more offences at my beck than I have thoughts to put them in, imagination to give them shape, or time to act them in. (3.1.121–6)

Hamlet thus locates himself as the site of the problem, while the audience are offered the curious paradox of an explicitly predatory perspective over one with whom their sympathies rest. They share the venal position of the informer, but possess a knowledge superior to those hidden onstage of the actual subject. Such metadramatic irony allows them the privileged position of being able to look with derision on the figure of the informer, in the persons of both the King and his proxy, and this then becomes a factor in shaping their responses to authority in the play. The fact that the audience has paid to see this nuances their perspective further.

The reactions of the King and Polonius to the information they have acquired from their activities differ, and the audience is now positioned either to collude with or critique their conclusions. Claudius immediately moots his scheme to send Hamlet to England, though we do not know at this point that this includes his intended murder; Polonius' reaction, however, is to set up another scenario to take place after the inner play, this time with Gertrude, where he can again be the hidden audience to Hamlet's 'madness.' Hamlet must not be 'unwatch'd' the King agrees (3.1.188), as, birdlike, over 'something in his soul [. . .] his melancholy sits on brood' (3.1.163–4). Polonius then suggests to the King 'I'll be placed, so please you, in the ear / Of all their conference' (3.1.183–4). Given the play's imagery of the ear, we are invited to see him in this case not merely as intrusive but even as an actively poisonous audience. As a result of this encounter, Gertrude is enjoined by Hamlet to act a new role, but the ambiguity and complicity of her own position may be seen in the fact that she also informs Claudius about Hamlet's conduct in the closet scene, though even her testimony may be suspect. Misinformation and misrepresentation seem to flow in every second breath of this play and the audience is increasingly well placed to perceive this.

Accordingly, closer to the play's metadramatic centre, Hamlet's injunction to the players to 'Suit the action to the word, the word to the action' (3.2.17–18) turns out to be deeply ironic. It reflects upon, as it informs, his assertion of the 'purpose of playing [as] [. . .] to hold as 'twere the mirror up to Nature to show Virtue her feature, Scorn her own image, and the very age and body of the time his

form and pressure' (3.2.20–4). Contrary to the claim that this statement articulates 'Shakespeare's own theory of drama', or even 'the
mimesis of mimesis,' outlining some kind of dramatic ideal, a prop-
erly contextual reading suggests otherwise.[43] These metadramatic
passages must be read against Hamlet's own persistent reluctance
to suit the action to the word, a core issue of the text, which does
indeed hold 'the *mirror* up to *Nature*', and what it reflects upon is
the impossibility of anything but a distorted relationship between the
two. 'Virtue' may be shown 'her own feature', but her chief feature
is that, be she 'as chaste as ice, as pure as snow' (3.1.135), she shall
'not escape calumny' (3.1.136), in a radical disruption between reality and representation. The time may be shown 'his form' but his
form, as we have been told, is 'out of joint' (1.5.186); Claudius also
states that the young Fortinbras believes 'Our state to be disjoint and
out of frame' (1.2.20).[44] Therefore, Hamlet's injunctions to the trav-
elling players should be understood alongside other metadramatic
examples of representation which have become 'disjointed' from the
reality they attempt to mirror, through their connection with illegitimate authority. The play as a whole works as a general arraignment
of the disjunction between authority and true representation in the
interpretation of both drama and life. The nature of this disjunction also describes the potential for an authority disengaged from
its subjects by unreliable interlocution to become increasingly, and
potentially homicidally, distorted.

Exacerbated by Claudius' guilty conscience, Denmark's culture
of informing has produced just such a dangerously disjointed body
politic and Hamlet intends to attempt to use a play to begin to set
it right. Since his information about the murder he is supposed to
revenge comes from an informant whose status as a disembodied
spirit renders his testimony dubious – the ghost is only said to be
'like' the King (1.1.57), and Horatio refers to it as an 'illusion'
(1.1.126) – it is no wonder that Hamlet insists on 'grounds / More
relative than this' (2.2.538–9), that is, more relatable (or 'retailable'),
not only to test their veracity, but to place them in a discursive environment in which he is able to exert some control. However, though
perhaps artistically heroic, this will fail.

Central to *Hamlet*'s metadrama, its inner-play *The Murder of
Gonzago* has been amended by Hamlet for this purpose. His authorship here resounds with the older sense of the *auctor*, one who passes
on received knowledge. He is not the originator, but the rewriter of
memory bequeathed to him, like a family curse, from his dead father.
The fact that, after promising his father 'thy commandment all alone

shall live / Within the book and volume of my brain' (1.5.98–103), Hamlet is still constrained to materialise this bequest in an augmentative rewriting, is a gesture to the dependence of knowledge upon layers of representation and interpretation.[45]

Here Shakespeare the author/actor/director writes the part of Hamlet for an actor, acting a character, who is acting mad. This same character is writing, directing and watching actors acting as actors in a play within the play. This inner-play is being watched by the onstage King; and the play as a whole is being watched by the off-stage audience.[46] However, just as Claudius is watching the inner-play, Hamlet and Horatio are watching him. Connecting with all of these strata of dramatic surveillance, Hamlet plans, 'I'll observe his looks, / I'll tent him to the quick. If 'a do blench / I know my course' (2.2.531–3), and thus the dramatist gets to interpret audience reaction for himself, rather than being subject to the interpretations of an audience or the unreliable testimony of the informer. In order to effect this dramatic ideal, Hamlet recruits the apparently unimpeachable Horatio, and his appeal, that 'both our judgements join / In censure of his seeming' (3.2.82–3), casts Horatio as a fellow audience-member, not of course of the inner-play but of the primary onstage audience. Asked to observe his uncle, 'with the very comment of thy soul' (3.2.75), glossed here as 'the most concentrated attention of your entire being', Horatio plays the part of pure observer; he is not 'passion's slave' and as such models an ostensibly trustworthy audience.[47] Horatio's trustworthiness at this point of course suggests a contrast with Hamlet's avowed unreliability. However, even Horatio may be tainted by the compromised air of the Danish court: he is asked later by Claudius to give Ophelia 'good watch' (4.5.74) and, though we are not sure he acquiesces, the assumption is clearly there that he will.

As the metadrama disrupts the psychological boundary of the stage and, as the border-line shifts from scene to scene-within-scene, an audience mentally annexes space which was previously purely representative. The layered onstage audiences here offer abstractions of the offstage audience which might normally model various perspectives. An offstage audience might typically be drawn into the inmost perspective through simple scopic pulsion, losing sight of the outer frames and providing what William Nelles describes as a 'narrative embedding [which] has the paradoxical effect of producing the illusion of a more profound realism'.[48] But in this case that narrative embedding is disrupted as the offstage audience's attention is diverted by Hamlet's conversations and interjections. Initially,

Claudius is able to face the dumb show re-enactment of his crime because its signification is restrained within recognised and demarcated fictional parameters. He reacts violently only when Hamlet's narratological interpositionality breaks the dramatic frame and displays his own interpretative status as *auctor* by interjecting, 'You shall see anon how the murderer gets the love of Gonzago's wife' (3.2.256–7). When he is 'frighted with false fire' (F: 3.2.260) and exits calling for 'Lights! Lights! Lights!' (3.2.262), this recalls Hamlet's 'Words, words, words' (2.2.189) and reminds us that it is the dangerous meanings disinterred by Hamlet's rewriting that cause Claudius to leave the stage too soon, sloughing his façade of innocence as he goes. Claudius' failure is in being unable to maintain the primacy of his own essential authority over the discourse with which he is presented, a failure which is co-witnessed by both the onstage and offstage audiences. There is a faction of onstage audience which may remain in ignorance of the issues here; in this case the offstage audience is positioned to perceive and appreciate their own superior understanding of what is at play.

This metadrama facilitates a power-shift which is obvious to the offstage audience: Hamlet, the rightful king and *auctor*, becomes the nervous author or informer anxious to read a reaction, creating or discovering meaning, while the King (who might conventionally grant or withhold an audience) is simultaneously positioned as an audience and coerced into displaying a vulnerable interpretability more commonly experienced by the early modern actor or author.

Claudius' own perspective is clearly tainted, but also Hamlet's status as *auctor*, the bearer of received truth, and interpreting audience of Claudius' 'conscience', is complicated by his simultaneous occupation of the position of the conventional observing informer intending to wrest incriminating evidence from his subject. His supposed madness adds to the unreliability of his perspective.[49] He embodies, and is disempowered by, the contradictions inherent in a system of control barren of moral authority.[50] The fact that Lucianus, the inner-play's ear-poisoner, represents both Claudius and Hamlet, further suggests a moral conflation of their respective roles as murderer and revenger, with the recurring image of the poisoned ear the emblem of deception and misinformation. But, as we have seen, neither does Horatio escape this taint. In these ways, even the apparent dramatic ideal of Hamlet's making turns out to be corrupted by the miasma of Elsinore and his attempt at true interpretation infected with his society's fatal flaw.

Hamlet's metadrama thus represents the problematic power-relations of a state suffused with role-playing informers, headed by a murderous authority whose already dubious legitimacy they undermine with misinformation. But it suggests in addition the potential for drama to be complicit in this system, even as it offers a revealing depiction of it. By this point in the play the offstage audience is already sensitised to perceive compromised authority, so that when the metadrama here offers the vision of Hamlet also becoming a part of the same structure it may serve as an indication of the universality of informing and alert them to its corrupting force. Hamlet's interpretations, however, will lead only to self-reflection, not action, and therefore, although he models an informing audience, his own reluctance to acquiesce in the mess of state means that this remains a passive one. But again, his inaction is not a character flaw so much as it is simply the outworking of a system in which the combination of authoritative action and moral legitimacy is a logical impossibility. The *hamartia* lies in the system itself.

These issues, aptly exemplified in the obviously metadramatic parts of the play, are replicated throughout, often casting small overseen scenes as inset dramas and characters who are both audiences and actors, further associating the institution of the theatre with informing. Polonius provides plenty of examples. By his own confession he has been an actor in the past (see 3.2.99–100), and he sets up Ophelia as an actor also, to facilitate their spying on Hamlet, directing her: 'Read on this book / That show of such an exercise may colour / Your loneliness' (3.1.43–5). Ophelia is explicitly an informer too, as Polonius' possession of notes from Hamlet to her attests:

> This in obedience hath my daughter shown me;
> And more about hath his solicitings
> As they fell out, by time, by means and place,
> All given to my ear. (2.2.122–5)

In his state of 'madness' Hamlet openly accuses Polonius of being dishonest, punning on both Polonius' self-interested state-craft and the supposed generative capacities of fishmongers and their daughters, imaging the action of the sun breeding 'maggots in a dead dog' (2.2.178). This metaphor expresses a view of sickly reproduction in both sexual matters and those relating to the generation of information, which is Polonius' business as informer. Hamlet's metadramatic rejoinder to Polonius' separate statements, 'Then came the actors

[. . .] / Upon my honour' (2.2.329, 331) is to link them in parallel: 'Then came each actor on his ass' (2.2.332). Polonius is recognised as an actor and his honour is the ass. Standing for the state of informers generally, Polonius' immorality is established by the voyeuristic and incestuous sexual connotations of his plan to 'loose my daughter to [Hamlet]' as he arranges with the King, which combines spying and metadrama.[51] In this way the activities of an informer provide the material for the state of Denmark to be perceived metaphorically as the rotten flesh of a dead dog. The combination of sex and information here as generative activities continues with Hamlet's quibble: 'conception is a blessing but as your daughter may conceive, friend – look to't' (2.2.181–3). This suggests that Hamlet is aware that Ophelia is also an informer – possibly even that his love-letters to her may be a 'plant' designed to disguise his procrastination as love-madness. Polonius, moreover, even misrepresents his own dealings to the King and Queen when he reports that his response to Ophelia's revelation about Hamlet's attentions was 'Lord Hamlet is a prince out of thy star. / This must not be' (2.2.138–9), when in fact he has said nothing of the sort, instead telling Ophelia 'tender yourself more dearly' (1.3.104). This may be driven by necessity, but Polonius is familiar with the deployment of language to fulfil self-interested ends, as he makes clear to Ophelia in relation to Hamlet's vows: 'springes to catch woodcocks – I do know / When the blood burns how prodigal the soul / Lends the tongue vows' (1.3.114–16). Polonius then is a prime embodiment of authority structures which require duplicitous roles simultaneously demanding the functions of both informer and actor. The metadrama here is simply the most natural form in which to explore these issues of compromised authority.

As the King's chief informer, and his acting appendage in the scene in Gertrude's closet, Polonius' fate will be exemplary. The metadramatic structure here links an informer's coney-catching device with the authority of the husband and King; Polonius gives dramatic direction, sets up the action: 'Look you lay home to him. / Tell him his pranks have been too broad to bear with, / [. . .] Pray you be round' (3.4.1–2, 4), and then conceals himself. 'Coney-catching' was the Elizabethan phrase for robbery through the practice of sometimes elaborate devices of fraud and deception. 'Coney' was a name for a tame or docile rabbit and hence a dupe of some kind. It also implied simplicity, possibly through being young, or newly-arrived in the city. What he overhears in this metadrama is a potentially incriminating scene in which Hamlet directly accuses his mother of complicity in the crime Claudius has perpetrated. It is quite deservedly then that this

menacing watcher, separated from the protagonists by the woven artifice of the arras, receives the vital, fatal thrust in the place of Claudius,
as the concealing fabric is penetrated.[52] One implication of this is that
even in his wife's bedchamber the King is an illegitimate audience.
His right to interpret the scene in hand, even by proxy, is forcibly
questioned at the point of Hamlet's blade. Unless he is using the term
with irony, when Hamlet claims 'I took thee for thy better' (3.4.30),
he cannot mean this in a moral sense as a qualitative judgement of
relative worth. But, either way, whether he believes he is killing the
King as a menacingly hidden watcher or Polonius as his informer,
this pointed indeterminacy leads to him killing a form of authority,
and a model of a vicious and poisonous audience. When the dramatic fabrication separates the actor from the audience the potential
is always there to conceal the interpretative power which the audience holds. Figured so, where the nature of authority is obscured
by artifice the position of audience-member is potentially every bit
as dangerous as that of the author-actor. In this case metadramatic
modes which foreground the role of the audience may actually serve
to partially disarm them, bearing the principle in mind that a hidden
audience is always more threatening than a seen one.[53] This suggests
also that, where 'authority' hazards its legitimacy upon informing,
although an empowerment of the audience may result, those acting
as proxies for an absent, more authoritative 'audience' may be subject to a similar fate. Polonius is in effect another victim of Claudius'
original crime; the informer dies both in the course of his duty and
as proxy for his master, but it is the authority and jurisdiction of the
King, and the social malaise he represents, which are in question. As
Rosencrantz puts it, 'The cess of majesty / Dies not alone, but like a
gulf doth draw / What's near with it [. . .] Never alone / Did the King
sigh but with a general groan' (3.3.15–17, 22–3), which, more than
merely expressing the expected results of the King's death, displays an
anxious awareness of the ease with which the King's own corruption
becomes that of the system.[54]

The play's metadrama now takes a further authorial cast which
implicates authorship itself with the outcome of informing: murderous political expediency. Describing Hamlet's reaction to the ghost,
Horatio says, 'He waxes desperate with imagination' (1.4.87) and the
word 'imagination' at this time carries revolutionary undertones.[55]
Claudius, who has most to lose by Hamlet's interpretative activities,
wishes to put 'fetters [. . .] about this fear / Which now goes too free-
footed' (3.3.25–6) and thus writes Hamlet's death warrant and order
of betrayal to be enacted in a distant land (which is, of course, the

home of the theatre audience). Having had his own kingship deferred, Hamlet is now to be displaced and dispatched. Claudius is attempting to literally write Hamlet out of the plot, while shifting authorial responsibility for this by referring to the prince as 'most violent author / Of his own just remove' (4.5.80–1). It is in the closet scene that we first learn of the King's 'mandate', the 'letters seal'd' with his signet, borne by Rosencrantz and Guildenstern, and by which they intend to 'marshal [Hamlet] to knavery' (3.4.200–4). Hamlet, however, has other plans, to rewrite and augment their letters authorially. He thus becomes the metadramatic author of Rosencrantz and Guildenstern's demise as he later tells:

Being thus benetted round with villains,
Or I could make a prologue to my brains
They had begun the play. I sat me down,
Devised a new commission, wrote it fair. (5.2.29–32)

Hence, the closet scene does away with one informer, attempts to convert another and hints at the coming demise of two more. Despite his authorly self-assertion here, Hamlet also shifts responsibility partially onto Rosencrantz and Guildenstern for their own fates, arguing that their defeat grew 'by their own insinuation [. . .] / 'Tis dangerous when the baser nature comes / Between the pass and fell incensed points / Of mighty opposites' (5.2.57–61). Like Polonius, they have insinuated themselves into a position between opposite sword-points of political struggle. In their case, however, the sword is both an instrument and a metaphor for the point of Hamlet's authoring pen as he writes their doom at the hands of others and authorises it with his own rightful regal seal, the signet-ring of his father, a sign of his own legitimacy and authority. This metadramatic episode of self-referential authorship functions in a manner similar to the inner-play in that its authority to challenge one kingly authorship is derived from the trace of another.

Having written Rosencrantz and Guildenstern out of the plot, Hamlet then re-enters as actor in the final cataclysm, a cosening metadramatic 'device' (4.7.62) of the King's bloody authorship. Laertes also becomes an actor in this, but it is Hamlet who remains the central agent and controlling force of the narrative. Rosencrantz, Guildenstern, Polonius, Laertes and Claudius all die, directly or indirectly, at his hand and he leaves any revolutionary conclusions to be drawn by the liminal lurkers, Horatio and Fortinbras, respectively Hamlet's interpreter and successor.

All the discourses of authority, both social and dramatic, in this play, including the operation of informing as a cultural *hamartia*, pass through the personae of Hamlet. Hamlet is always acting but sometimes he is acting acting; his is always a metaperformance, a performance about performance: of acting roles, of public roles, of private roles, of duties to the self, family, friends, lovers, state, the dead, of duties and obligations of memory, of honour, of revenge, of succession, and of the possibility of questioning their obligatoriness. Internalising all of these discourses, he disturbs them as he forces the authorities to respond to his antic disposition, until he himself is compromised by his acquiescence in the self-destructive informing structures which infect his kingdom. As I have argued, *Hamlet's* Denmark is made rotten not by the murder of old Hamlet, in itself, but by the corrupting structures of authority which afford the murderer protection and threaten others. Denmark falls apart not merely because of personal ambition but also, significantly, through its reliance on informing that functions as a hyperbolic example of dramatic engagement with the real, and these concerns are felt throughout the period in different ways, as we will see. In any case Hamlet's acquiescence argues that theatre is complicit in this and thus the play claims no moral high ground on these issues.

In *Hamlet*, the social wrong to be addressed is extreme and pressing; the imperative of the ghostly author-informer is forceful since it is based on first-hand experience; as Prince, the interpreter is empowered, if hesitant; and his own dramatic production has the power to reveal guilt where it is hidden. This should be a recipe for a creative and authoritative theatrical critique of social issues. But it is the fatally flawed nature of the authority-structures themselves which ultimately accounts for the carnage of the play's ending. Functioning as a structural parallel of the ghost of old Hamlet, Fortinbras appears latterly like the incarnation of a rumour. The ghost is flesh-made-representation, a shadow which casts itself across the play, robbing Hamlet of his substance; Fortinbras is representation-made-flesh, a silhouette which inherits substance from the dead of the tragedy to make possible his manifestation. Far from reinstating the good order of things, however, Fortinbras merely begins the whole theatrical process anew, combining the roles of both actor and king when he asks Horatio to 'call the noblest to audience' (5.2.371) while Horatio reinvents himself as a metanarrator who will bear the tale on and 'truly deliver' (5.2.369) the narrative of the bodies on display 'high on a stage' (5.2.362). Given the prevailing predatory imagery associated with the informer, it is entirely apposite that Fortinbras refers to these bodies as a 'quarry' (5.2.348), the contemporary term for a pile of deer killed in the hunt. Horatio's promised interpretation of the newly-formed tableau, self-consciously metadramatic and written in the intermingled blood of author, informer, audience and authority, will, moreover, merely replicate these destructive structures in its performance beyond the onstage narrative, despite his assurance of true delivery. Implicit in all of *Hamlet*'s metadramatic discourse by its very absence is a nostalgia, or hope, for a model of authority, and of authorship, which is free from the constraints of a predatory political imperative. We will see this given a much more explicit formative role in the metadrama of Ben Jonson.

Notes

1. Edward Guilpin, *Skialetheia. Or, A shadowe of truth* (London: I[ames] R[oberts] for Nicholas Ling, 1598), <http://gateway.proquest.com/openurl?ctx_ver=Z39.88-2003&res_id=xri:eebo&rft_id=xri:eebo:citation:99841568> (last accessed 8 December 2015).
2. Jacques Derrida, *Specters of Marx: The State of Debt, the Work of Mourning and the New International*, trans. Peggy Kamuf (London: Routledge, 1994), p. 6.
3. Unless otherwise noted, as here, all line and other references are to William Shakespeare, *Hamlet*, ed. Ann Thompson and Neil Taylor (London: Arden Shakespeare, 2006), which uses the Second Quarto (Q2) of 1604–5; where the First Quarto and Folio are used, (Q1) and (F) respectively, the text consulted is William Shakespeare, *Hamlet: The Texts of 1603 and 1623*, ed. Ann Thompson and Neil Taylor (London: Arden Shakespeare, 2006).
4. Weimann, *Shakespeare and the Popular Tradition*, p. 131.
5. Richard Fly, 'The Evolution of Shakespearean Metadrama: Abel, Burckhardt and Calderwood', *Comparative Drama*, Vol. 20, No. 2 (1986), pp. 124–39, 126.
6. 'Sterility' obviously indicating barrenness here, and with no sense of cleanliness as in its modern usage.
7. Stephen Gosson, *The Schoole of Abuse* (London: Thomas Woodcocke, 1579), n.p. <http://gateway.proquest.com/openurl?ctx_ver=Z39.88 2003&res_id=xri:eebo&rft_id=xri:eebo:citation:99899035> (last accessed 2 December 2015).
8. Ibid. n.p.
9. Robert Greene, *Groats-worth of witte* (London: [J. Wolfe and J. Danter] for William Wright, 1592), <http://gateway.proquest.com/openurl?ctx_ver=Z39.88-2003&res_id=xri:eebo&rft_id=xri:eebo:citation:99852791> (last accessed 8 December 2015).

10. Ibid. n.p.
11. Ibid. n.p.
12. William Shakespeare, *Hamlet*, ed. Harold Jenkins (London: Arden, 2000), p. 20ff.; see William Shakespeare, *Hamlet*, ed. Ann Thompson and Neil Taylor, p. 85 for an outline of the debate on memorial reconstruction.
13. Thomas Dekker, *The Guls Horne-booke* (London: Nicholas Okes, 1609), p. 28, <http://gateway.proquest.com/openurl?ctx_ver=Z39.88-2003&res_id=xri:eebo&rft_id=xri:eebo:citation:99840980> (last accessed 23 November 2015).
14. Ibid. p. 28.
15. See William Shakespeare, *Hamlet*, p. 254, n. 224. For the constant undertones of reference to female genitalia and their preoccupation with revealing what is hidden, see the excellent and fascinating study by Patricia Parker, 'Othello and Hamlet: Dilation, Spying, and the "Secret Place" of Woman', *Representations*, Vol. 44 (Autumn 1993), pp. 60–95. The imagery of informing more generally, I argue, produces not so much a picture of invasive exposure of what is occulted or mystified, as, rather, a predatory appetite for the life of another, suggesting murder rather than rape. Parker seems to be detecting in these plays a particular sexualisation of what is a general social malaise. See also p. 63 of Parker's article for more on Shakespearean informers.
16. ['Toute autorité politique se définit par son regard exorbité, avide de renseignements']; my translation. Banu, p. 21.
17. See, respectively, Shakespeare, *Hamlet*, p. 239, n. 38, p. 404, n. 136 and Shakespeare, *Hamlet*, ed. Jenkins, p. 238, n. 38.
18. Shakespeare, *Hamlet*, ed. Jenkins, p. 254, n. 316.
19. 'Eyas': 'young hawk taken from the nest for the purpose of training, or one whose training is incomplete', *OED*, 2nd edn. See also William E. Miller, 'Little Eyases', *Shakespeare Quarterly*, Vol. 28, No. 1 (1977), pp. 87–8, where Miller notes the 'disagreeable quality of eyases' simply as birds. Note also this reference was cut from the 1604–5 Quarto (Q2) by which time these child actors were under the patronage of Queen Anne as The Children of Her Majesty's Chapel: a ' "diplomatic" cut' – see Shakespeare, *Hamlet*, p. 52.
20. Shakespeare, *Hamlet*, ed. Jenkins, p. 255, n. 338.
21. For a later date, and other controversies involving these child actors, see Roslyn L. Knutson, 'Falconer to the Little Eyases: A New Date and Commercial Agenda for the "Little Eyases" Passage in *Hamlet*', *Shakespeare Quarterly*, Vol. 46, No. 1 (Spring 1995), pp. 1–31.
22. Shakespeare may have had more to do with the controversy than has been thought; see Jonson, *Poetaster*, pp. 36–7.
23. Thompson and Taylor accord with Jenkins's note that the other usages of the word 'tar' in Shakespeare (*King John*, 4.1.117 and *Troilus and Cressida*, 1.3.392) both have to do with inciting dogs to fight. See

Shakespeare, *Hamlet: The Texts of 1603 and 1623*, p. 244, n. 351 and Shakespeare, *Hamlet*, ed. Jenkins, p. 256, n. 351.

24. Thompson and Taylor discard Jenkins's suggestion that the 'innovation' refers to the Essex rebellion, and question the likely reference to the *poetomachia* in favour of a more diplomatic imperative: see Shakespeare, *Hamlet: The Texts of 1603 and 1623*, p. 242, n. 328–60 and Shakespeare, *Hamlet*, ed. Jenkins, pp. 3, 470–2. Perhaps these views are not mutually exclusive.

25. Another hint at this concern is Claudius' desire to control the representation of the killing of Polonius, thus avoiding slanderous representation. Jenkins's necessary addition to the text of Q2 at 4.1.40, 'So envious slander', before the lines

> Whose whisper o'er the world's diameter,
> As level as the cannon to his blank,
> Transports his poison'd shot, may miss our name
> And hit the woundless air

is a six-syllable phrase (or still five with 'env'ious') whose switch to dactylic form introduces a falling metre that sits awkwardly with the momentum of this passage. I would suggest that this insertion should be a four syllable phrase, to fit in with the confident iambic pentameter. Additionally 'envy' seems inapt under the circumstances; the phrases 'So sland'rous fame' or 'So sland'rous news' may be more applicable. A better possibility, I suggest, would be 'So shame's report'. Not only does this sit well with the surrounding text's imagery of gunfire, but the echoing 'report' of both cannon and slanderer also accords with the common view of the dangerous mouth of the passer-on of 'information'. For other contemporary examples relating such mouths to cannons see Ben Jonson, *Every Man Out of His Humour*, ed. Helen Ostovich (Manchester: Manchester University Press, 2001) (1.2.216–20); Shakespeare, *King John* (2.1.462–5).

26. Thomas Nashe, *The vnfortunate traueller* (London: Thomas Scarlet for Cuthbert Burby, 1594), <http://gateway.proquest.com/openurl?ctx_ver=Z39.88-2003&res_id=xri:eebo&rft_id=xri:eebo:citation:99841227> (last accessed 27 November 2015).

27. Thomas Nashe, *Summers last will and testament* (London: Thomas Scarlet for Cuthbert Burby, 1600), <http://gateway.proquest.com/openurl?ctx_ver=Z39.88-2003&xri:pqil:res_ver=0.2&res_id=xri:lion&rft_id=xri:lion:ft:dr:Z100106638:1> (last accessed 7 December 2015).

28. Besides the hawk, Shakespeare favours the chough as a type of chattering bird, as with the ephemeral courtier Osric (5.2.74), also linking it with augury and the discovery of guilt in *Macbeth* where Macbeth asserts that 'Augures, and understood relations, have / By Magot-pies,

and choughs, and rooks, brought forth / The secret'st man of blood'
(3.4.123–5); see William Shakespeare, *Macbeth*, ed. Kenneth Muir
(London: Arden, 1980), p. 97, n. 124.

29. Hamlet's use of the bird of prey image in his statement 'I should ha' fatted all the region kites / With this slave's offal' (2.2.514–15) is, I think, only obliquely related to these themes.

30. See Shakespeare, *Hamlet*, ed. Jenkins, p. 287, n. 4.

31. Forker notes that most of Shakespeare's references to actors are pejorative; see Charles R. Forker, 'Shakespeare's Theatrical Symbolism and its Function in Hamlet', *Shakespeare Quarterly*, Vol. 14, No. 3 (Summer 1963), pp. 215–29. Claudius himself fears his own 'bad performance' (4.7.149).

32. For further details see my article, Bill Angus, ' "A hawk from a handsaw": A New Contextualisation', *Notes and Queries*, Vol. 56, No. 1 (March 2009), pp. 60–2.

33. Since the phrase alludes to both duplicitous associates and to bad acting, the connection between this and Falstaff's description of his sword which 'hack'd like a handsaw' (*1 Henry IV*, 2.4.161) may not be quite as far-fetched as has been thought. Falstaff uses the phrase when, like a ham actor, he re-enacts and exaggerates his encounter with the hundred 'rogues in buckram' (2.4.200) and the parallels here should be obvious in performance.

34. For an exploration of the effeminacy of the penetrable ear see Hutson, p. 15ff.

35. Graham Holderness, *Shakespeare: The Histories* (Basingstoke: Macmillan, 2000), pp. 59–60.

36. Shakespeare, *Macbeth* (1.5.25–8).

37. Shakespeare, *Hamlet*, ed. Jenkins, p. 186, n. 116.

38. Archer, p. 122.

39. For this last it references the following ambiguous usage: '1616 SHAKESPEARE *Jul. C.* (1623) I. ii. 203 He is a great Obseruer, and he lookes Quite through the Deeds of men.' *OED*, 2nd edn.

40. Referencing '1611 *Bible* (A.V.): *Deut.* xviii. 10 An obseruer of times, or an inchanter, or a witch. 1698 J. FRYER *New Acct. E.-India & Persia* 193 Strict Observers of Omens'. *OED*, 2nd edn.

41. Daniel, p. 229.

42. When Jonson discusses slander he often uses eye imagery which is skewed in some way; see Meskill, pp. 86, 88–9, 129.

43. See Weimann, *Shakespeare and the Popular Tradition*, p. 199 and Parker, p. 281, respectively.

44. This is echoed in *Macbeth*'s 'But let the frame of things disjoint' (3.2.16–17).

45. See Shakespeare, *Hamlet*, ed. Jenkins, 'Writes': stage direction (1.5.109).

46. See Weimann, *Shakespeare and the Popular Tradition*, p. 172.

47. Shakespeare, *Hamlet*, p. 301, n. 75.

48. William Nelles, 'Stories within Stories: Narrative Levels and Embedded Narrative', *Studies in the Literary Imagination*, Vol. 25, No. 1 (1992), pp. 61–74, 70.

49. Hamlet's intention to provoke Claudius into a readable reaction is based on various contemporaneous examples of the convicting power of drama. Jenkins notes such in relation to various plays, including *A Warning for Fair Women* (1599), where a woman confessed to the murder of her own husband after seeing a similar crime depicted. Shakespeare's company had recently performed this play. As in Heywood's *Apology for Actors*, these examples were offered as evidence of the usefulness of dramatic representation in the face of cultural opposition. Here, however, the very conventions of dramatic apologetics to which the whole scene alludes are associated with Hamlet's compromised perspective. In this case, Shakespeare's negative capability perhaps works against his own theatrical interest. See Shakespeare, *Hamlet*, ed. Jenkins, p. 482.

50. Reluctantly, perhaps, he embodies what Weimann calls 'the late ritual heritage of those "doble dealing ambodexters" to whom the Puritans so deeply objected'. Weimann, *Shakespeare and the Popular Tradition*, p. 171.

51. Shakespeare, *Hamlet*, p. 249, n. 159; Shakespeare, *Hamlet*, ed. Jenkins, p. 245, n. 162. Again in this connection see Patricia Parker.

52. Incidentally, stabbing fatalities were quite common to both European royalty and actors at this time. For an interesting overview of this, offered as a contextualisation of a contemporary dagger and rapier found near the site of the Globe in Southwark, see Neil MacGregor, *Shakespeare's Restless World* (London: Allen Lane, 2012), pp. 61–73.

53. In this regard, the onstage audience-member of Dekker's *The Guls Horne-booke*, who is told 'to creep from behind the arras, with your tripos or three-footed stool in one hand, and a teston mounted between a forefinger and a thumb in the other' may be a target for parody, but is nevertheless relatively disempowered by their very visibility; see p. 30.

54. It is ironic that Rosencrantz and Guildenstern are themselves part of this 'cess of majesty' as two of the 'many bodies [. . .] / That live and feed upon your majesty' (3.3.9–10), hence are two of the 'ten thousand lesser things' which are 'mortis'd and adjoin'd' to the spokes of the 'massy wheel / [. . .] which when it falls / Each small annexment, petty consequence, / Attends the boist'rous ruin' (see 3.3.11–23). They are certainly partakers of the 'general groan' which might accompany the King's 'sigh'.

55. This is one sense in five of this vintage, as *OED* notes, including 'the mental consideration of actions or events not yet in existence. a. scheming or devising; a device, contrivance, plan, scheme, plot [. . .] 1523 *Hypsip.*, with-outen any othir affeccioun of loue or euyl ymagynacyoun. *c*1400 Mandeville (1839) xxiii. 251 alle here lust and alle

here ymaginacioun is for to putten alle londes undre hire subieccioun. 1535 Coverdale *Lam.* iii. 60 thou hast herde their despytefull wordes (o lorde) yee and all their ymaginacions agaynst me. 1548 Hall *Chron., Rich. iii* 47b, that mischevous ymaginacion whiche he nowe newely beganne and attempted. 1660 *Trial Regic.* 9 in no case else imagination, or compassing, without an actual effect of it, was punishable by our law', *OED*, 2nd edn.

Chapter 2

Every Man In and *Out:*
Metadramatic Ideals and
Harsh Realities

The two *Every Man* plays, though separated in their writing and performance by only a short period of time, show a development within Jonson's work towards an increasingly critical depiction of the self-interested interpreter and the corrupting influence of the informer. This growing tendency will form a significant element in many of Jonson's later plays, especially where they deal with issues of social and cultural authority, and this is very often expressed through metadramatic forms.

Every Man In His Humour: 'a stir of art and devices'

Every Man In His Humour, initially performed in 1598 and Jonson's first big theatrical success, is a play whose metadrama reproduces structures of surveillance and informing while also proposing an explicit ideal of interpretative practice. In its revision of 1616, the subject of this study, the play's relocation in London allows for a fuller sense of local identification with plot and character than the earlier Italianate version. Here the intermingling of informer, audience and authority, though troubled, ultimately produces an interpretative model that recognises the artistic authority of the author, and over-rides the play's tensions between legitimate and illegitimate authorities, creative, personal and civic.

The play describes how an intercepted letter enables the elder Knowell to follow his supposedly studious son, Edward, to London and there spy upon his life of debauchery with the gallants and poetasters of the time. Knowell's servant Brainworm acts as his informer upon Edward. But Jonson is equivocal about the nature of authority this implies. The deliberate breach of the privacy of the letter obviously entails a betrayal, but it is couched within a legitimising patriarchal oversight. The father's wish to curb the son's propensity for poetic licentiousness displays a general antitheatricality but even more so shares Jonson's specific distaste for poetasters. This social critique, which exposes the surveillance inherent in the system of patronage, is not without some equivocation about its devices and motives. The informing servant Brainworm, one of the many misusers of information, secretive note-takers and informers, which Hutson agrees 'haunt Jonson's writing', of course, turns out to be troublingly subversive.[1] But there is also an interpretative ideal tied in with this, based in what Victoria Moul calls Jonson's 'idealised Augustan patronage'.[2] That is, the older man does not ultimately wish to frustrate the younger, rather asserting, 'There is a way of winning more by love, / And urging of the modesty, than fear; / Force works on servile natures, not the free' (1.2.114–16).[3] In the end, however, all the characters' farcical complaints, including a merchant's fears of cuckoldry by riotous abusers of his hospitality, will be laid at the feet of the benign authority of a Justice whose clemency will be exemplary, though this will not extend to the worst misusers of language. Thus the comedy here reverberates within an unresolved cultural tension between legitimate and illegitimate authorities, and between the roles of truly authoritative interpreter and plotting, informing, device-maker, each of which Jonson understands and constantly reworks.

Every Man In's metadramatic prologue is both self-advertisement and apologia. It implicitly criticises inadequate poets and rejects their 'foot-and-half-foot words' (Prol. 10) in favour of 'deeds and language such as men do use' (Prol. 21), in the hope that the audiences 'that have so graced monsters may like men' (Prol. 30).[4] The appeal to the audience which this contains, however, is also qualified by the assurance that the play's 'image of the times' will deal only with 'follies' not with 'crimes' (Prol. 23–4), aiming to pre-empt any negative interpretation and limit its own potential for playing into the hands of informers. This is all the more necessary because the play's aspiration to a plain-dealing Horatian realism dramatises and satirises a practical cultural imperative: to avoid the damaging accusation of having produced a damaging accusation. However, there is, as always for Jonson, at the heart of this a recognition of his own inevitable complicity in such representative cultural practices and an underlying link between the author and the informer. In this way the dramatic artifice of others is linked not merely with bad poetry but also with slander, or 'traducing', as it is often termed at the time, the work of the informer, which is something for the ambitious satirist to avoid at all costs. Jonson thus always seems to walk a tightrope beneath which is his own critique of the dramatic incompetence of lesser poets who are tainted by this association, stepping off when it suits his need for self-deprecation. So, Captain Bobadill, a fashionable 'Paul's Man', both advances and models a critique of poetasters, that they 'prate and swagger and keep a stir of art and devices, when [. . .] reade 'em, they are the most shallow, pitiful, barren fellows that live upon the face of the earth' (1.5.43–5). This gallant, who apparently thinks that *The Spanish Tragedy* is a new play, is in agreement here with the most egregious poetaster and gull of the play, Master Matthew. Furthermore he is almost instantly distracted into appreciating how his boot becomes his leg, all of which ironically undermines this incompetent's observation. In a play which relies on the kind of 'devices' Bobadill describes, this comment on poetasters as unreliable 'barren' interpreters works as a point of defensive metadramatic self-deprecation. Here, as is often the case, Jonson's Horatian aspirations are contextualised by the parodic depiction of the conditions within which knowledge, authority and artistic credibility are fashioned.[5]

In this way issues relating to poetic authority and the general atmosphere of informing underpin the metadramatic structures in this text. These are often specifically linked to themes of predation, involving overhearing, slander and political plotting. So, when the poetic son Edward asks his cousin Mr Stephen, the country gull, to come 'over the fields to Moorgate' (1.3.71) to join his poetasting friends, he feels the need to emphasise that 'it is not to draw you into bond, or any plot against the state, coz' (1.3.72–3), the satire here indicating the currency of such fears.[6] In this play Jonson deals with plotting and informing, the fear of slander, venal interpretation and cuckoldry as a microcosmic conspiracy against the state, by placing them within self-referential frameworks. Thus the metadrama becomes more pronounced where the subplot's merchant Kitely (a name with predatory connotations) links theatre imagery with his tenant Wellbred's licentiousness:

> He makes my house here common as a mart,
> A theatre, a public receptacle
> For giddy humour, and diseasèd riot.
> And here, as in a tavern, or a stews,
> He and his wild associates spend their hours
> In repetition of lascivious jests. (2.1.57–62)

This theatrical self-parody is developed further into what Kitely is really paranoid about: the loose tongue of slander, and, in particular, the fear that Wellbred will, like a deceiving informer, 'blow the ears of his familiars / With the false breath of telling what disgraces / And low disparagements I had put upon him' (2.1.95–7). Furthermore Kitely is concerned that this misinformation, exaggerated in interpretation, might have wider consequences for his reputation, saying they make 'loose comments upon every word, / Gesture, or look I use', and expresses his trepidation that they may 'Beget some slander that shall dwell with me' (2.1.99–100, 103) and ruin his social position. So the theatrical repetition of 'lascivious jests' is the driver to their loose tongues and may lead to the very kind of traducing discourse that the Prologue wishes to distance himself from, as the province of 'other' poets. There is more than one reputation at stake here.

For his own part, Kitely figures his fear of being cuckolded as a kind of plot, asserting that when 'spirits of one kind and quality / Come once to parley in the pride of blood; / It is no slow conspiracy that follows' (2.3.19–21). Further, he alludes to familiar hunting imagery in which he perceives himself to be prey whose scent carries on the wind to the aptly named predator-wife, Dame Kitely; she says, 'good sweetheart, come in. The air will do you harm', and he replies as a metadramatic aside to the offstage audience, ' "The air"! She has me i' the wind!' (2.3.51–3). However Kitely tries to hope for better, he cannot escape the 'black poison of suspect' (2.3.68) which clouds his judgement, and perhaps with reason. Discussing a disturbance at Kitely's house, the licentious Wellbred quibbles upon the meaning of what Dame Kitely states 'might' have resulted from the quarrel, 'Might, sister? So, might the good warm clothes your husband wears be poisoned, for anything he knows' (4.8.14–15). Kitely's reaction to this perceived plot, possibly delivered again in an aside, is comedically extreme:

> Now, God forbid! Oh, me, now I remember:
> My wife drunk to me last and changed the cup,
> And bade me wear this cursèd suit today.
> See if heav'n suffer murder undiscovered! –
> [. . .] Oh, I am sick at heart! I burn, I burn. (4.8.17–20, 23)

With metadramatic self-reference, Wellbred responds, 'My very breath has poisoned him [. . .] Will he be poisoned with a simile? – Brother Kitely, what a strange and idle imagination is this!' (4.8.25, 30–1). Kitely is confounded, asking, 'Am I not sick? How am I then not poisoned? Am I not poisoned? How am I then so sick?' (4.8.33–4);

Dame Kitely tells him that his problem is of his own making: 'If you be sick, your own thoughts make you sick', with Wellbred adding, moralistically, 'His jealousy is the poison he has taken' (4.8.35–6). Kitely is thus shown up as an excessive and prejudiced interpreter of words; he is Jonson's bugbear: one who refuses to think well enough of himself to avoid seeing himself as the subject of all critical or satirical discourse.[7] Jonson is still exercised by this in 1632 in *The Magnetic Lady*, where such people are referred to as 'narrow and shrunk natures, shrivelled up poor things that cannot think well of themselves, who dare to detract others' (Chorus 2, 37–8).[8] This insight into the workings of Kitely's suspicious mind operates as a self-referential metadramatic device for displaying the interpretative anxieties of Jonson's theatrical production in a field so open to the imagination of the informer, whose 'malice of misapplying', in the terminology of the rack, 'deforms the figure of many a fair scene' to commit 'civil murder' (*The Magnetic Lady*, Chorus 2, 27–8). Thus these dramatised microcosmic household anxieties are related to the moral state of the wider field of the nation and its own tainted authority structures under whose material pressure drama is produced.

One significant author of the play's metadramatic devices is the character Brainworm, Knowell's rebellious servant, a self-interested and self-fashioning interloper in the business of the *senex* spying upon the son, and an authorised informer. Brainworm, however, exemplifies the lightness of touch which Jonson applies to these serious social issues in this play. The play's cross-generational conflict, which Brainworm calls 'this hunting-match, or rather conspiracy' (2.4.8), is another power-game couched in the imagery of predation and plotting, and thus, to intercept Edward on his way to London, he asserts that he must assume a 'borrowed shape' (2.4.6), acting within the act in a deceptive informing role. Moreover, disguised thus as the maimed soldier Fitzsword, Brainworm becomes a kind of creator, an author of the metadramatic scene he is directing from within, as he laughs to see himself 'translated thus, from a poor creature to a creator; for now must I create an intolerable sort of lies, or my present profession loses the grace' (2.4.1–3).[9] Since he is alone onstage at this time, the 'true counterfeit' (2.4.17) he produces is opened to the offstage audience, who are therefore drawn into sharing his perspective as he 'stands aside' (s.d. 2.4.17), informer-like, and through this framing they see the working of the device itself. The effect of his speech is to draw attention to the artifice of the device, its actedness, and both the creative and deceptive natures of Brainworm's 'present profession'. This, however, is quite the question: is his 'profession' at this point to be taken as servant, soldier, actor, or lying informer? His bawdy but otherwise seemingly innocuous allusion to a lie being so 'ominous a fruit as the *fico*' (2.4.4), that is the fig, actually points to classical and contemporary associations between this fruit and the sycophant and informer.[10] The theatrical, metadramatic 'lie' he is about to perpetrate, in the company of the offstage audience, is therefore one associated with self-interested informing. Nevertheless he cuts an ambiguous figure, appealing to an offstage audience.

Brainworm's further suggestion that 'we may wear motley at the year's end, and who wears motley, you know' (2.4.10–11), alludes of course to the motley-wearing fool, but there are also older traditions of vice figures and devils wearing motley, perhaps originally related to the biblical injunction not to 'wear clothing woven of two kinds of material'.[11] There is also the possibility that the idea of motley itself has some pejorative idiomatic currency at this time. Guilpin uses it in *Skialetheia* (1598) with the same associations that are implied in Jonson's text:

> Thus all our actions in a simpathy,
> Doe daunce an anticke with hypocrisie
> And motley fac'd Dissimulation,
> Is crept into our euery fashion.[12]

So, in this part of the play, Brainworm is casting himself within and around tried and tested theatrical types: the Vice, the dissimulating informer, but also, increasingly, he evokes the Jonson-like self-authored man. It is in this complex conceptual garb that he interrupts Edward and Stephen's trivial discussion about the poesies of various rings with something of more substance: his own material performance. This coney-catching role-play disguised as Fitzsword operates as both a plot device and a metadramatic technique. It is a role-play within a role-play which creates a level of dramatic irony that encourages the offstage audience to share his perspective on the foolish gulls.

Bizarrely, in his disguise and assumed role, Brainworm also falls in with the prowling Knowell senior, and therefore becomes doubled as servant to his own master, which emphasises the instability of his identity. Knowell's name is of course ironic; he knows nothing of what is going on here. Brainworm's intention is, in fact, to use this defensive and offensive masquing to gain information to benefit himself and Edward, who is about to be let in on the act. In a highly self-conscious metadramatic vein, when discovered by Wellbred and asked how he came to be 'transmuted thus', Brainworm declares, 'Faith, a device, a device' (3.2.50). This usage of the word 'device' persists, and carries contemporary senses of a 'plan [. . .] scheme, project [. . .] one of an underhand or evil character; a plot, stratagem, trick, something devised [. . .] for dramatic representation; "a mask played by private persons", or the like.'[13] Here the device's 'art', its constructedness, is foregrounded, as Wellbred asks, 'Why, Brainworm, who would have thought thou hadst been such an artificer?'; Edward adds to the field of connection between the authoring of language and deceptive role-play, declaring, 'Except a man had [. . .] been a weaver of language from his infancy for the clothing of it, I never saw his rival' (3.5.18–22).

This predatory theatrical weaving of language continues, as does the audience's awareness of its nature, when Brainworm returns to Knowell to report that Edward has discovered his role as informer, acting as Fitzsword. Having been locked up, he has escaped and now informs upon Edward's forthcoming meeting with a woman. Brainworm wants to oversee the result of this, promising the departing Knowell, 'I have another trick to act yet' (4.6.47). Brainworm next disguises himself as Formal, the legal novice, to wreak further gainful havoc on the plot, extorting more material to use in a further disguise, this time as a City Sergeant. Brainworm thus combines in himself the familiar worlds of the informer, the actor and the author. In these cases the audience sees clear connections between theatrical representation and informing. This presents a very equivocal picture of the informer, and especially in relation to the potential for self-forming the depiction is almost positive. Either way, metadrama is the natural dramatic habitat for such a figure, and his succession of roles leads him and the offstage audience, drawn into collusion by their shared awareness of his role-play, ever more surely towards the inevitable clash with the authority-figure of Justice Clement.

In the latter part of the play, immense farcical confusion arises over Kitely's cuckolding and Knowell's spying on his son as the plots become intertwined through Brainworm's work. This serves to link informing devices with predatory acting, drama with falsehood, and illegitimate authority with all, but especially with poetasters. As the characters finally approach Justice Clement for his arbitration, Clement realises something is wrong with the performance of these role-players. With something of the Jonsonian ideal observer's acuity, he declares the plain truth of the matter, 'Why, this is a mere trick, a device. You are gulled in this most grossly, all' (5.1.29–30), using 'device' to mean both theatrical construct and deceptive trap. Again, where Brainworm is exposed as the author, agent and instigator of much of the action of the play, Clement asserts his own interpretative authority, saying, 'I told you all there was some device' (5.3.53). In this way the association of authorship with informing is again confirmed through metadrama, but now with the promise that somehow the overseeing authority will bring clarity and resolution in place of equivocation.

Though Brainworm is initially made a scapegoat, and must suffer for the sake of the devices he has wrought, he is finally forgiven for the sake of his wit, and suspicion is cast elsewhere, with Justice Clement finally adjudging, 'Thou hast done or assisted to nothing, in my judgement, but deserves to be pardoned for the wit o'the offence' (5.3.91–2). He adds, 'If thy master, or any man here, be angry with thee, I shall suspect his ingine' (5.3.93), that is, his natural ability or intellect. Thus Justice Clement models a typically Jonsonian interpretative ideal: one which holds in intellectual contempt any judgement which excludes the theatrical privilege of wit, and the licensed space of the weavers of language. Clement emphasises this when he also discovers the lack-wit poetaster Mr Matthew's plagiarism and has it publicly burnt. He finally exits with a metadramatical encomium to Brainworm, '[w]hose adventures this day, when our grandchildren shall hear to be made a fable, I doubt not but it shall find both spectators and applause' (5.5.74–6).

So Jonson makes this mild arbiter an apologist of the devices of metadramatic plotting and poetic integrity in an epilogue which recommends this mode of interpretation to the audience by example. Clement's relative harshness with the gulls may be, as Russ McDonald suggests, evidence of both Jonson's 'emerging didactic bent and artistic inexperience', but even so, Clement exemplifies a judicial and interpretative ideal under whose oversight the legitimacy of theatrical 'devices', and the illegitimacy of other kinds, may be explored, in the self-referential metadramatic manner which most befits them, without anyone needing to be excessively punished.[14] On the contrary, those, like Jonson himself, who would create a 'stir of art and devices', are made the subjects of true discernment, and 'wit' is attributed and rewarded accordingly, even, quite remarkably, in the case of the informer. *Every Man In His Humour* thus reproduces its own material conditions of production in the tension between the social authority of the genuine Horatian satirist, of the lack-wit poetasters, and of other misusers of information, while advancing an interpretative ideal in which even the material reality of oversight by potentially predatory authorities is made to appreciate creative wit. Though the ideal seems to have been warmly received, Jonson's subsequent career gives us some understanding of the extent to which this remains a fantasy.

Veracity and Voracity: *Every Man Out* and the Duality of the Author

Let me be censured, by th'austerest brow
Where I want art or judgement. Tax me freely.
Let envious critics with their broadest eyes
Look through and through me. (Ind. 58–61)[15]

Every Man Out of His Humour (1600, first performed 1599) is a play in which conceited and pretentious character types parade exaggerated humours that are ultimately exposed and cured. This curative process takes place through a series of often structurally metadramatic social scenes in which ambitious social climbers seek love, fame and fortune via various kinds of self-performance. The very necessity for a cure here implies a sickness which is both personal and social, one that exists within networks of signification and is in need of treatment. The 'plot' of this text is less significant than the dramatic structures within which the characters' excesses are discovered, and through which they learn to temper their personality disorders, and hence the maladies of the dysfunctional society they represent. These are dominated by metadrama.

Throughout, a choric onstage audience representing both audience and author provides a critical commentary designed to forestall self-interested and venal critical interpretation of the play. This authorial audience amounts to far more than what earlier critiques thought of as mere 'experiments in perspective' and in fact makes explicit the tension upon which both this and *Every Man In* base their comedy, created by an environment of interpretative paranoia and litigious lack-wits.[16] As Mitis of the chorus advises, 'the days are dangerous, full of exception, / And men are grown impatient of reproof' (Ind. 121–2). These choric incursions are meant to 'orient the audience morally and aesthetically' as McDonald suggests but I would add that they are also meant to orient them politically and interpretatively.[17] The concern to model an appropriate audience reaction here is certainly far less playful than that found in *Every Man In*, produced just the previous year. Given this play's fraught reception (meeting with hostility at The Globe and possibly official censure) the effectiveness of the technique may be in question.[18] But the fact that Jonson's social satire explicitly includes the troubling potential of the interpreter is of critical interest, since, as a chief interpreter of the times, the author may be implicated in this as much as the informer.

Something of the duality of this connection may be perceived when Asper, 'the Presenter' character, states his metadramatic and satiric intention to, 'scourge those apes, / And to these courteous eyes [*indicating audience*] oppose a mirror, / As large as is the stage whereon we act', in order to show them 'the time's deformity / Anatomised' (Ind. 115–19). His need to emphasise his 'constant courage, and contempt of fear' (Ind. 120) in stating this, and specify exactly what he is not afraid of, alludes to the potentially violent nature of prospective responses to his satire:

I fear no mood stamped in a private brow,
When I am pleased t'unmask a public vice.
I fear no strumpet's drugs, nor ruffian's stab,
Should I detect their hateful luxuries. (Ind. 19–22)[19]

These fictional threats play into a narrative of real punishment which may, as we have seen, be equally vicious. This play was written against the backdrop of the proscription of satire by the Archbishop of Canterbury and the Bishop of London in 1599, a ban which led to popular incidents of book burning.[20] Unlike Justice Clement's poetry burning, this was not limited to plagiarised works, and it seems in direct defiance of the ban that Jonson specifically calls *Every Man Out* a 'comical satire'.[21] As M. Lindsay Kaplan points out, satire at this time was regarded as potentially seditious criticism, always in danger of slippage into the realms of defamation, and perceived possibly even as an 'arrogation of royal authority'.[22] It is remarkable and somewhat audacious then that, within this testing critical atmosphere, the play risks establishing direct connections between its own metadrama and the portrayal of the dangers of the act of interpretation, and that it is forthright in doing so. Recent Jonson criticism has developed a response to metadrama which focuses on Jonson's undoubted desire to establish the primacy of satire as a necessary corrective to social ills. This present study would suggest that behind the concern to establish satire as socially authoritative lies a structure of social control which the drama wittingly or unwittingly replicates. The means of expression in this case mirror one of the very social ills which Jonson's satire critiques, and this obviously is a cause for concern within that project. These issues are at play in *Every Man Out*'s approach to authority, which is ostensibly more nuanced by scepticism than the lighter, relatively conservative approach of *Every Man In*.

As part of the play's direct metadramatic mode, the authorial character Asper sets up the chorus, the characters Cordatus and

Mitis, onstage, as model interpreters, commanding them, 'as censors to sit here, / Observe what I present, and liberally / Speak your opinions upon every scene' (Ind. 152–4). They are referred to as the 'Grex' (defined by *OED* as 'a herd, flock, drove; of people [. . .] esp. a philosophical sect') and hence this choric form resonates with both satirical commonality and interpretative nous.[23] At the heart of this onstage audience is Cordatus, described by Jonson as 'the author's friend; a man inly acquainted with the scope and drift of his plot; of [. . .] understanding judgement [. . .] a moderator' (Characters, 105–8).[24] This structure produces a very acute form of metadrama which refers to its own status both as a medium of interpretation and as matter for interpretation; that is, simultaneously as both the subject and object of interpretation. Here the metadrama conceals nothing; on the contrary, it openly offers the very act of interpretation back to its offstage audience for interpretation in its turn. Helen Ostovich sees the Grex as an Aristophanic chorus intended to 'include the audience in the play both as objects of satiric attack and as sharers of an in-joke at the expense of society at large'.[25] Given the serious material consequences such interpretation could have for authors, as a joke it constitutes what we might call dark humour.

In the case of *Every Man Out*'s interpretation, there was clearly an issue of censure at the point of performance, though it is not clear what form this took. The quarto versions of the play (1600 onwards) contain the following disclaimer:

> It was not near his thoughts that hath published this either to traduce the author, or to make vulgar and cheap any the peculiar and sufficient deserts of the actors; but rather (whereas many censures fluttered about it) to give all leave and leisure to judge with distinction. (Characters, 113–17)[26]

Jonson refers to issues raised with the portrayal of Macilente and the Queen in the original ending, and clearly there has been a necessity to negotiate with its interpretations in a similar manner to *Staple of News*'s later issues in this regard.[27] Whatever the exact nature of these 'censures' were that 'fluttered about it', Ostovich suggests that they indicate at least a robust response to the play, which was clearly considered somehow risky in content or intention.[28] Thus, when at the outset Asper declares openly his aggressive critical and satirical intentions to 'strip the ragged follies of the time / Naked as at their birth – / [. . .] and with a whip of steel / Print wounding lashes in their iron ribs' (Ind. 15–18), Cordatus and Mitis, the official onstage interpreters, object to this and attempt to rein him in, warning, 'Unless your breath had power / To melt the world and mould it new again / It is in vain to spend it in these moods' (Ind. 46–8). The intransigence of a censorious authority thus informs this metadramatic exchange. But equally, potentially liberating connections between metadrama and interpretative openness are established when Asper turns to the offstage audience, as he must at this point, and exclaims,

> I not observed this throngèd round till now.
> Gracious and kind spectators, you are welcome.
> [. . .] Yet here mistake me not, judicious friends:
> I do not this to beg your patience,
> Or servilely to fawn on your applause,
> Like some dry brain despairing in his merit (Ind. 49–50, 54–7)

Here he establishes his authorial integrity by contrasting allusion to the above-mentioned Jonsonian bugbear: one who, 'despairing in his merit', sees himself mirrored in whatever is being critiqued. The visual element is significant here also, where Asper continues, provocatively, 'Let me be censured by th'austerest brow [. . .] / Let envious critics with their broadest eyes / Look through and through me' (Ind. 58, 60–1), figuring a piercing, penetrative gaze from the threatening interpreter, which he, in the person of the author, explicitly invites, and braves. Asper's metadrama thus models what Jonson hopes will elicit the correct response of offstage interpreters, inviting their critique with the self-assurance of his burgeoning artistic authority. The interpreters in turn are potentially linked with the play's critical treatment of the excessively 'humorous': Cordatus agrees with Asper that, 'if an idiot / Have but an apish or fantastic strain' he blames it on his 'humour' (Ind. 113–15). Developing this critique, Asper asks rhetorically who could possibly take exception to him, answering himself, 'None but a sort of fools, so sick in taste / That they contemn all physic of the mind / And like galled camels kick at every touch' (130–2). In these ways, the introductory passages of the play aim both to prescribe modes of interpretation to an offstage audience and to shape their response accordingly. Within this interpretative framework, the image of the touchy 'galled camel' sticks, and fits into a recognisable picture of the informer and his over-sensitive patron.

Before declaring metadramatically, 'I go / To turn an actor and a humorist' (211–12) and merging vice-like into the performance, Asper expresses another of Jonson's interpretative concerns: that audiences may feel they have the right to wrest his meanings to suit themselves, and that this might be catching. He asks Mitis to observe the offstage audience, and to note any who 'Cries mew, and nods, then shakes his empty head, / [. . .] A fellow that has neither art nor brain, / [. . .] Taking men's lines with a tobacco face' (Ind. 161, 177, 179): one who, informer-like,

> us[es] his wried looks,
> In nature of a vice, to wrest and turn
> The good aspect of those that shall sit near him
> From what they do behold! [. . .] (Ind. 180–4)

The fictional undesirable audience-figure is imagined here 'In nature of a vice', an interestingly demonic theatrical metaphor for the role of audience malcontent, especially since Asper himself may be seen to fill this role himself. However, these passages also frame an interpretative ideal: good spectators, we are told, have 'serious and intentive eyes' (Ind. 137); they are 'attentive auditors' (Ind. 199). They do not try to corrupt their fellows. These obvious attempts at framing or modelling responses before the fact of course indicate the inevitability that interpretations are to be made. Indeed during one incursion of the Grex, Cordatus makes it clear to Mitis that it is 'the special intent of the author you should [make objections], for thereby others that are present may as well be satisfied, who happily would object the same you do' (2.2.590–3). Mitis and Cordatus thus help to sustain the carefully balanced critical atmosphere which Jonson aims to create and cultivate. As models of an audience they constantly remind us of 'the problem of satiric mimesis', as McDonald argues, and they do this by attempting to define the terms within which legitimate interpretation of that satire may be made.[29] But more than this, they display a growing concern over legitimate interpretation, which, despite the humour, is driven by a deep unease over the possibilities of malignant misinterpretation.

So far we have considered how the metadrama works to set up an openly interpretative audience; but the play also offers us another kind of observer, one far more explicitly malign in his intentions. At his first appearance, Carlo Buffone, a 'public, scurrilous, and profane jester [. . .] [whose] religion is railing' (Characters, 22, 30–1), inveigles himself into the metadrama, addressing both those onstage, and the audience offstage: 'Boy, fetch me a glass quickly, I may bid these gentlemen welcome, give 'em a health here' (Ind. 314–16). He also alludes to the author with: 'I mar'l whose wit 'twas to put a prologue in yond sackbut's mouth' (Ind. 317–18), exemplifying Jonsonian self-deprecation through the use of a critical character; here, as is often the case, this seems to be a defensive manoeuvre. Carlo then drinks to the audience and refers directly to 'our poet' (Ind. 329) making 'a good meal among players, where he has *caninem appetitum* [. . .] [will drink] three, four, five of these [draughts of Canary]' (Ind. 331–2, 334–5), and afterwards 'look villainously [. . .] like a one-headed Cerberus' (Ind. 335–6), adding, '(he do' not hear me, I hope)' (Ind. 336–7). Curiously, since he is the author, Jonson is depicted here not merely as dog-like and monstrous in his appetites but also as a dangerous listener to the discourse he has authored. Carlo effectively sets him up as the dubious interpreter of Carlo's own metadramatic act; doing so of course only serves to draw attention to Carlo's own doubtful nature. Already more than three hundred lines into the play, Carlo introduces it with its title: 'He has made a play here, and he calls it *Every Man Out of His Humour*' (Ind. 339–40), and, with this metadramatic implication that the Induction has not been scripted, Carlo sets up a rapport with the audience, addressing them in such a direct manner that his fictional status becomes a fading matter. When he tells them that he wishes to be part of the audience but cannot, since this would involve him in praising himself, 'I could wish my bottle here amongst you, but there's an old rule: "No pledging your own health"' (Ind. 343–5), this indicates an expected positive response from the audience – the delivery here might determine any weight of irony behind the statement. And when he closes by enjoining silence and passivity in the audience, advising them to 'sit still, seal up their lips, and drink so much of the play in at their eares' (Ind. 346–7), he figures their reception of the play as a matter of appetite, with the drinking ear disturbingly reminiscent of other ear–mouth imagery, including that surrounding Lady Macbeth and the poisoning of old Hamlet. This approach connects early modern regimens of appetite and self-control with imagery surrounding informing, and offers the audience Carlo's own boisterous perspective, which, as already mentioned, will turn out to be the view of an informer.[30]

At the next Grex, Carlo's moral and interpretative voracity is emphasised as Mitis and Cordatus discuss how the author describes him as a 'violent railer' (Ind. 351) who traduces all that 'come within the reach of his eye' (Ind. 356); Mitis says, 'You paint forth a monster' (Ind. 358). Jonson is indeed painting a kind of social monster, and the audience should soon see this. John Marston's offence at being caricatured as Carlo was evidently a trigger for the internecine poetic strife in which *Cynthia's Revels* and *Poetaster* figured over the next few years.[31] But there is a far more significant original model for Carlo, as Herford and Simpson, and more recently Matthew Steggle, have convincingly argued, and this is at the real heart of the offence which Marston quite rightly takes at this mockery of his honour.[32] John Aubrey's *Brief Lives*, written towards the end of the seventeenth century, describes one Charles Chester, an annoyingly verbose associate of Ralegh. As Aubrey recounts, 'one time at a tavern Sir Walter Ralegh beats him and seals up his mouth (i.e., his upper and nether beard) with hard wax. From him Ben Jonson takes his Carlo Buffono' [sic].[33] Steggle also notes that Harington's 1596 *An Apology* links Chester to the archetypal harsh interpreters Momus and Zoilus, as critics of his own writing.[34] However, rather than simply being a critical raconteur and well known man-about-town, Chester (and hence Carlo Buffone) was a notorious informer. He is on record writing to Cecil specifically commending his own informing in Cecil's service.[35] He is also named in at least one case of passing information to the Inquisition, and is noted to be carrying letters and informing in the service of Walsingham.[36] Also, as Ostovich notes, 'Buffone' means not only 'clown' but also has a root in 'bufe', the thieves' cant term for a dog, another connection with typical imagery for informers.[37] This typology may help to elucidate a John Davies epigram that Steggle mentions, in the preface to *Coryat's Crudities*, which depicts Chester as a predatory devourer.[38] Living in that world of predation, his own turn of course came, and on 20 August 1600 Chester was himself informed against for 'having been heard making unfavourable comments upon the queen and upon Cecil'.[39] Somehow escaping this charge, he died in 1604 leaving £400, a considerable sum for a man of his means, the residual sum perhaps of fees accrued through his lucrative time as an informer. How much the original audiences would have known of this is anybody's guess, but even as a stock character Carlo's real nature would be familiar to them.

Thus far, the real author has interposed Asper, Cordatus and Mitis between himself and the offstage interpreters, and has complicated that relationship with the introduction of the critically dangerous figure of Carlo, who will pass, like Asper, into and out of the world of the inner-play. After a vast metadramatic preamble the action passes to Act 1, Scene 1, an elaborate, protracted framing even in comparison to the lengthy introductory passages of *Bartholomew Fair*. And so the stage is thoroughly set for the entrance of Macilente, the stock brooding malcontent and melancholic, with his own personal social disease, his 'wounded soul' and Juvenalian 'cor'sive' thoughts (1.1.5, 7). He is perhaps, as W. David Kay suggests, 'yet another thinly-disguised version of Jonson'.[40]

No love is lost between Macilente and Carlo, although they are both in their own way representative of personal and social dysfunction. When Carlo greets Macilente, he replies by calling him 'good Janus' (1.2.204), the two-faced god, and to the aspirant Sogliardo, he describes him as a 'lean mongrel, [who] looks as if he were chap-fallen with barking at other men's good fortunes' (1.2.214–16). Carlo goes on, 'he carries oil and fire in his pen, will scald where it drops. His spirit's like powder, quick, violent: he'll blow a man up with a jest. I feare him worse then a rotten wall does the cannon, shake an hour after at the report' (1.2.216–20). Macilente is described here as a barking dog and a writer of earth-shaking slanders, with a play on the word 'report' indicating the explosive power of his criticism.[41] Meanwhile Macilente tells the offstage audience directly that Carlo is 'an open-throated, black-mouthed cur / That bites at all, but eats on those that feed him'; moreover he will, 'serpent-like, / Creep on the ground, as he would eat the dust, / And to your back will turn the tail and sting / More deadly than a scorpion' (1.2.234–9). This accusation of deceptive two-faced social performance recalls the role-play of both theatre and informer and it reflects back also on Macilente who, as a melancholic is also implicitly self-theatricalised, indicated by such metadramatic asides to the audience as, 'I know my cue, I think' (2.2.22). The metadramatic references here describe a conceptual field encompassing the duplicity of role-play in the world and in the theatre, fawning policy and the dangerous nature of the slanderous user of information. Indeed both are accused of being traitors to friends. As metadramatic characters, Macilente and Carlo personate the two faces of the informer; they are the explicit and the hidden menaces of the predatory slanderer, precisely the duplicitous hate-figure whose influence the opening passages of the play are designed to obviate. However, of the two, Carlo's disease cuts closer to the core of venality and corrupt patronage: later in the play, the typical courtier Puntarvolo advises the vainglorious knight Fastidius Briske to disregard Carlo's 'blasphemy' because, as he says, 'it is in the power of my purse to make him speak well or ill of me' (2.1.495–8). It appears Carlo is not merely a voracious barking and poisonous interpreter, but further that he is also known to sell his slanders for hard cash.

In this thoroughly metadramatic atmosphere, many of the play's characters seem to share between them the attributes of the popular vision of the informer, the kind of dog-imagery which is very often associated with informing abounds and often connects with metadramatic self-reference. The scurrilous Carlo, who 'with absurd similes will transform any person into deformity' is described as a 'feast-hound or banquet-beagle' (Characters, 23–5). Meanwhile Carlo, in the terminology of hunting, accuses Deliro of being a 'good bloodhound, a close-mouthed dog' adding 'he follows the scent well. Marry, he's at fault now' (4.3.121–3); Puntarvolo replies, 'I should wonder at that creature is free from the danger of thy tongue' (4.4.124–5). Further, the malicious nature of the dog's tongue is also bound up with the authorial nature of the plotter: Cordatus says of Macilente, 'Now does he [. . .] plot and store up a world of malicious thoughts' (4.5.153–5), and Carlo accuses him of 'plotting some mischievous device' (5.3.25–6). Carlo is sensitised to such artifice in his own respect of course, but also because he has witnessed Puntarvolo's punctilious performance of his own character, which Carlo, in the language of informing and theatre, calls 'a project, a designment of his own, a thing studied and rehearsed as ordinarily at his coming from hawking or hunting as a jig after a play' (2.1.223–5). The venal Sogliardo, who is 'so enamoured of the name of a gentleman that he will have it though he buys it', we are told, has a theatrical bent, since he 'comes up every term to [. . .] see new motions' (Characters, 74–7). Fungoso 'follows the fashion afar off like a spy' (Characters, 68); Clove and Orange work here as conies to be caught – they are 'fit for nothing but to be practised upon. Being well flattered, they'll lend money [. . .] Their glory is to feast players' (Characters, 96–9).

Such self-referential moments create a conceptual framework within which metadramatic structures reproduce the conditions of hidden watching or hearing and dubious interpretation. These facilitate a ubiquitous information-gathering and come to seem inevitable, even finally touching the divine. So, when the transgressive Sordido arrives reading an almanack, Macilente speaks aside to the audience, 'Stay. Who's this? / Now, for my soul, another minion / Of the old lady Chance's: I'll observe him' (1.2.239–41). Simply stepping aside (or in this case remaining lying down) in this manner, Macilente constructs an empowered perspective which the audience, by virtue of the aside, is invited to share. The diegetic gravity here must work through four levels: offstage audience > onstage audience (Cordatus and Mitis) > the observer (Macilente) > the action/dialogue. The tendency of scopic pulsion is to draw the spectator into the innermost metadramatic level of the play and thus to elide the outer frames, this frame-blindness creating a shared critical perspective for both the offstage and onstage audiences. Depending on the production, this perspective may be primarily conceptual rather than visual, but is no less real for all that. Either way, the overview Macilente provides here ridicules Sordido's credulity. Laughing, Macilente asks (directly or indirectly of the offstage audience), 'Is 't possible that such a spacious villain / Should live and not be plagued? Or lies he hid / Within the wrinkled bosom of the world, / Where heaven cannot see him?' (1.3.67–70). In this universalised imagery of the malcontent, even God is an overlooker, waiting to punish 'villains' unless they hide their evil doings in the bosom of the earth.

Sordido's particular villainy is that he is a hoarder. Despite being ordered to relieve the sufferings of the starving poor, he deliberately withholds and conceals his farm produce, and speaking this aloud he is advised by Hind, his servant, 'O but master, / Take heed they hear you not [. . .] / They will exclaim against you' (1.3.114–16). But these are informers whom Sordido rashly deprecates, saying 'their exclaims / Move me as much as thy breath moves a mountain!' (1.3.116–17). Here the offstage audience's response is influenced not only by the fact of their inclusion within Hind's 'they', who might overhear and 'exclaim' against the hoarder, but also by this deprecation, which is deepened when Sordido refers to the starving multitude as 'that many-mouthèd vulgar dog [. . .] baying at my door' (1.3.134–5). In this way the audience is implicated in opposition to Sordido's crime. Always implicitly overhearers, here they are also specifically cast as potential informers, conventionally depicted with canine voracity. Of course, Sordido's scorn of the material effects of such an exclamation against him is mere bravado, and fitting with the venal and foolish nature of his character. And the audience's informing in this case would carry a sense of righteous justice. But even so, this sense of predatory voracity is reflected throughout the play: at the next interjection of the Grex, Cordatus calls Sordido 'a wolf i' the commonwealth' (1.3.163); later, Carlo is asked by Puntarvolo, when being beaten, 'are you howling, you wolf?' (5.3.244). These canine and lupine references reflect the play's firmer sense of critique of contemporary personal and social ills in the area of authority and informing. The co-opting of the offstage audience into this critique affords them a perspective whose ambiguity the author shares.

The elaboration and questioning of this ambiguous framework of interpretation develops throughout, with Mitis and Cordatus as the most obvious elements in the picture. Discussing the potential reception of the play, Mitis expresses the belief that 'this last scene will endure some grievous torture'; Cordatus asks in reply, 'How? You fear 'twill be racked by some hard construction?' (2.2.358–61).

Drawing parodic attention to the appetite of certain audience-members for the 'wresting' of meanings of their own from the themes and persons of the play, particularly the foolish would-be courtier Fastidius Briske, both Mitis and Cordatus go on to attempt to pre-empt possible misinterpretation in either city or court, making absolutely explicit the general concerns over the issue of self-interested interpretation that pervade the play and society at large. For this purpose Cordatus asks rhetorically, 'can you imagine that any noble or true spirit in the court [. . .] will make any exception at the opening of such an empty trunk as this Brisk is? Or think his own worth impeached by beholding his motley inside?' (2.2.373–8); Mitis, of course, answers, 'No, sir, I do not' (2.2.379). Cordatus continues didactically, on behalf of Jonson, that such erroneous interpretations would mean that 'a man writing of Nero should mean all emperors; or speaking of Machiavel, comprehend all statesmen; or in our Sordido, all farmers; and so of the rest – than which nothing can be uttered more malicious and absurd' (2.2.383–7). Displacing thus the malice of utterance from the stage to its interpreters, Cordatus further describes the kind of wresting constructions that the text as a whole is directed against, calling these venal types, 'narrow-eyed decipherers [. . .] that will extort strange and abstruse meanings out of any subject, be it never so conspicuous and innocently delivered' (2.2.388–90). It is difficult not to hear Jonson's own rebuke in this, and indeed impossible where he is directly referenced by Cordatus in a metadramatic statement that resonates with authorial anger at these hidden perverters of meaning:

> to such – where'er they sit concealed – let them know the author defies them and their writing-tables, and hopes no sound or safe judgment will infect itself with their contagious comments, who, indeed, come here only to pervert and poison the sense of what they hear, and for nought else. (2.2.390–6)

This obviously also contains an implicit warning to the ordinary audience-members about the need for their use of 'safe judgement' to avoid the kind of toxic wresting typical of despised informers. It contains therefore a strong appeal for veracity over voracity.

However, despite the desire to resolve these ambiguities and cure this social malady, the text is not reluctant to admit the potential for theatre's complicity in these deceptive processes. For example, the threat of duplicitous hypocrisy is bound up both with acting and cannibalistic appetite in Carlo's advice to Sogliardo on his becoming a gentleman: 'Speak ill of no man to his face, nor well of any man behind his back. Salute fairly on the front, and wish 'em hanged upon the turn. Spread your self upon his bosom publicly, whose heart you would eat in private' (3.1.267–70). Here Carlo is of course really talking about himself; he has already alluded metadramatically to theatre also when he advised Sogliardo against dealing with prison dwellers, 'poor needy Ludgathians [who] care not what violent tragedies they stir' (1.2.124, 126). With one eye on Jonson's own recent prison experience for his part in *The Isle of Dogs*, this suggestion of authorial violence accords with the image of the gentleman-informer eating the heart of his rival in private. Carlo's earlier instructions to Sogliardo on 'gentlemanly' behaviour at the theatre: 'look with a good starched face, and ruffle your brow like a new boot; laugh at nothing but your own jests [. . .] and sit o' the stage, and flout' (1.2.61–3, 66) provide a larger context to his conflation of theatre with his own dubious social role. Since it is possible that the Globe did not usually allow stage-seating at this time, this may work primarily as a gibe at the private theatres.[42] In any case, it might be safe to assume that public stage-seats would be restricted for metadramatic plays of this kind, due simply to the difficulties of staging an onstage audience in addition to such a presence. Where there were seats available onstage this may be doubly metadramatic, referring to both as frames of interpretation.

At the next appearance of the 'staged' onstage audience of the Grex, Mitis has clearly been made anxious by Carlo's imputations of such casual social duplicity, and declares metadramatically that he fears another objection which 'will be enforced against the author ere I can be delivered of it' (3.1.512–14). He explains that the comedy might have been safer if it were about love-tangles, which he refers to as 'cross-wooing' (3.1.520), and argues that this would be less risky than 'to be thus near, and familiarly allied to the time' (3.1.520–1). There is, of course, a pre-emptive admission here. Cordatus responds, however, by citing Cicero's dramatic ideal and concludes, 'if the maker have failed in any particle of this, they may worthily tax him, but if not, why, be you (that are for them) silent, as I will be for him; and give way to the actors' (3.1.529–32). Cordatus is 'for' (i.e. represents) the author and Mitis in this sense is 'for' the audience, and this accounts for both Cordatus's apologetic function and Mitis's relative passivity.[43] In this case it is significant that the figure of the author is also a figure of an ideal audience; the author's own potential for informer-like voracity and misinterpretation of the times is mitigated by his association with this ideal, which simultaneously undercuts any potential accusation of slanderous representation.

Whether in slander or sycophancy, the fear is that the informer deals in misinformation. Moul is not the first to note Jonson's Juvenalian disgust at the 'ceaseless round of pandering and flattery' in a society corrupted by informing, and here Jonson draws together an awareness of dishonest 'practice' of all kinds with the world of the player.[44] The lying Cavalier Shift is an interesting character in this respect. He is described as 'a threadbare shark [. . .] [whose] profession is skeldring [. . .] odling [. . .] and making privy searches for imparters' (Characters, 80–1, 93). The first of these terms, 'skeldring', is glossed by *OED* as 'to swindle, cheat, defraud (a person)'; 'odling' is more obscure, but may refer either to 'ogling' or having dealings with 'odalisques', though *OED* dates the first usage of this as 1681. *OED* offers no illumination on precisely what an 'imparter' might impart at this time; I would suggest they are either imparters of information or, like the easy prey Clove and Orange, of money, as Ostovich has it.[45] Therefore, as Shift enters, Mitis frames him in metadrama, saying, 'Stay. What new mute is this that walks so suspiciously?' (2.2.397). Cordatus replies, 'O, marry, this is one for whose better illustration we must desire you to presuppose the stage the middle aisle in Paul's' (3.1.1–3). Staged thus, Shift talks of having taken 'an ounce of tobacco' with a gentleman and how he is now 'come to spit private in Paul's' (3.1.26–7). Since Paul's is very much a public space, the 'spitting' of whatever has passed between himself and the 'gentleman' suggests a reasonable metaphor for informing. His shady nature as a putative dweller in the underworld, emphasised when Sogliardo accuses him of having done 'five hundred robberies' (4.3.274), underscores this tendency. As a malcontent, Macilente is also just such an ambiguous character, described as a 'well parted [. . .] scholar', though his judgement is 'dazzled' (Characters, 7, 10). To add to Macilente's characterisation as an informer, wise Cordatus likens his ongoing 'cold passion' (1.1.31) to the '*sudat frigidus*' (1.1.34), the cold sweat which is the sign of the sighing poet.

Connections are drawn then between the poet and the melancholic or malcontent, with the melancholic playing the author, the malcontent playing the informer and both playing the plotter. Throughout the play, Macilente increasingly expresses this ambiguity, developing a pseudo-moralist character, and his 'devices' (for instance promising to reconcile Deliro with his unappreciative wife while arranging for her to meet Fastidius Briske, his real intention being to trick Deliro into realising his wife's potential for infidelity) give him authorial status as a plotter. It is little surprise then when he turns out to be Asper, the metadramatic presenter of the Induction. Harsh by name, Asper, the self-conscious onstage figure of the author, is both character and critical commentator. Like the ideal satirist, his character description declares he is 'constant in reproof, without fear controlling the world's abuses', yet is careful to assert that he is 'one whom no servile hope of gain [. . .] can make to be a parasite either to time, place or opinion' (Characters, 1–5). As both author and plotter, this is a very important distinction to draw.[46]

Towards the end of the play, although the forces of law do eventually arrive to deal with the riotous behaviour which has culminated in Carlo the informer having his incontinent mouth waxed shut, there is no sense of closure here, no Justice Clement to correct the pretentious or excessive behaviour of the unbalanced characters. It is in fact Macilente-Asper who is found metadramatically directing a 'stir of arts and devices' to bring resolution of a kind to the separate scenes: informing the Drawer of Fungoso's hiding place and leaving him to pay the tavern bill; sending Deliro to rescue him; telling Fallace this was 'a device to remove your husband hence' (5.3.400–1), using this as a pretext for her to rescue Fastidius Brisk from gaol at the Counter; directing Deliro to prosecute Brisk, knowing that he will find Fallace there (framing her own drama self-consciously in relation to the unfashionable elaboration of Lyly's *Euphues*). Throughout this plotting facilitation of the general dishumouring process, another interpretative framework seems to be offered to the audience, who, guided by the interjections of the Grex, are then left to interpret as they see fit. At the conclusion of the play, Macilente-Asper immediately turns to the onstage audience of the Grex and asks, 'How now, sirs? How like you it? Has't not been tedious? (5.4.41–2). Cordatus denies him a response, saying, 'Nay, we ha' done censuring now' (5.4.43), and defers judgement in favour of the offstage audience: 'here are those round about you of more ability in censure than we, whose judgements can give it a more satisfying allowance. We'll refer you to them' (5.4.47–50). This is done in the hope that the plot, characterisation and structure of the play as a whole will have conditioned the audience's responses in accordance with Cordatus's description, again producing an interpretative ideal which recognises the creative veracity of the author. Curiously, in his conventional appeal Macilente-Asper tells the offstage audience that if they will bestow 'plaudite' they may 'make lean Macilente as fat as Sir John Falstaff' (5.4.60, 62–3). This seems like a tenuous connection with a merely proverbial opposite in body size, but I would suggest that the association is a broader one, and Chapter 5 will explore the relationship of Falstaff to metadramatic self-performance in more detail. But again, this leaves the resolution inconclusive and plays into the interpretative hands of the offstage audience.

In *Every Man Out*, Jonson puts his own ideal of the author as interpreter of the times into the hermeneutic scene and he has it walk a tightrope over a network of popular conceptual connections between a model of authorly veracity and the potential voracity of the interpreter and informer. Perhaps the lack of success of this sequel is due to the fact that good comedy relies upon playing with an acknowledged but often unstated tension, which is released in laughter. Here the tensions involved in the interrelations of ideal author, informer and audience are simply made too obvious, and though in their own terms they reveal much, they finally leave little to be released as humour. The only strong hint of resolution is the dissolution of Macilente-Asper's own malice in the presence of the Queen, as he declares that in her graces, 'All my malicious powers have lost their stings. / Envy is fled my soul at sight of her, / And she hath chased all black thoughts from my bosom' (5.4.6–9).[47] In the sun-like presence of ultimate authority, melancholy itself is cured. However, in his final response he bestows a significant blessing on her court,

> where never may there come
> Suspect or Danger, but all Trust and Safety.
> Let Flattery be dumb and Envy blind
> In her dread presence. (5.4.33–6)

Despite his understanding of his own complicity in some of the same mechanisms, Jonson's recommendation as author always emphasises the value of veracity as against the informing machinations of the malcontent, the sycophancy of the fawning courtier and the poisonous words of the melancholic. Offering a stronger critique of the pressures of authority on theatre and authorship than is found in *Every Man In*, it is most significant that the abiding image of this text is that of the enforced sealing of the informer's voracious and incontinent mouth.

Notes

1. Hutson, 'Civility', p. 6.
2. Victoria Moul, *Jonson, Horace and the Classical Tradition* (Cambridge: Cambridge University Press, 2010), p. 108.
3. Unless otherwise noted, all line references refer to Ben Jonson, *Every Man In His Humour*, ed. David Bevington, in *The Cambridge Edition of the Works of Ben Jonson*, Vol. 4.
4. This has been read as a critique of Shakespeare's dramatic artifice, although in September 1598 it was played at the Curtain by the Lord Chamberlain's Company, a production in which Shakespeare acted a part, possibly that of Knowell. See Russ McDonald, *Shakespeare and Jonson, Jonson and Shakespeare* (Lincoln and London: University of Nebraska Press, 1988), pp. 5–7; also Ben Jonson, *Bartholomew Fair*, in Arthur F. Kinney (ed.), *Renaissance Drama: An Anthology of Plays and Entertainments* (Oxford: Blackwell, 1999), Induction 127–30.
5. For the association between 'poetry and governance' see James Loxley, *The Complete Critical Guide to Ben Jonson* (London and New York: Routledge, 2002), p. 48.
6. Mr Stephen will later be encouraged by the poetaster Mr Matthew to be a hidden audience as they over-listen Captain Bobadill's military boasting as an example of gentlemanly behaviour: 'Matthew: 'Pray you, mark this discourse, sir / Stephen: So I do' (3.1.123–4).
7. The roots of this are in the preface to Martial; see Ben Jonson, *Bartholomew* Fair, ed. John Creaser, in *The Cambridge Edition of the Works of Ben Jonson*, Vol. 4, p. 271, n. 10.
8. Jonson, *The Magnetic Lady*, ed. Ostovich, in *The Cambridge Edition of the Works of Ben Jonson*, Vol. 6.
9. *OED* lists this as one of the earliest secular usages of the word 'creator', in this context as '2. a. *gen.* One who, or that which, creates or gives origin to', though it might be argued that Brainworm is also alluding to his creation of his own role, thus also giving this the earliest sense, unlisted in *OED*, of 'b. One who 'creates' a dramatic character or role'.
10. From the Greek συκοφάντης, sykophántēs, an informer; specifically one who informed upon anyone found to be illegally exporting figs: Plutarch, *Plutarch's Lives*, Life of Solon, 24, 2, <http://www.gutenberg.org/dirs/etext96/plivs10.txt> (last accessed 3 December 2015). *OED* argues that the Greek origin of this word, derived from συκος, sykos, 'fig', and φανης, fanēs, 'to show', as 'fig-shower', 'has not been satisfactorily accounted for', though these possible etymological difficulties would not preclude the currency of this seventeenth-century usage. See also Ben Jonson, *Poetaster*, 'An honest sycophant-like slave' (5.3.112).

11. Bible (Lev. 19: 19) and see Vicki K. Janik and Emmanuel Sampath Nelson, *Fools and Jesters in Literature, Art, and History* (Westport, CT: Greenwood, 1998), p. 5ff.
12. Guilpin, n.p.
13. As *OED*, carrying contemporary senses: 'Something devised or contrived for bringing about some end or result; an arrangement, plan, scheme, project, contrivance; an ingenious or clever expedient; often one of an underhand or evil character; a plot, stratagem, trick [. . .] b. Used of things non-material [. . .] fancifully invented for dramatic representation [. . .] a mask'.
14. McDonald, *Shakespeare and Jonson*, p. 51.
15. Unless otherwise noted, all line references refer to Ben Jonson, *Every Man Out of His Humour*, ed. Helen Ostovich (Manchester: Manchester University Press, 2001). This edition is based on Jonson's 1600 Quarto 1.
16. Edward B. Partridge, 'Ben Jonson: The Making of the Dramatist (1597–1602)', in John Russel Brown and Bernard Harris (eds), *Elizabethan Theatre* (London: Edward Arnold, 1966), pp. 221–44, 231.
17. McDonald, *Shakespeare and Jonson*, p. 58.
18. Ben Jonson, *Every Man Out of His Humour*, ed. Randall Martin, in *The Cambridge Edition of the Works of Ben Jonson*, Vol. 1, p. 235.
19. For the Juvenalian characterisation of Asper here, see Moul, p. 101.
20. Loxley, p. 22.
21. Donaldson, p. 153. Martin points out that Jonson does, however, avoid the scatological content which was also at issue in the Bishops' ban; see *The Cambridge Edition of the Works of Ben Jonson*, Vol. 1, p. 237.
22. M. Lindsay Kaplan, *The Culture of Slander in Early Modern England* (Cambridge: Cambridge University Press, 1997), p. 80.
23. See also *Volpone*'s 'Grege' (2.2.28).
24. 'Moderator' here has virtually the same sense as the modern usage, with perhaps a more literal emphasis on 'A person who [. . .] mitigates something or makes something moderate', *OED*.
25. Jonson, *Every Man Out*, pp. 19–20. For similar choric insets see also Kyd's *Spanish Tragedy*, Peele's *The Old Wives' Tale* and Greene's *James IV*.
26. See also McDonald, *Shakespeare and Jonson*, p. 58.
27. See Jonson, *Every Man Out*, p. 111, n. 112–17.
28. Ibid. p. 38.
29. McDonald, *Shakespeare and Jonson*, p. 58.
30. See Elizabeth Herbert McAvoy, *Consuming Narratives: Gender and Monstrous Appetite in the Middle Ages and the Renaissance* (Cardiff: University of Wales Press, 2002).
31. See Chapter 5, herein.
32. See *Ben Jonson*, ed. C. H. Herford, P. Simpson, E. Simpson, 11 vols (Oxford: Oxford University Press, 1925–51), Vol. 9, p. 405; and Matthew Steggle, 'Charles Chester and Ben Jonson', *Studies in English Literature, 1500–1900*, Vol. 39, No. 2, Tudor and Stuart Drama (Spring 1999), pp. 313–26.

33. John Aubrey, *Brief Lives*, ed. Richard Barber (Woodbridge: Boydell and Brewer, 1982), p. 264.

34. Steggle, p. 316. For earlier concerns about such critics, see H. S. Bennet, *English Books and Readers 1475 to 1557* (Cambridge: Cambridge University Press, 1969), p. 50.

35. Steggle, p. 315.

36. Matthew Steggle, 'Charles Chester and Richard Hakluyt', *Studies in English Literature, 1500–1900*, Vol. 43, No. 1, The English Renaissance (Winter 2003), pp. 65–81, 66, 72.

37. Jonson, *Every Man Out*, p. 103, n. 22.

38. Steggle, 'Charles Chester and Ben Jonson', p. 319.

39. Ibid. p. 317.

40. W. David Kay, *Ben Jonson, A Literary Life* (New York: St Martin's Press, 1995), p. 50.

41. See Chapter 1, n. 25 for connection between a cannon's report and those attributable to humans.

42. Jonson, *Every Man Out*, p. 141, n. 66.

43. Cordatus later cites Plautus' use of suicidal intentions in a comedy, asking 'is not his authority of power to give our scene approbation?' (3.2.155–6).

44. Moul, p. 108.

45. Jonson, *Every Man Out*, p. 109, n. 93.

46. McDonald also notes that both Asper and Macilente (see 1.2.157–62), like Hamlet, are intriguers, involved in 'laying plots'; see McDonald, *Shakespeare and Jonson*, p. 81.

47. For discussion of the alternative endings and the possible presence of Elizabeth here, see Martin (ed.), in *The Cambridge Edition of the Works of Ben Jonson*, Vol. 6, p. 239ff.

Chapter 3

Sympathy for the Informer: Iago, Volpone and Other Metadramatic Authors

Like the informer, any artist is essentially an interpreter, whether the interpretation is of a political reality, a nuance of culture, an emotion, or a handkerchief. That act of interpretation, which generates an origination or a reworking to produce a text, always places the artist in some alethic relation to the original. The dramatic author is perceived to be both storyteller and interpreter, an originator and an augmentative passer-on of stories. But in the English language a tale-teller very closely resembles the more incontinent tell-tale (the earliest recorded usage of the term 'tell-tale', meaning one who 'maliciously discloses private or secret matters' is 1548).[1] There is an example of this usage in Nashe's *The vnfortunate traueller* (1594) where one is 'privily informed' upon by 'hungry tale-tellers'.[2] In fact, though all tale-tellers may not be tell-tales, all tell-tales are tale-tellers. In contemporaneous terms, the concept of the *auctor* obviates this connection to some extent with its adherence to a recognised authority-structure accepted as a guarantee of truthfulness. The breakdown or shift in this convention of authentication and authorisation, to a significant extent caused by the upheavals of the Reformation and the development of print culture, is in part the source of the tension within which at least Jonson's relationship with the reception of his plays is to be understood. Jonson deals with this shift often in directly didactic and structurally metadramatic terms, asserting himself as author in the transactions of authority and the authentic. Shakespeare, however, appears to lack Jonson's agitation about the perception of his authenticity, or possibly the same very public kinds of ambition, so where he deals with this it tends to be at a distance from his authorial self, his metadrama most often being manifested in the generative narrative interplay of his characters.

For both Shakespeare and Jonson, the self-referential nature of the metadrama we have looked at so far reveals a field of interconnections relating to issues of authority, authorship, interpretation and informing, and it is evident that in each case an identifiable dramatic figure emerges from them. This figure, usually male, is a combination of character types, and he crosses or transgresses various typical boundaries. He is a scheming, predatory, liminal shadow-dweller; a man bound by relationship to systems of patronage, though suspected of being masterless in his own mind. He is typically theatrically self-analytical, displaying the excessive outward form of a suspect interiority. He is an over-empowered audience, the embodiment of the perverse interpretation of the authentic. The manifestation of a fear of misprision, he is melancholic, Machiavellian and malcontented. He is the instigator of a dystopian present, the parasitic plotter, the maker of tragedy. He is both author and informer, the epitome of metadramatic characterisation.

Given early modern discourses around loose-tongued women, it is perhaps surprising that these informer figures do tend to be male (a possible exception being Livia in Middleton's *Women Beware Women*). Although this is the case, there seems to be no dominant field of imagery which suggests they are commonly feminised by their loose tongues. Perhaps this is because informing is not only a fundamental element in the maintenance of the patriarchal structures of government, but is also an obligation underpinning the whole milieu of patronage. Though masculine, they are also typically foreign, a conventional defensive theatrical device which displaces a discourse into less sensitive fields where it may be framed as pertaining to the delinquency of foreign states, or states of being. The imperative of deniability at work here combines with the pull of the exotic to produce, for instance, a narrative set within a generally rotten Denmark, or in a tainted Venetian 'court'. This convention may ultimately cause a kind of metadramatic frame-blindness on the part of the audience such that any narrative associations are in any case perceived in relation to their own social issues, regardless of the setting. But in any setting, the plays of Shakespeare and Jonson's era, as Weimann argues, contain 'submerged echoes of an older social existence', their inversions the '"devilish" heritage of a pagan past', and the roots of this ubiquitous figure are to be found tangled with those of an older character which provided its own stimulus to dramatic action.[3]

In early morality plays the Devil's influence is felt in the representation of individually personified vices, but by the middle of the sixteenth century, a single figure, the Vice, begins to emerge, representing something rather more complex than simply sin incarnate. Its dramaturgy, as Antony Hammond writes, revolves around acts of 'deceit and guile' attracting the audience's attention and sympathy, 'both by embodying its own destructive and anti-authoritarian impulses, and by engaging the audience in a conspiratorial relationship'.[4] As the drama evolved a progressively secular character this relationship became increasingly empathetic.[5] Conventional wisdom holds that the Vice then mutated into the stage villain, but this is not quite as straightforward as it seems.

In Jonson's *Volpone*, it is chiefly in Volpone and Mosca's metadramatic celebration of masquerading and misbehaviour for its own sake that Parker and others identify their 'strong resemblances to late morality "Vices"'.[6] Ronald Broude identifies the 'vice-like' nature of the 'secret criminals' of *Volpone* and Marlowe's *Jew of Malta*.[7] Rainer Pineas holds disguise as a central characteristic of the Vice, drawing the conclusion that Volpone has no specific vice because he is one himself.[8] For Shakespeare, Richard III's admission of duplicity, given of course as a metadramatic aside to the audience, makes plain the roots of his own villainy: 'Thus, like the formal Vice, Iniquity, / I moralize two meanings in one word' (3.1.82–3).[9] Iago echoes and internalises this same idea when he lies that he lacks 'iniquity' to do him service (1.2.3–4). But also the irrepressible Falstaff carries aspects of the Vice, and is called 'grey iniquity' (*HIV1*, 2.4.442), though he is certainly no villain.[10] In Jonson's *The Devil is an Ass* (1616), Satan suggests that the old-fashioned vices, like the character Iniquity in this play, would be fit only for comedy and that today's dramatic requirements necessitate 'extraordinary subtle ones' (1.1.116). He suggests that contemporary Vices are,

> most like to vertues;
> You cannot know 'em apart by any difference.
> They wear the same clothes, eat the same meat,
> Sleep i' the self-same beds, ride i' those coaches. (1.1.121–4)[11]

Jonson repeats this sentiment in *The Staple of News* where Mirth laments, 'now they are attired like men and women o' the time, the Vices' (2 Int. 13–14).[12] In short, for Jonson, and for Shakespeare, these excessive Vices are now so firmly integrated into society that they can hardly be differentiated from the people they are preying upon.

Moreover, as contemporary awareness of, and cultural reference to, Niccolò Machiavelli's *The Prince* increased throughout the period, perceptions of the Machiavel and the Vice developed together.[13] George Abbot's exposition of 1600 indicates the popular reputation Machiavelli was developing around this time: describing him as 'by the abundance of his wit, most fit for euill [. . .] a professed politician, whose preceptes closely couched, haue filled the world with the deuill'.[14] In contemporary mores, Machiavellian realpolitik is perceived as specifically anti-Christian.[15] The Elizabethan and Jacobean stage Machiavel sits well with our description of the figure who emerges within metadramatic structures: often discontented, ruthless, unscrupulous, scheming and underhand, he is also a malcontent, who, though commonly bent on revenge, often also voices strong satiric or corrective views about the decadence of society and typically confides in the audience with conspiratorial and metadramatic asides.[16]

The self-serving tyranny of this figure also involves an implication of excess which gives further impetus to these elements. Robert Burton's *The Anatomy of Melancholy* (1621) describes this particular excess as 'the Devil's bath': that is, a humoural imbalance which provides a foothold for the activities of that old informer the Devil in tempting people to do evil, specifically subjecting them to illusions.[17] Volpone's description of Mosca as his 'fine devil' (5.3.46) mirrors Iago's 'demi-devil' (5.2.298), as Parker notes.[18] Later in the century George Fox will assert this connection with force: 'He that is an *Informer*, is a Persecutor, and Spoiler, and a Destroyer; and the DEVIL is the Head of all Informers.'[19] Parker sees historical connections between Mosca and the *commedia dell'arte*'s *zanni* Arlecchino, which is in turn derived from the medieval devil Harlequin, or Hellequin.[20] This is also a possible source for *MND*'s Puck, another informer of a kind.[21] The theatrical figures who inherit the Vice tradition thus resonate with the malcontent's moral outrage and theatrical critique, with the Machiavel's vicious, immoral politician and desire for authority at any cost, and with the melancholic's vulnerability to temptation and black thoughts. The malcontented melancholic Machiavellian Vice, our informer, although he carries the sulphurous odour of the Devil, now looks just like us, and metadrama is the air that he breathes.

Jonson's vision of the function of theatre as a Horatian corrective to oppressive or immoral social structures is complicated by the fact that since theatre depicts itself as the tale-teller to the state, to some extent it necessarily conflates the role of the author with that of the

informer. Thus these structures are not only depicted but often repro-
duced in the metadramatic forms of the theatre. But the opposite of
this conflation is equally true, as onstage informers often also take on
authorial roles within the texts which depict them. Their actions are
on many occasions used as catalysts to action. Thus, for instance, the
dramatic action of *Othello* (1602) is also a 'plot' (self-consciously
so), and Iago, with his 'imputation and strong circumstances / Which
lead directly to the door of truth' (*Othello*, 3.3.409–10), though
clearly evil, functions as the shadow of an authorial manipulator, the
creator of the whole tragedy.[22] Perhaps the most significant informer
figure on the early modern stage, he is simultaneously 'a malcontent and exposer of Jacobean ideologies', as Hugh Grady says.[23]
And, as he weaves his own mendacious web, he negatively models a
venal interpretation to the offstage audience. As John Bernard notes,
Iago is both the play's 'prime shaper' and its interpreter; he not only
invites the audience 'to view the ensuing action from his own quasi-
directorial perspective' but also models their 'potential role in constructing the meaning of the dramatic action'.[24] His relationship with
the offstage audience is facilitated by the metadrama which his dual
role causes to manifest around him.

There are many other such insidious figures in Shakespeare:
Macbeth is groomed by Lady Macbeth, Brutus by Cassius; while
Richard III and *Titus Andronicus*' Aaron the Moor also cut Iago-
like figures in the narratives they generate. These give some indication of Shakespeare's concern over, or familiarity with, this type of
character and he often plays creatively upon its resemblance to the
author as tale-teller. They stand among numerous other contemporary onstage authors of tragic 'plots', ranging from Carisophus in
Richard Edwards' *Damon and Pithias*, and Barabas in Marlowe's
The Jew of Malta, through to Bosola in Webster's *Duchess of Malfi*,
among many others. Jonson's *Volpone* offers us Mosca, with whom
we will deal shortly. In each case these metadramatic informers produce narrative action from manipulative and illicit uses of information. And, as in Iago's case, the metadrama they inhabit offers the
audience the perspective of this seductive figure as a negative model
for their own interpretative practices.

Iago then is an informer-author, who, without the authority of a
Richard III to plot and shape events, nevertheless succeeds in exercising his Machiavellian will through metadramatic devices facilitated
by the credulity of others. His duplicity is introduced to us with his
invocation of the two-faced god, 'By Janus' (1.2.33) and his anti-
Christian statement, 'I am not what I am' (1.1.64).[25] Since he is an

ensign, or standard bearer, his role as informer simply goes with the job; his persona as a manipulative author of tragedy is developed throughout the play, along with a sense of his own power. There is nevertheless something metatheatrical about even his first simple stirring-up of Brabantio's camp, playing the unwelcome informer whose information about Othello and Desdemona is also an accusation. We get a taste of the treachery to come with Brabantio's arrival, as Iago warns Othello, 'be advised, / He comes to bad intent' (1.2.55–6). This malicious linguistic juggling is an element of Iago's practice throughout: a very authorial trait. When he sees Roderigo aligned with the accusing party, he apparently draws his sword and says with mock surprise, 'You, Roderigo! come sir, I am for you' (1.2.58). This 'I am for you' is deliberately ambiguous, meaning both 'I am with you' and 'I will fight you'. Having authored this little scene, Iago is willing and able to ride the narrative and follow its outcome either way. In this metadramatic milieu, Brabantio's charging of Othello with witchcraft is framed by accusations more fitting to aberrant theatrical authorship or acting: 'I [. . .] attach thee / For an abuser of the world, a practiser / Of arts inhibited and out of warrant' (1.2.77–9). Othello's apt reaction to this is also suitably metadramatic as he addresses the swords of authority: 'were it my cue to fight, I should have known it / Without a prompter' (1.2.83–4); his restraint here is perhaps something of a theatrical ideal, or necessity.

It is in the exchanges where Iago weaves his false information into a full narrative for Othello that his skill as an author is most obvious, whilst his ironic pose as one who thinks badly of himself for being suspicious in the first place marks out his simultaneous acting ability as both tempter and dissimulator. The shared awareness between Iago and the offstage audience throughout this play is a generator of both tension and moments of temporary release: for instance, when Othello suspects that Iago has a 'monster in [his] thought / Too hideous to be shown', Iago soon turns this around to warn Othello himself against the 'green-eyed monster' jealousy (3.3.110–11, 168). The metadramatic irony which this generates perhaps lies heaviest when Iago manipulates Othello into having to persuade him to tell his destructive tale, and even more so because Othello does this in the language of the plotting informer: 'thou dost conspire against thy friend, Iago, / If thou but think'st him wronged and mak'st his ear / A stranger to thy thoughts' (3.3.145–7). The audience offstage are aware of Iago's devices in the obvious sense that Othello is missing, as he contrasts a 'false disloyal knave['s] / [. . .] tricks of custom' (3.3.124–5) with Iago's 'honesty', but by this point in the play there is also a growing awareness of Iago in a larger sense as the originator, the controller, the author of this unfolding tragedy.[26] Iago's boastingly apologetic statement, 'I confess it is my nature's plague / To spy into abuses, and oft my jealousy / Shapes faults that are not' (3.3.149–51), while echoing the satirist, voices the conventional pejorative opinion of the informer. His 'scattering and unsure observance' (3.3.154) is precisely the kind of random applica-tion of authority many fear their lives or livelihoods are subject to, because of informers, and this must go some way towards shaping the response of the original audience accordingly. The fact that the paranoia Iago's 'observance' generates causes Othello to order more of the same ('set on thy wife to observe' [3.3.244]) would cause an early modern audience no surprise; it would simply be expected that Othello would reinforce his position of authority by this supposedly advantageous function of the patronage system. Here of course this metadramatic tactic merely plays into the very unsafe hands of this vicious and manipulative author-informer, as the audience is aware.

These informing structures appear again when Othello's mounting paranoia and anger cause him to demand ocular proof of Desdemona's unfaithfulness, and Iago tempts Othello with the role of 'supervisor' to 'grossly gape on' while she is 'topped' by Cassio (3.3.398–9). In fact what he offers is a homoerotic scene of his own imagining in which a sleeping Cassio, taking his temporary bed-mate Iago for Desdemona, cried out,

> 'O sweet creature!' and then kiss me hard
> As if he plucked up kisses by the roots
> That grew upon my lips, lay his leg o'er my thigh,
> And sigh, and kiss, and then cry 'Cursed fate
> That gave thee to the Moor!' (3.3.424–8)

Iago's utilisation of such 'dangerous conceits' (3.3.329) enables him to set up Othello to produce the 'reading' of the handkerchief which he intends. The usual predatory imagery appears where Othello's memory of the portentous handkerchief is termed 'the raven o'er the infectious house / Boding to all' (4.1.21–2).[27] Here Iago has been the author and augur of ill tidings, and his wrested and highly augmen-tative interpretation causes another which produces a tragic ending that exceeds even his own twisted intentions.[28]

Alone in consciousness on the stage as Othello falls into his epi-leptic fit, Iago muses, 'work on, / My medicine, work! Thus credu-lous fools are caught' (4.1.44–5), relishing his role as the provider of the poisonous bait of misinformation. When Othello comes round, Iago immediately sets him up metadramatically as hidden audience to his arranged conversation with Cassio, inviting him, 'Will you withdraw?' The stage directions state simply '*Othello retires*' (s.d. 4.1.93). While he is doing so Iago confesses directly to the offstage audience that he will deceive Othello by questioning Cassio about the prostitute Bianca instead. Othello apparently begins listening in (at line 110) and shares his own commentary on Iago and Cassio's 'inner' conversation with the offstage audience in asides which disrupt the scopic pulsion of the exchange: 'Iago beckons me: now he begins the story' (4.1.131). He even interprets Cassio's gestures as supposedly relating to Desdemona, elaborating on them in situ, imagining her 'Crying 'O dear Cassio!' as it were: his gesture imports it' (4.1.136–7). In this way Iago's metadrama causes Othello to become the audience to his own downfall; the false interpreter of his own annihilation, which is ultimately based on his credulous misprision. For an offstage audience, the disruption of diegetic gravity here tends to destroy any frame-blindness, producing a dramatic irony which counters the pull of any obvious subject-position; although their sympathies are surely with Othello, their interpretative perspective has been seduced by Iago. So Iago's role as the author here has a clear metadramatic quality to it, which fuses a pure and darkly appealing self-reference with the specifically predatory approach of the politic informer. This combination highlights the complexities of interpretation for an audience who are invited to share his malicious perspective.

Iago's dealings with Roderigo are also unsurprisingly lacking in honesty, and the informer's plotting and politicking exploit the venality of the patronage system in such a way that money is always an issue. In return for Iago's false promises of access to Desdemona, Roderigo has been supplying jewels that 'would have half corrupted a votarist' (4.2.189–90), but to no avail, as he complains, 'Every day thou doff'st me with some device' (4.2.177). Iago's use of Roderigo as a cash cow has no doubt enabled the very 'devices' Roderigo complains Iago has visited upon him. When Iago asks him for a hearing, Roderigo alludes to his dishonest theatricality, declaring, 'I have heard too much; and your words and performances are no kin together' (4.2.184–5). Ever the inveigler, Iago admits to him 'your suspicion is not without wit and judgement' (4.2.212–13), and his authorial response is to thicken the plot by conspiring with Roderigo upon Cassio's life. In this short passage, many of the typical elements connecting metadrama to representations of informing are present:

the all-corrupting influence of money, the suspect devices of the politic informer, the metadramatic performativity of the lying inveigler, and the driven plotting of the tragic author.

The outcome of Iago's authorly machinations is that the murder-bed becomes a stage within a stage, emphasising its centrality to the plot; furthermore its tableau of blood is the material remains of the informer's metadramatic carnage. In this way it serves as a darkly emblematic representation of the central message of this book: that metadrama and informing go hand in hand. But, although Othello and Desdemona die due to Iago's informing devices having 'set the murder on' (5.2.183), he too is to suffer, to be punished with 'cunning cruelty' (5.2.331), and here we might hope to find some sense of redress against the informer, some definitive authorly abjuration of these practices. In the end, however, the ubiquity of these destructive authority structures quickly reasserts itself as Lodovico, like *Hamlet*'s Horatio, offers to be the passer-on of this heavy 'act', promising in his turn to tell the tale to the relevant authorities. Having got 'straight aboard', this interpreter will 'relate' the information to the state (5.2.368–9), no doubt not without some compensation for his trouble. Thus, in a display of typical Shakespearean negative capacity, if not equivocation on this matter, the metadramatic form and informing content of the play facilitate both the radical exposure of this destructive social force and its continuity in the perpetuity of the tongue of the teller. For the audience, whose perception throughout is of both the material malevolence of the informer's trade and the great skill of the author in telling this tale, having perhaps experienced sympathy for each, this registers in the end as critical self-awareness.

Jonson's *Volpone* (1607) has many resonances with *Othello*, especially in relation to the character of Mosca, who, like Iago, is both metadramatic informer and an internal author.[29] Connections between the plays also extend through these characters into the significance of role-playing, the predatory nature of vice and commerce, and authority destabilised by its excessive desire for power at any cost.[30] *Volpone* is, as Ostovich argues, a play that 'satirises social venality', and, although it does this perhaps to address the sin of avarice rather than the envy and sheer appetite for deception which animates Iago's *Othello*, I suggest that the particular kind of avarice targeted is still that which animates what are perceived to be corrupt authority structures.[31] But even if we read *Volpone* as an apology for entrepreneurial meritocracy and social mobility these are still nonetheless tainted by the kinds of deception common to the worlds of informing, dramatic writing and performance discussed so far.

It is tempting to read *Volpone* in relation to Jonson's own often dubious social position, always bound up with his writing, which leads him towards both legal troubles and personal involvement with the world of informing. At this stage in his life he was still to some extent scrabbling for a meaningful position in what Parker calls 'a society that he had good reason to know was venal and treacherous'.[32] Donaldson sees the play's concern with social duplicity and plotting as a reaction to contemporary anxieties in the aftershock of the Gunpowder Plot.[33] On a personal level, these may include those arising from Jonson's own latest arraignment, this time along with his wife, for recusancy.[34] His personal experience of arraignment and prison had hardened him to the processes of power, and his history of run-ins with the authorities may have prompted *Volpone*'s Venetian setting; as Dutton notes, Venice was a writers' haven where no censorship was effective – surely an intriguing prospect to Jonson.[35] Furthermore, as Dutton points out, any beast tale such as this also has a crucial advantage, one which metadrama shares, that is, its 'deniability'.[36] This may be especially necessary if the fox indeed alludes to one of the Cecils, as has been suggested. These were a particular focus of antipathy to recusants like Jonson through what Dutton calls the 'venal hypocrisy' of their religious policy.[37] Parker notes a web of connections associating the fox with both the Machiavel and the Devil;[38] and, in a further connection with informing, 'the old fox' was what Essex called Cecil's father Lord Burghley, for reasons not merely to do with cunning.[39] Also, in this reading the characters of the metempsychosis (1.2.1–82) may parody the Cecil children, just as the dwarf Nano might be read as representing Cecil himself.[40] Such social contexts provide the comedic territory in which Jonson's parodic metadramatic device-authors can ply their disreputable trade, but besides possible specific references to individuals, the necessary connections between the play's metadrama and the world of informing may well have provided the impetus for *Volpone*'s geographical and conceptual displacement.

Besides his need to account for the play's acerbic comedy, the socially sensitive nature of these characters may be one reason for Jonson's preliminary cautionary epistle to *Volpone*. In this he is adamant that he has never in the past used 'broad reproofs' or been 'particular' or 'personal' except to 'a mimic, cheater, bawd, or buffoon' (51–2). He continues fervently,

> I know that nothing can be so innocently writ or carried but may be made obnoxious to construction [. . .] Application is now grown a trade with many, and there are that profess to have a key for the deciphering

of everything; but let wise and noble persons take heed how they be too credulous, or give leave to these invading interpreters to be overfamiliar with their fames, who cunningly, and often, utter their own virulent malice under other men's simplest meanings. (56–64)

Jonson here clearly feels, and makes explicit, the pressures of dramatic production in a world of 'too credulous' individuals who may be gulled by those 'invading interpreters' who are unscrupulous with the truth, hungry for gain and make application their 'trade'. This points not only to the potentially venal audience of Jonson's preoccupation, but more specifically to the amply-rewarded informing practice in which Volpone's metadramatic gulling plays a part as the subject of the play's critique. The easily misled 'gull' figure is another of the period's obsessions and is of course an element in the deep concern authors have for a process whereby the authorities which oversee them are potentially gulled by deceiving informers.

Volpone himself claims that the pleasure of his coney-catching life is not so much in the gold as in the malicious plotting itself; as he says, he delights 'more in the cunning purchase of my wealth / Than in the glad possession' (1.1.31–2). In his initial genuflection to the money shrine, however, he states that riches are 'the dumb god that giv'st all men tongues' (1.1.22). Though set within a parodic religious framework where money is both 'the world's soul' (1.1.3) and 'the price of souls' (1.1.24), it seems likely that the central thrust of this metaphor is the hired loquacity of the sycophant or loose-tongued informer.[41] James Loxley sees this as pertaining to the general standard of money as a root of evil, 'a strange principle of transgression and transformation to which no limits can be put, twisting and warping the world into ever-shifting shapes'.[42] Contemporary discourses around the tongue centre on biblical injunctions such as James 3: 6, 'And the tongue is a fire, a world of iniquity: so is the tongue among our members that it defileth the whole body, and setteth on fire the course of nature; and it is set on fire of hell.'[43] The Vice was of course as typically loquacious as it was metadramatic, and Mosca and Volpone represent this tradition as much as does Iago.

In his paean of praise for Volpone's own employment of money, Mosca refers to himself as Volpone's 'poor observer' (1.1.63); this resounds with conventions of dutiful service and religious observance, but also carries an indication of the metadramatic oversight and promise of venal self-service recognisable as the characteristics of the informer. Conflating its distinct senses makes a point about the nature of the observation as noted above in Ophelia's description of Hamlet, 'the observed of all observers' (3.1.156). Appropriately, Volpone's thoughts turn immediately to those 'envious' persons who accuse Mosca of being a 'parasite' (1.1.68), and in denying it he establishes Mosca's 'truth', the trustworthiness of an 'honest Iago'; indeed, it was a conventional characteristic of the morality Vice to be considered honest.[44] Mosca, it may be observed, gets money out of Volpone for these statements of 'truth'. When Mosca exits, Volpone adds to the venal significance of the term 'observer' by telling the offstage audience in a metadramatic aside that his lack of an heir also causes predatory legacy hunters to 'observe' him (1.1.75).

Throughout the play, metadrama is associated with venal plotting and informing. Volpone himself is the onstage audience of the first act's frequently cut interlude with the dwarf, eunuch and hermaphrodite and since the performance pleases Volpone, Mosca admits authorship (1.2.65). But this inner play of the fools is interrupted by another, heralded by the arrival of Voltore at the door, causing Mosca to have to dress Volpone for his own role as 'carcass' in waiting (1.2.90). These visitation scenes (1.3–5) each work as plays-within-the-play in which both Volpone and Mosca have metadramatic roles in the presentation of a scene for the benefit, or detriment, of their clients. These operate with asides to the offstage audience (1.3.18, 1.4.18, 67, 124–30), which draw them psychologically into the world of the play as colluders in the dramatical gambits of these self-interested tale-tellers. Somewhat paradoxically, the sympathy this generates may be directed as animosity towards their clients for popular sins, especially in the realm of the tongue, as, for instance, where Mosca mocks Voltore, in praising him, that he can 'Give forkéd counsel [and] take provoking gold / On either hand' (1.3.58–9). Thus the accusation is felt when Mosca says Voltore is 'of so perplexed a tongue, / [. . .] that would not wag, nor scarce / Lie still, without a fee' (1.3.63–5), with a pun on the word 'lie'. After all this improvised metadramatic invention, Mosca still gives Volpone the impression that he is in charge as author of these inner-play devices: 'Alas, sir, I but do as I am taught; / Follow your grave instructions; give 'em words; / Pour oil into their ears, and send them hence' (1.4.139–41); Volpone of course concurs.

Other characters are also implicated in the world of informing. Of the legacy-hunters, Voltore the lawyer is both tongue-wielding advocate and bird of prey, echoing connections between informers and the law; Corbaccio is the self-deceiving raven, who appropriates Mosca's 'plot' as his own, claiming 'this plot / Did I think on before' (1.4.109–10), linking money with both illegitimate devices and authorship; and Corvino is the crow who becomes 'a chimera of wittol, fool, and knave' (5.12.91), another bird of ill-omen.[45] The character of Sir Politic Would-be, however, shifts the discourse of acting, informing and self-authorship into another, more politically dangerous register. It may be for this reason that 'Pol', as he is known, is made to bear such a light characterisation of his type. Ostovich argues that contemporary audiences would recognise Pol as a 'busybody, and know-it-all whose trendy ambitions and asinine pronouncements on state affairs make him a byword of sophisticated fatuity', though they also might share his 'alarmist belief in plots within plots and his conviction that secret agents are undermining the governments of Europe'.[46] I would argue that the more sensitive might also detect something even more sinister underlying this fatuity. In denying any disaffection with his home country, he puns that it is 'to the state / Where I was bred [that] I owe / My dearest plots' (2.1.6–8). The more astute Peregrine acts as a foil to his idiocy, though his own name implies a predatory avian nature, which is evident in his encouraging Pol's ridiculous discourse over the news from home. The inside knowledge Pol claims of Stone the fool's role as an informer who 'received weekly intelligence' (2.1.68) from foreign countries hidden inside cabbages, and which he would pass on inside oysters and cockles, tempers his own slightly more serious claim to dangerous connection with the Turkish '*Mamaluchi*' (2.1.90).[47] Ostovich suggests that the model for Pol may well have been one Sir Anthony Shirley, an informer to James I/VI, Cecil and Essex, who operated mainly on the continent.[48] Peregrine's metadramatic aside about Pol may allude to authorial anxieties over representing such a character, who,

> Were he well known, would be a precious thing
> To fit our English stage: he that should write
> But such a fellow, should be thought to feign
> Extremely, if not maliciously. (2.1.57–60)

But also, Pol himself mirrors the role of the dramatic author as much as he does Mosca's invidious informer when he claims 'I do love / To note and to observe [and to] mark / The currents and the passages of things', including 'the ebbs / And flows of state', even if it were, as he claims, 'For mine own private use' (2.1.100–5). The offstage audience is thus sensitised to these connections as a requisite for their interpretation of similar issues surrounding Volpone and Mosca.

In such a universally suspect metadramatic environment, Volpone's performance of the role of Scoto in pursuit of Celia is recognised for its politicking, along with that of his assistant: they are, Peregrine says, 'beliers / Of great men's favours' (2.2.15–16); Pol in his unintended fashion calls them 'admired statesmen' (2.2.11), with 'statesmen' here meaning primarily 'politicking informers'. Before the onstage audience, on his inner stage, the disguised Volpone's first instinct is to distance himself from the lesser 'fabulist' (2.2.54), whose tales twist the truth about their own travails.[49] Considering Pol's opinion of the status of such mountebanks, there is some ambiguity in Volpone/Scoto's boast of 'mine own excellency in matter of rare and unknown secrets' (2.2.145–6). Corvino meanwhile situates the whole of the mountebank scene within a recognisable metadramatic frame when he refers to the stage set-up as Volpone's 'properties' (2.3.6), and expresses anxiety over being cast by it as *Pantalone di Besogniosi* (2.3.8) of the *commedia*.[50] The metadrama here may be informed by contemporary suspicions about actors working as informers for the authorities, exacerbating fears about subsequent theatrical representation of prominent citizens' secrets before a public made receptive by means of dramatic devices. Indeed, Pol's reaction to this interruption, that it may be 'some trick of state' (2.3.10), is indicative of these paranoid conjectures, as is his next thought: 'this three weeks all my advices, all my letters, / They have been intercepted' (2.3.13–14). Peregrine's ironic encouragement of his paranoia: 'it may be some design upon you' (2.3.11), indicates Jonson's concern with fair interpretation, and defines a reasonable audience reaction, in a far subtler didactic mode than is usual for Jonson. Volpone himself is as concerned about his performance as any actor might be; he values Mosca's reassurance but misses the latent menace in Mosca's metadramatic wish that he might 'escape [Volpone's] epilogue' (2.4.34). Corvino's angry response to the inner play meanwhile is to suggest that Celia has been complicit as an 'actor' (2.5.40), drawn into the 'action' (2.5.4) by a 'whistle' (2.5.10), as a hawk might be; he threatens to penetrate her with a dagger, with 'as many stabs / As thou wert gazed upon with goatish eyes' (2.5.33–4), and finally to open her whole body to interpretation in the theatre of 'anatomy' (70). It is surprising therefore that Mosca's weak argument of misinformation should so readily convince him to prostitute his wife to Volpone in the hope of gold, and this further indicates the generally excessive nature of greed in the play and its destructive potential in such an environment.

Mosca's own vain soliloquy, meanwhile, is an apology for the trade of 'parasite' (3.1.7ff.), a virtual synonym for 'informer' at this time. Though it is, as he says 'so liberally professed!' (3.1.11), his is not merely the 'town-art' of tale-telling for victuals (3.1.14) nor yet the 'court-dog-tricks' (3.1.20) of flattery and fawning, though it certainly includes each of these, despite such assertions. Rather, he sees himself as a shooting star in the Machiavellian firmament. It has been said that, 'Volpone is first of all an actor; Mosca is first of all a con-man',[51] but, with his parasite's ability 'to change a visor swifter than a thought' (3.1.29), Mosca clearly believes himself by far the better actor, one born to the art, compared to others, Volpone included, who are mere *zannis*.

Subsequently, Mosca's metadramatic acting hooks Bonario into his private scheming, and, bizarrely, produces an unprompted confession of the very informing activities that he has just claimed are beneath him:

> I have done
> Base offices in rending friends asunder,
> Dividing families, betraying counsels,
> Whispering false lies, or mining men with praises,
> Trained their credulity with perjuries. (3.2.25–9)

Once he has ensnared Bonario with his dramatical skills, he immediately begins to practise these dangerous devices upon him, taking him home to situate him as an unseen audience to his father's betrayal, and holding him in suspension while he stage-manages another metadramatic scene. There the inner stage will again be Volpone's bed, to which Corvino brings Celia as an unwilling actor. Mosca's Iago-like stage-machinations now involve ridding the scene of Corvino, but his attempt at manipulating an onstage audience in Bonario is about to backfire. In his attempt to prove to Celia that his decrepitude is just an act, Volpone boasts of his youthful dramatic triumph, when he 'acted young Antinöus' (3.7.162) and was attractive to 'the ladies present' (3.7.163); indeed, there is much metadramatic irony in using the evidence of one role to refute the reality of another.[52] In any case, whatever the acting pedigree of the would-be rapist that Volpone now reveals himself to be, Celia eloquently refuses the role that Mosca has authorised for her. Volpone's own Ovidian eloquence is soon exhausted and his resort to force proves the unruly nature of the hidden audience as Bonario emerges to be Celia's rescuer, leaving Volpone 'unmasked' (3.7.277), Mosca '*bleeding*' (s.d. 3.8.1), and the entire scheme in jeopardy. Bonario therefore works as a metadramatic model of a dangerous audience, although it is Mosca's temporary carelessness in allowing him this role that has threatened to blow the plot wide open.

Throughout all of this, Mosca occupies a liminal position somewhere between being Volpone's 'good angel' (3.4.115), his rescuing 'power [. . .] fate [. . .] fortune' (3.4.126), and merely 'this fellow / Whose lips are i' my pocket' (3.7.50–1), the informer that Corvino thinks him to be. If Volpone is a Vice continually in need of redemption, Mosca's agency of salvation can only be seen as a very ironic and temporary form, one which recalls the didactic structures of the morality play, with Mosca as the fly-demon Beelzebub.[53] Having apparently learned his lesson in attempting to control interpretation, Mosca deals with the next unexpected emergence of a hidden audience with far more authority. When the relatively astute Voltore indicates that he has overheard Mosca's conversation with Corbaccio about the will, asking 'What device is this [. . .] ?', Mosca is quick to reply 'A plot for you, sir', claiming Corbaccio has made Volpone his heir, 'By my device, drawn to it by my plot' (3.9.20, 21, 25), and uses it as an occasion to weave his lies around Corvino, Celia and Bonario. These machinations are obliquely parodied in the following scenes, in Sir Pol's perception of a 'plot' (4.1.1) and Peregrine's chagrined 'counterplot' (4.3.24), with the plotting of 'devices' again redolent of the activities of both author and informer.

After the court scenes, and putting out the news of Volpone's death, the pair are soon preparing to receive their visitors again with Mosca gowned and playing the role of successful heir (5.2.69–70), while Volpone now takes the metadramatic role of hidden audience: 'I'll get up / Behind the curtain, on a stool, and hearken' (5.2.83–4). Here, Volpone's eavesdropping mirrors that of the *commedia*'s Pantalone: a recognised metadramatic convention of the character type. Parker notes that the staging here requires a curtained area of the kind that is very probably necessary for many of the other plays which require hidden audiences.[54] At this point it seems that Volpone is in control of the metadrama, as he encourages Mosca to 'play the artificer now; torture 'em rarely' (5.2.111). But by this point Mosca barely needs his licence to become the performer on the inner stage. Volpone's 'Ay, now they muster' (5.3.8), as he '*peeps from behind a traverse*' (s.d. 5.3.8), inviting the audience, 'Look, see, see, see!' (5.3.17), are collusive asides from an effectively hidden audience to the offstage audience. As with any aside, their effect is to draw the offstage audience into a common perspective with Volpone, but here the hiddenness itself produces another dynamic. As he watches these predators picking over the carcass of his possessions, both he and the offstage audience, who have now been drawn into his perspective, are staged as predators themselves. Obviously this has been the position of Volpone and Mosca throughout, and this scene makes explicit the many points of connection between themselves and the offstage audience which have been established through their sympathetic treatment in the play. Thus when Mosca threatens to inform on Lady Pol, to 'tell some riddles' (5.3.45) about what she has offered Mosca to be entered as an heir, the audience also feels privy to this empowering information. Mosca's curse to her, 'go be melancholic' has Volpone respond, in another aside, with his 'O, my fine devil!' (5.3.45–6). The offstage audience are therefore privileged through the metadramatic structure to share the ambiguous subject-positions of Mosca and Volpone as the predators of predators.

When Mosca orders Corvino to go and be melancholic too (5.3.60), there is an implied threat obvious in the informer's offhand assertion, 'I'll not betray you' (5.3.57). To Corbaccio also there is the threat of public exposure: 'Go home, and die, and stink. / If you but croak a syllable, all comes out' (5.3.74–5). Voltore, the most able of the suitors, thinks that all of this is for his own benefit, but he is soon sent packing after a passage of eloquent invective in which Mosca acts, authorially, as the scourge of the social vices Voltore represents (5.3.80–101). Mosca's threat of informing on each of these legacy hunters is enough in itself to frighten them away, without a word of response. The offstage audience here, through their very complicity in these metadramatic devices, get to share the traditional and vital paradoxical moral force of the Vice; indeed, the Devil preaches with authority because he is uniquely placed to understand the temptations he admonishes.[55] However, his practical hermeneutics are bound to leave his disciples both melancholic and malcontented, and this is a lesson that the audience are now placed to understand.

In the next scene, another often omitted from modern productions, Pol continues to exaggerate his self-appointed role as a statesman-spy, as Peregrine sets up a disguised encounter with accomplices to teach Pol a lesson. Under pressure of the accusation of plotting, Pol admits metadramatically that he has no suspect papers, 'but notes / Drawn out of playbooks' (5.4.41–2), and retreats into his tortoise shell, which he calls 'mine own device' (5.4.60), to attempt to avoid Peregrine's dramatic snare, and failing, obviously. Pol is a 'politician' in the seventeenth-century sense, which includes both plotting and informing; his wife's politicking (as a 'she-wolf' [5.2.66]) links her inevitably to the role of would-be courtesan. Together, what Parker calls their 'would be Machiavellianism'[56] is even more comedic than that of Mosca and Volpone, both mirroring its metadramatic nature and offsetting its potential for 'application' with their own 'incompetent theatricality'.[57] Ultimately the instructive destiny of Pol as would-be politician is to become fodder for the very fables he is fond of telling (5.4.82–4).

Pushing their dramatic luck now, Volpone dresses as a *commendatore*, a law court deputy, and Mosca as a *clarissimo* aristocrat, in order to pursue their already-beaten prey. Here for the first time Mosca's Machiavellian intentions towards Volpone become explicit as he begins to tell a new tale:

> My Fox
> Is out on his hole, and ere he shall re-enter,
> I'll make him languish in his borrowed case [. . .]
> To cozen him of all were but a cheat
> Well placed; no man would cònstrue it a sin:
> Let his sport pay for't. This is called the Fox trap. (5.5.6–8, 16–18)

Tortured by their mockery, Voltore identifies the disguised Volpone as Mosca's 'familiar' (5.9.8), and Volpone maintains the ambiguity of his role throughout the court-scenes that follow. In Mosca's and Volpone's role-reversal at the end, Volpone loses mastery of the story, which passes to Mosca. However, Mosca's attempt to brazen out the court narrative of Volpone's death eventually pushes Volpone out of the other side of his snare (5.12.85), revealing his own venality in the process. The First Avocatore accuses Mosca of having been 'the chiefest minister, if not plotter, / In all these lewd impostures' (5.12.108–9), and he is therefore sentenced to be a 'perpetual prisoner in our galleys' (5.12.114). As Volpone thanks the court, Mosca draws on the more usual lupine imagery for the predatory inventor of cozening devices, cursing him, 'Bane to thy wolfish nature!' (5.12.115); as he shows his true voracious colours, thus the fox becomes the wolf.

These many metadramatic devices, authored principally by Mosca and authorised largely by Volpone, are inner dramatic interludes which reveal serious flaws in the social fabric, energised by avarice. The bond between Corvino and his wife is destroyed in his venal pursuit of wealth. Corbaccio breaks the bonds of the father and son for the same reason. Voltore the lawyer breaks with recognised standards of conduct. Even the Avocatori are not impartial to the temptations of wealth, thus indicating that the categories of the economic and the political are clearly linked. But Mosca and Volpone are also themselves emblems of social disintegration: they are a Vice split or doubled for the modern age. Volpone is a parody of true authority, selling an imaginary inheritance, the false rights to piles of gold, metadramatically exposing the venality of the would-be-powerful. Even as he feigns illness and death, he holds firmly onto the reins of power through his informing agent. Mosca then appears to be the real beneficiary of this arrangement; he is empowered by his informing agency in gathering intelligence information and engaging in Machiavellian plotting against not only his victims, but also his master. He is the Machiavel to Volpone's parodic study of illness and melancholy, yet he carries the malcontent within him too. He is the operative element of Volpone's cunning and his role as informer to the higher power gives him the privileged position of interpreter to that power, ultimately authoring circumstances to its detriment.

The connection with Macbeth is notable here, since his ambition is initially stimulated by allegiance to Duncan whom he will, of course, later betray and murder. Mosca's dramatis persona recalls this comedically, at least in reference to the destructive energy of such excessive ambition. Most significantly, though, Mosca's metadramatic authorship of the plots in this play parallels Iago's own, which similarly forms the action of *Othello*. Mosca too will suffer for his plotting, who is unable to foresee the consequences of his latest plot and ends up pushing his and Volpone's act too far, the author of his own demise.[58] As a figure of authority himself, Volpone self-destructs through the excessive nature of his obsession with the devices of play-acting and his reliance on the informer.

Speaking of *The Duchess of Malfi*'s informer Bosola, C. G. Thayer says tragedy is 'concerned with the problem of self-fulfilment, of achieving one's destiny [. . .] [which] cannot occur [. . .] if he is merely playing a role in someone else's play: the play must be his own'.[59] He must, in effect, tell his own authentic tale. One wonders what such a consummate actor, dealer in misinformation, and author-figure as Iago might achieve in a play called *Iago*. This play is Volpone's own but its status as a comedy does not allow the character the luxury of a fully introspective personal journey of any kind and his destiny is generously left in the interpreting hands of the offstage audience when he returns as the Epilogue. Here theatre judges theatre in his apologetic appeal: 'He yet doth hope there is no suff'ring due / For any fact which he hath done 'gainst you' (Epi. 3–4), and this is indeed a theatrical ideal.

Although ultimately he becomes in fact what hitherto he has 'feigned', in terms of the judgement of the court, Volpone fares better than Mosca simply because of his superior social position.[60] Parker suggests that the fox survives to make his apology because 'he represents something permanent in all of us, a corruption that is closely linked to our vitality'.[61] If this were the case it would require a vitality that recognised its own self-performance within a vicious economy which allowed for no flaw in the universal role-play, and forgave any corruption but one which revealed itself. But this economy is not yet in place. In fact Volpone survives to apologise simply because comedy demands it, and because, in a person of his rank, his acquisitive gulling of the credulous in legal matters seems a parody of mere policy, in any case the employment of an informer is commonplace.

As the metadramatic strategies of these plays' authorial Vices echo the power-structures of their culture, and the instability of an authority based on such devices, the interaction between the functions of author and informer produces salutary examples of the destructive results of excessive envy and avarice. This allows audiences who shared the perspectives of these appealing tale-tellers, and found their sympathies rankly abused, to be conscious of their own interpretative practices and hopefully sensitised to their propensity for the same excesses. The complicating factor here, in a world as heavily dramatised as that of Iago, Volpone and Mosca, is that dramatic roles themselves risk taking on the character of social misdemeanours.

Notes

1. *OED* has 'One who tells tales; one who idly or maliciously discloses private or secret matters; a tale-bearer, a tattler.' It cites the following:

   > 1548 *Hall's Vnion: Henry IV* f. ij^v, He..was very glad (as tell tales and scicophantes bee..) to declare to the kyng what he had heard. *a*1639 W. Whately *Prototypes* (1640) iii. xxxix. 4 Most men will hate such as complaine of them, and call them tel-tales.

2. Thomas Nashe, *The vnfortunate traueller*, pp. 6, 8, <http://www.oxford-shakespeare.com/Nashe/Unfortunate_Traveller.pdf> (last accessed 16 December 2015).

3. Weimann, *Shakespeare and the Popular Tradition*, pp. 19, 22, 157. For a reasoned descriptive overview of the transition between vice and parasite, see Robert Withington, ' "Vice" and "Parasite." A Note on the Evolution of the Elizabethan Villain', *PMLA*, Vol. 49, No. 3 (September 1934), pp. 743–51.

4. William Shakespeare, *Richard III*, ed. Antony Hammond (London: Methuen, 1981), p. 100.

5. Ibid. p. 100.

6. Jonson, *Volpone*, p. 13. Enck meanwhile notes similarities between Mosca and the morality Vice; see John J. Enck, *Jonson and the Comic Truth* (Madison: University of Wisconsin Press, 1957), pp. 34–5, 123.

7. Ronald Broude, 'Volpone and the Triumph of Truth: Some Antecedents and Analogues of the Main Plot in *Volpone*', *Studies in Philology*, Vol. 77, No. 3 (Summer 1980), pp. 227–46, esp. 238.

8. Rainer Pineas, 'The Morality Vice in Volpone', *Discourse: A Review of the Liberal Arts*, Vol. 5 (1962), pp. 451–9, 452–3.

9. William Shakespeare, *Richard III*, ed. E. A. J. Honigmann (London: Penguin, 1995).

10. See herein Chapter 5.

11. Ben Jonson, *The Devil Is an Ass*, ed. Anthony Parr, in *The Cambridge Edition of the Works of Ben Jonson*, Vol. 4.

12. Ben Jonson, *The Staple of News*, ed. Joseph Loewenstein, in *The Cambridge Edition of the Works of Ben Jonson*, Vol. 6.

13. See Niccolò Machiavelli, *The Prince* (1514), trans. George Bull (Harmondsworth: Penguin, 1961).

14. George Abbot, *An exposition upon the prophet Jonah* (1600) <http://gateway.proquest.com/openurl?ctx_ver=Z39.88-2003&res_id=xri:eebo&rft_id=xri:eebo:citation:99836358> (last accessed 11 December 2015).

15. For the influence of other Machiavellian ideas and rhetoric on Iago, see Ken Jacobsen, 'Iago's Art of War: The "Machiavellian Moment" in *Othello*', *Modern Philology*, Vol. 106, No. 3 (February 2009), pp. 497–529.

16. Somewhat ironically, Machiavelli himself warns about malcontents in his advice about conspiracies: 'he that conspires, cannot be alone', but must recruit malcontents, 'and so soon as thou hast discover'd thy self to a malcontent, thou giv'st him means to work his own content, for by revealing thy treason, he may well hope for all manner of favour'. See Niccolò Machiavelli, *The Prince* (1640), p. 148, <http://gateway. proquest.com/openurl?ctx_ver=Z39.88-2003&res_id=xri:eebo&rft_id=xri:eebo:image:12126:8> (last accessed 12 December 2015).

17. Robert Burton, *The Anatomy of Melancholy*, ed. Floyd Dell and Paul Jordon Smith (New York: Tudor, 1948), p. 938.

18. Jonson, *Volpone*; see pp. 14–15, notes esp. 46–56.

19. Fox, n.p.

20. Jonson, *Volpone*, p. 23. Weimann argues that figures like Arlecchino, 'might be traced back to the possessed ritual leader of magic processions': see Weimann, *Shakespeare and the Popular Tradition*, p. 32. The figure of Pol connects perhaps also with roots in another figure of the *commedia dell'arte*, the obstreperous fool Pulchinello. See Maurice Sand, *The History of the Harlequinade* (London: 1915), pp. 1, 117–18.

21. See Winifried Schleiner, 'Imaginative Sources for Shakespeare's Puck', *Shakespeare Quarterly*, Vol. 36, No. 1 (Spring 1985), pp. 65–8, esp. 68.

22. Shakespeare, *Othello*, ed. E. A. J. Honigmann (London: Arden, 2006). Unless otherwise noted all references are to this text. For Iago's 'evil' and connections with the Vice figure see Bernard Spivak, *Shakespeare and the Analogy of Evil: The History of a Metaphor in Relation to his Major Villains* (New York: Columbia University Press, 1958) or Leah Scraggs, 'Iago – Vice or Devil?', *Shakespeare Survey*, Vol. 21 (1968), pp. 53–65.

23. Hugh Grady, 'Iago and the Dialectic of Enlightenment: Reason, Will, and Desire in *Othello*', *Criticism*, Vol. 37, No. 4 (Fall 1995), pp. 537–58, 538.

24. John Bernard, 'Theatricality and Textuality: The Example of *Othello*', *New Literary History*, Vol. 26, No. 4 (1995), pp. 931–49, esp. 938–9.

25. According to Varro, Janus is referred to as the creator and originator of the world; see *De Lingua Latina*, VII. For Iago's 'I am [. . .]', see Bible, Exodus 3: 14 and John 8: 58.

26. Iago later asks Desdemona, 'How comes this trick upon him?' (4.2.128).

27. Roderigo adds hell to the animal picture with, 'O damned Iago! O inhuman dog' (5.1.62).

28. For further connections between 'augur' and 'author' see, B. Angus, '"A hawk from a hand-saw"', Thesis, p. 293ff.

29. Carr calls them 'distant cousins'; see Carol A. Carr, 'Volpone and Mosca: Two Styles of Roguery', *College Literature*, Vol. 8, No. 2 (Spring 1981), pp. 144–57, 156.

30. The significance of the handkerchief (s.d. 2.2.226) is also notable in drawing parallels between Volpone and Othello, as are similarities in the relationships between Iago and Roderigo, and Mosca and Voltore. For other connections see Bryan F. Tyson, 'Ben Jonson's Black Comedy: A Connection between *Othello* and *Volpone*', *Shakespeare Quarterly*, Vol. 29, No. 1 (Winter 1978) pp. 60–6. In this connection, Tyson notes also the classical precedent for turning a tragedy into a comedy.

31. See Helen Ostovich (ed.), *Ben Jonson, Four Comedies*, p. 9, where she also notes possible connections with the contemporary businessman Thomas Sutton.

32. Jonson, *Volpone*, p. 10.

33. Donaldson, p. 230.

34. See Ben Jonson, *Volpone*, ed. Richard Dutton, in *The Cambridge Edition of the Works of Ben Jonson*, Vol. 3, p. 5.

35. Richard Dutton, '*Volpone* and Beast Fable: Early Modern Analogic Reading', *Huntington Library Quarterly*, Vol. 67, No. 3 (September 2004), pp. 347–70, 360.

36. Ibid. p. 367.

37. Ibid. p. 369.

38. Jonson, *Volpone*, p. 14.

39. See Anthony G. Petti, 'Beasts and Politics in Elizabethan Literature', *Essays and Studies* (1963), pp. 68–90, at 78–9.

40. Dutton, '*Volpone*', pp. 369–70.
41. See, for instance, Giacomo Affinati, *The dumbe diuine speaker*, trans. Anthony Munday (1605), <http://gateway.proquest.com/openurl?ctx_ver =Z39.88-2003&res_id=xri:eebo&rft_id=xri:eebo:citation:99851157> (last accessed 8 December 2015).
42. Loxley, p. 71.
43. Bible, King James Version (1611), James 3: 2–12, esp. 6.
44. Pineas, pp. 455–6.
45. Among sources for these are the legacy hunters in Horace's *Satires*, see Jonson, *Volpone*, pp. 11, 299–320.
46. Ostovich (ed.), *Ben Jonson, Four Comedies*, pp. 11–12.
47. See Jonson, *Volpone*, p. 137, n. 90 where Parker notes the Mameluchi 'after 1517 served as beys [. . .] for the Turkish empire [. . .] the term was also used in the sixteenth century to describe fighting slaves of the Pope'.
48. Ostovich (ed.), *Ben Jonson, Four Comedies*, p. 13.
49. The assembled 'Grege' here brings to mind the interpretative 'Grex' of *Every Man Out*.
50. See Jonson, *Volpone*, p. 155, n. 8.
51. Carol A. Carr, p. 152.
52. For connections between this reference and the puritan debate about 'stage plays', see J. L. Simmons, 'Volpone as Antinous: Jonson and " 'Th'overthrow of Stage-Plays" ', *Modern Language Review*, Vol. 70, No. 1 (Jan. 1975), pp. 13–19.
53. Jonson, *Volpone*, p. 80, n. 2.
54. Ibid. p. 43.
55. For more information on the traditional role of the Vice as preacher, see Pineas, p. 456.
56. Jonson, *Volpone*, p. 38.
57. Ibid. p. 39.
58. See Pineas, pp. 453–4.
59. C. G. Thayer, 'The Ambiguity of Bosola', *Studies in Philology*, Vol. 54, No. 2 (Apr. 1957), pp. 162–71, esp. 169.
60. As does Vindice in *Revenger's Tragedy*. See J. L. Simmons, p. 16.
61. Jonson, *Volpone*, p. 42.

Chapter 4

'Masters both of arts and lies': Metadrama and the Informer in *Poetaster* and *Sejanus*

In *Poetaster* (1601) and *Sejanus* (1603), Ben Jonson's metadramatic technique addresses the legitimacy of both poetic and political authority in relation to types of self-performance. Jonson's explicit concern in *Poetaster* is the position of poetry in a healthy society; for him this entails self-promotion, with the added imperative of specifically lampooning the failings of rivals. *Sejanus* meanwhile offers a critique of corrupt ambition. But at the edges of these fields of poetic apology and social invective the metadrama shades into another, more disturbing narrative. Here again the despised figure of the informer lurks, as a significant element in both *Sejanus*'s satire of vicious authority and *Poetaster*'s deprecation of artistic adversaries. In each case, a particular kind of authority is tainted by the connection. In 'An Epistle to a Friend', Jonson expresses his concern over the fact that 'flatterers, spies, / Informers, masters both of arts and lies, / [are] [. . .] easier far to find / Than once to number.'[1] This perception is borne out in wider society, as we have seen, and Jonson's defensive concern to establish the role of the poetic satirist as a Horatian ideal may in part result from his dealings with authorities contaminated by this association.

Critics have noted the echoes of these issues. Speaking generally, Kaplan notes that Jonson always reserves the poet's right 'to identify and condemn official corruption'.[2] More specifically, Donaldson relates the informing in *Sejanus* to the intimidation of contemporary London Catholic communities, which were under what he describes as the 'constant threat of surveillance'.[3] Kay's biography also notes Jonson's indignation at this 'prevailing atmosphere of intrigue and fear' and relates this to *Sejanus*'s nightmare vision, where, as he says, all live 'in terror of informers, arbitrary justice and the executioner'.[4] Though Meskill's reading of Jonson tends to suggest that poetic reputation was chiefly what was at stake, she also concedes the 'frightening power of [the spectator] to affect the poet's earthly fate'.[5] I would like to suggest that connections with the poet's earthly fate are of primary importance in these matters, with future reputation following after. But rather than simply seeing the figure of the informer as carrying a convenient pejorative association in these plays, of particular interest here is the way in which metadrama and the structures of informing fit so integrally together, and, further, whether or not, in the end, Jonson himself is able to escape the same associations.

As is well attested, Jonson uses *Poetaster* to deliver a series of satirical blows to figures associated with Marston and Dekker for failing to produce truly Horatian satire. That both *Poetaster* and *Sejanus* reference specific individuals is indicative of Jonson's characteristic metadramatic technique, that affords the butts of his negative characterisations the opportunity to respond in kind. As the combative exchanges of the so-called *poetomachia* ensue, Jonson spends much imaginative energy on attempting to differentiate himself qualitatively from illegitimate poetic authority.[6] His satiric ideal manifests itself in what Tom Cain calls 'an acute moral sensibility that must speak out [. . .] [being] the natural expression of the man of 'merit' [. . .] whose integrity cannot be compromised'.[7] Jonson, he argues, 'draws a powerful distinction between this and the false satire which comes from the "grosser spirit", whose "bleared and offended sense" (5.3.345–6) [. . .] cannot recognise such merit, and so calumniates it out of spite and envy'.[8] Not only is he adamant that the subjects of the title are not to be regarded as true 'satyrs', but his inset metadramas employ the imagery many contemporary sources associate with the despised informer, connoting the bestial voracity, sycophancy and amorality of the self-interested user of information. Here, he not only mocks their individual qualities, pointing out their failure to attain to his ideal of the satirical poet, but he also imagines them in direct collusion with the mechanisms of oppressive authority and with examples of deliberate self-interested misinterpretation. This functions as an attempt both to manipulate the authoritative viewpoint of his audience, and to enhance his own dramaturgical and social authority.

Moreover, we may find these same mechanisms of oppressive authority replicated in Jonson's own metadramatic structures, accompanied by the bestial imagery which is often connected with informers.

Indeed, David Riggs notes the similarities between Jonson's own *Isle of Dogs* prison experience of informers just four years earlier and the informing practice in *Poetaster*.[9] Jonson's metadramatic poet-baiting thus reflects upon wider issues of authority and morality in a world of uneasy representation, but it also does so in a way that implicates Jonson himself in the workings of that world. The accusation against Dekker as the poetaster Demetrius, that he has 'one of the most over-flowing, rank wits in Rome' and will 'slander any man that breathes' (3.4.337–8), including simply inventing slurs on Horace (3.4.322–33), is an example of this. Also, his harrying of these exemplary victims often causes him to extend his critique to anyone perceived to oppose his poetic and social idealism, very much including his audience. We do not know the bearing this approach had on his success in offend-ing public opinion for *Poetaster* (for which he was constrained to issue his *Apologetical Dialogue*) or for the disastrous performance of *Sejanus* in 1604 at the Globe, where it was 'greeted by the hostility of its audience' to the point of being 'hissed off the stage', as Philip J. Ayres notes.[10] However, it may not be merely coincidental that other Jonson plays we know were regarded as having been offensive to their audience (rather than merely ineffective, as was *Epicoene*), *Every Man Out* and *The Staple of News*, are both highly metadramatic.

In *Poetaster*'s Induction, Envy provocatively addresses a central interpretative issue relating to three groups of interest: the player-poetaster, the audience member and the informer. Of the content of the play, she asks,

> How might I force this to the present state?
> Are there no players here? No poet-apes,
> [. . .] whose forkèd tongues
> Are steeped in venom, as their hearts in gall?
> Either of these would help me; they could wrest,
> Pervert, and poison all they hear or see (Ind. 33–9)

This draws metadramatic attention to the audience, and calls its char-acter into question. Its ostensible targets are the false 'poet-apes', but implied within this is a warning – that perversion of meaning for pri-vate gain leads to a bestial condition – which expresses a preoccupation on a wider level with the figure of the informer. The terms of reference which frame this accusation of calumny are of primary interest here. Envy's snakes have 'forced stings', which, she says, 'hide themselves within his maliced sides / To whom I shall apply you' (Ind. 9–11); these we might fear as she has 'vigilant thoughts / In expectation of this hated play' (Ind. 16–17).[11] She adds that she covets a hope to destroy their pleasures with 'wrestings, comments, applications, / Spy-like suggestions, privy whisperings, / And thousand such promoting sleights' (Ind. 23–6). These wrested comments are the twisted interpretations by which Envy intends to 'force' the meaning of the play to apply 'to the present state' (Ind. 34) in order to denounce it to the authorities.[12] Within the narrative itself, Envy may be ultimately frustrated in this desire, but outside the frame of drama Jonson's 'new-found [satirical] freedom' in these plays was not to be untroubled by real wresting detractors.[13]

Envy here is not merely the image of malignant reading, who poses a danger to literary reputation; if this were the case why would there be such a preoccupation with informers?[14] Envy, indeed, represents a wider culture of informing which disrupts the very social legitimacy that Jonson is aiming for. In Meskill's reading of *Poetaster*, the fear of misreading is seen as reflecting 'conspiracies and groups of slanderers in court' whose lives are in danger, but no connection is drawn with the real lives of authors.[15] In fact, not only did *Poetaster*'s poor reception force Jonson to add his apology to the printed text for the sake of clarity, but in the case of *Sejanus* he was summoned before the Privy Council to explain himself. *Sejanus* was, as Parker says, 'violently unpopular with the audience' but it also allowed the Earl of Northampton to cite Jonson for 'popery and treason'.[16] The play, in fact, might have provoked ire not so much through insult to individuals as through its representation of a corrupt court, which as Donaldson suggests 'closely resembled their own system of governance'.[17] This reaction may well have been exacerbated by the fact that Northampton's own 'wresting' of the plot to his political world connected *Sejanus* with the high-profile treason trials of 1603, and most particularly because Ralegh's sensational trial took place only weeks before its first production.[18] Besides Envy's noted warning in *Poetaster* against the 'application' of drama to present situations, the 'present state' is also referred to in *Sejanus*, where the protagonist and scheming informer Sejanus describes Cordus the historian as

> a writing fellow they have got
> To gather notes of the precedent times,
> And make them into annals – a most tart
> And bitter spirit, I hear, who, under colour
> Of praising those, doth tax the present state,
> Censures the men, the actions, leaves no trick,
> No practice unexamined, parallels
> The times, the governments. (2.304–11)

The key to this passage, and of immense significance to both dramatists and audiences, is the simple phrase at its centre: 'I hear.' This
puts the information given in the rest of the passage substantially
into question and, given Jonson's imaginative assault on wresting
'application' in this play, there is some metadramatic irony in the
fact that Northampton, or his informer, might hear this as a kind of
coded authorial confession.[19]

This species of interpretation is practised by the informer Momus
in Thomas Carew's masque *Coelum Brittanicum*, who confesses, 'a
Prærogative of wresting [. . .] to any whatsoever interpretation' and
describes himself as 'Arch-Informer, Dilator Generall, Universall
Calumniator'.[20] His informing privileges, meanwhile, are 'ubiqui-
tary [. . .] speculatory, interrogatory [. . .] over all the privy lodgings,
behind hangings, doores, curtaines, through key-holes, chinkes, win-
dowes [. . .] at all Courts [. . .] Counsels [. . .] and [. . .] Assemblies'.
Both the insidious ubiquity and the interpretative empowerment
of this 'Arch-Informer' are most emphatic. Jonson uses the name
Momus in *Poetaster* to describe the critical courtier Hermogenes
(4.5.6). While, in *Sejanus*, the general Caius Silius makes explicit his
anger against the 'Malicious and manifold applying, / Foul wresting, and impossible construction' (3.228–9) of informers, it is Sejanus
himself who is the very picture of the informer that Envy has in mind,
forcing a writer's meaning to fit his own ends. Envy's proposed 'spy-
like suggestions' go hand-in-hand with such 'privy whisperings' in
expressing malicious intent, recalling the leech-like 'soft whisperers
that let blood / [. . .] life, and fame-veins' of Jonson's 'Epistle to a
Friend'.[21] The informer's 'evidence' of course has a judicial function,
but its potential for Iago-like perversions of legal process is what is
of deep concern here. These circumstances help to reveal the powerful currency of the accusation contained within the phrase 'thousand
such promoting sleights' with which this personification of the poetasters promises to spoil the party, and this self-referential metadrama
can only, therefore, be intended to cast poetasters themselves in the
whispering and wresting roles of informers.[22]

Though Jonson stops short of accusing anyone directly of being
an informer to the state, his associations indicate that he perceives
a correlation between the envious poetaster and the dangerous
informer which he might turn to his own advantage. This connection
is also to be found in *Timber, or, Discoveries* (1640), where despite
the fact that Jonson's own voice is dispersed to a certain extent, in
the commonplace book tradition, among the strata of his sources,
he nevertheless manipulates them to support various propositions.[23]
Here, for instance, in the words of Scaliger, he expounds on what a

barbarous envy it is 'to take from those mens vertues [. . .] whom you cannot equall [. . .] you would destroy, or ruine with evill speaking'.[24] Through the voices of his *auctors*, Jonson then begins to apply this accusation of envy and slander to a specific type of detractor he calls 'Alastor', a tormenting spirit who has 'left nothing unsearch'd, or unassayl'd, by his [. . .] licentious lying in his aguish writings'; he calls him 'a troublesome base curre' who has 'bark'd, and made a noyse a farre off' and concludes, optimistically, 'they are rather enemies of my fame, then me, these Barkers'.[25] In his critique of this 'Nation of Barkers, that let out their tongues to lick others sores'[26] he extends the compass of his earlier accusations in *Poetaster*, against the 'barking students of Bears-college, / [who] swallow up the garbage of the time' (*Poetaster*, A.D. 32–3), to include surreptitious observers of all kinds.

When *Poetaster*'s serpentine Envy asks for those with 'forkèd tongues [. . .] steeped in venom' (Prol. 33–6), this, as we have seen, is an appeal for fellow interpretative monsters, either actor or poetaster-author, to aid her poisonous wresting. However, she goes on to taunt the audience with their own potential for corruption and offers to increase its effect: 'Here, take my snakes among you [. . .] / Help me to damn the Author. Spit it forth / Upon his lines [. . .] / [. . .] to hiss, sting and tear / His work and him; to forge, and then declaim, / Traduce, corrupt, apply, inform (Prol. 44, 46–7, 52–4).[27] From the outset of this intensely metadramatic play, the audience is thus fore-warned that, should they choose the subject-position of traducing, corrupting informer, which is intrinsically linked with that of the poetaster, they will draw the play's fire onto themselves and justify its insulting suggestions. In this forceful way the authoritative viewpoint remains very much with Jonson, who is then safe to indulge in a little self-deprecation while establishing his own critical perspective, com-manding the deference of both poetasters and audience. This require-ment of deference is perhaps not without some justification – after all, the potential cost to the author of any such damning 'applica-tion' is high enough – but it does make Jonson's metadramatic style seem peculiarly hostile, as may be seen when he sends on the second Prologue in armour, reasoning that

> 'tis a dangerous age,
> Wherein who writes had need present his scenes
> Forty-fold proof against the conjuring means
> Of base detractors and illiterate apes. (Prol. 66–9)

This prophylactic Prologue exposes the danger inherent in a metadra-matic exchange, where a text is often at its most open to audience participation in the interpretative process, and it seems that Jonson wants to prescribe, and thus control, the involvement of these interpretative monsters in his 'noble industry' (Prol. 65). This mistrust must relate to the mad world of preferred misinterpretation he describes in *Timber*, 'a field so fruitfull of slanders', where 'the diet of the times' is that the author 'must lye, and the gentle Reader rests happy, to heare the worthiest workes mis-interpreted; the clearest actions obscured: the innocent'st life traduc'd'.[28] In this respect, it is interesting to note that Jonson and Nashe's own 1597 play, *The Isle of Dogs*, was denounced to the Privy Council as containing 'very seditious & sclandrous matter', which Jonson clearly thought was not the only worthy work to be 'mis-interpreted' thus.[29]

Sejanus portrays just such a field full of slander, and Sejanus himself functions clearly in it as both lying author and slanderous informer. His own plotting is conflated with the play's plot as he sends Posthumus to Augusta with instructions to augment what information he has on Silius:

> Tell the words
> You brought me, th'other day [. . .]
> Add somewhat to 'em [. . .]
> Give Arruntius words
> Of malice against Caesar [. . .]
> You can best enlarge it
> As you find audience. (2.350–2, 354–6, 374–5)

In this authorial elaboration, Tiberius, 'the epitome of astute Machiavellian manipulation',[30] yields to the author Sejanus' 'design' (3.502) and Sejanus prospers where 'the innocent'st life [is] traduc'd' through this augmentation of truth. Tiberius goes on to confirm that Sejanus' machinations are based on false and self-interested information, 'offered [. . .] on the lives of the informers' (5.610–11). Such illegitimate information, poorly interpreted or deliberately augmented in the process of reception, is of concern to Jonson throughout his career. Cain notes connections between *Poetaster* and the background to the Essex rebellion in which 'letters reputedly written by Essex [. . .] were stolen, then had forged passages added'.[31] Sejanus' desire to 'present the shapes / Of dangers greater than they are [. . .] / [and] to feign / Where there are none' (2.384–7) also resounds with the self-interested augmentation which connects author and informer, as it does where Silius warns Agrippina that

> every second guest your tables take
> Is a fee'd spy, t'observe [. . .]

What conference you have, with whom, where, when;
What the discourse is, what the looks, the thoughts
Of every person there, they do extract,
And make into a substance. (2.444–9)

The metadramatic suggestion here is that her guests play the part of
venal audience members, making their own meaning and augmenting
their own observations for financial reward. This freedom to augment is echoed further in Tiberius' instructions to Macro: 'Inform,
and chastise. Think, and use thy means [. . .] / Explore, plot, practise'
(3.702, 704). Macro, not unlike the figure of Reynaldo in *Hamlet*, is
thus licensed to be creative in his informing. By way of a little philoso-
phising, in Macro's voice, Jonson explicitly alludes to the immorality
of such opportunism, asserting,

He that will thrive in state, he must neglect
The trodden paths that truth and right respect,
And prove new, wilder ways; for virtue, there,
Is not that narrow thing she is elsewhere. (3.736–9)

This perception of moral compromise also recalls Polonius' 'bait of
falsehood' (2.1.60), and the choice of a venal path is something the
statesman has in common with the later informer figure voiced in
the pamphlet *The Informer's answer*, who, lacking 'courage enough
to venture on the Road for a supply' opts to 'Imp the wings of our
broken fortunes with plumes of a safer plunder'.[32] Whether practical Machiavellianism or outright criminality, these 'wilder ways'
would certainly provide 'plumes of a safer plunder' for fortunes of
all kinds.

In *Sejanus* the betrayed general Silius refers to such plunder when
he calls his accusers 'wolf-turned men' (3.251), asking, 'Have I or
treasure, jewels, land, or houses / That some informer gapes for?'
(3.170–1). Silius is right to be concerned, pointing to the potentially
substantial rewards due to these voracious types, referred to later
as 'that fourth / Part, [of the guilty party's property] which the law
doth cast on the informers' (3.359–60). We are reminded here of
the very good purse the successful informer might indeed receive
in the period: a significant portion of whatever fine was imposed.[33]
This predatory world is imagined after Silius' suicide, where
Arruntius says of Tiberius in a metadramatic aside to the audience,
'Excellent wolf! / Now he is full, he howls' (3.347–8). All the way to
the top, those whose 'privy whisperings' result not only in financial

advantage but also in the consumption of human lives are characterised in this lupine or canine manner, with the ill-advised Emperor sharing this designation with his informing minions. In *Poetaster*, it is the 'turbulent informer' (5.3.15) Lupus, overtly the wolf, who accuses Horace (representing Jonson) of treason and is reminded by Tucca to 'beg their lands betimes, before some of these hungry court-hounds scent it out' (5.3.48–9).[34]

Further connections between venal statecraft and theatre are drawn when this imagery is also applied to various self-referentially metadramatic scenes. When Tucca positions Histrio the player (possibly representing the Chamberlain's Men, who commissioned *Satiromastix*) as audience to the Pyrgi's parodic playing, it is also with commerce in mind. He wants Histrio to hire the Pyrgi as actors, asking, 'What wilt thou give me a week for my brace of beagles here?' (3.4.208–9). Apart from the literal meaning, *OED* defines a 'beagle' at this time as one who scents out or hunts down; 'a spy or informer', recalling James I/VI's description of Cecil as his 'little beagle that lies by the fire'.[35] This connection between acting and informing is borne out at the banquet of the 'gods' where the first Pyrgus tells Tucca of Julia's 'inquisition' of him: Tucca's response is 'Well said [. . .] / inform, inform' (4.5.106–7). Meanwhile, in *Sejanus*, Silius declares that the 'beagles' Secundus and Natta habitually

> Flatter, and swear, forswear, deprave, inform,
> Smile, and betray; make guilty men; then beg
> The forfeit lives, to get the livings; cut
> Men's throats with whisp'rings; sell to gaping suitors
> The empty smoke that flies about the palace. (1.28–32)

This strong imagery of throats cut with whispers and the selling of 'empty smoke' draws on classical satire and contemporary political commentary to emphasise the vicious and duplicitous nature of the business in hand. The connection of informing with acting which this implies often uses canine or lupine imagery, and is fundamental to the metadramatic framework of insult Jonson directs at both rival poets and compromised authorities. Moreover, this applies by extension to those in the audience who might wish to emulate them. Dekker's *Guls Horne-booke* (1609) also describes audience-members coming 'with a hungry appetite [to] disgrace the author' as hounds whose tongues are out of control, one sycophantically copying another; he curses them, 'be thou a beagle to them all, and never lin snuffing till you have scented them'.[36] These are the dogs of patronage, an image

Dekker also applies to Jonson in *Satiromastix*, which adopts *Poet-aster*'s Crispinus, Demetrius and Tucca.[37] Playing on Jonson's own poetic failure, Tucca also accuses Horace of canine behaviour: 'when the Stagerites banisht thee into the Ile of Dogs, thou turn'dst Ban-dog [. . .] and euer since bitest [. . .] I aske if th'ast been at Parris-garden, because thou hast such a good mouth, thou baitst well'.[38] Here, as G. K. Hunter says, Jonson-as-Horace is presented as a 'toady' whose writing is 'corrupt' and self-interestedly 'concocted to exploit social possibilities, though he represents it as an essential part of a well-regulated state'.[39] In these ways, the *poetomachia* trades in metadramatic insults which reciprocate the accusation of either mindless or active complicity in sycophantic informing. However, it is not the system of authority per se that Jonson objects to, but its corruption by immoral or unworthy influences; ironically, however, his use of metadrama to depict this, fitting as it is, tends to implicate him in the same kinds of mechanism as employed by the chief culprit: the informer. His fervent wish to distance himself from these figures thus merely serves to index the minimal nature of the differences, an uncomfortable affinity which Horace also appears to have felt.[40]

In *Sejanus*, Silius laments the interpretative atmosphere of this compromised authority-structure:

> Every minist'ring spy
> That will accuse and swear is lord of you,
> Of me, of all, our fortunes, and our lives.
> Our looks are called to question, and our words,
> How innocent soever, are made crimes. (1.64–8)

Sabinus agrees that 'Tyrants' arts / Are to give flatterers grace, accusers power' (1.70–1). This ubiquitous paranoia over these tyrannous eyes and ears of the state is apparent also where the senator Lepidus is made to endorse inaction through fear of their activities:

> To suffer, and be silent; never stretch
> These arms against the torrent; live at home,
> With my own thoughts, and innocence about me,
> Not tempting the wolves' jaws: these are my arts. (4.295–8)

Jonson is apparently suggesting that the only alternative to being in the sighting-line of informers is a political quietism which is not possible for the kind of author he aspires to be. In contrast to the ideal silence of the audience required by the accusing Envy, the ideal

Horatian author here is one that will not 'suffer and be silent', who will stretch his 'arms against the torrent', and who, by refusing to keep his 'own thoughts and innocence' about him, will implicitly tempt 'the wolves' jaws'. *Sejanus*, however, makes clear the consequences to be expected from the practice of such an ideal in a state where informers have the ear of the highest authority. As Arruntius asks rhetorically in response to Lepidus, 'may I think, / And not be racked?' (4.304–5), concluding 'nothing hath privilege 'gainst the violent ear' (4.311).

These connections are explored in more detail in the earlier *Poetaster* where Jonson makes Tucca accuse him, as Horace, of being 'all dog and scorpion', carrying 'poison in his teeth and a sting in his tail' (4.3.115–16), an insult meant to backfire, since this is the traditional depiction of the satirist.[41] The passage, however, convinces Crispinus and Demetrius to join Tucca as both poetasters and informers upon Horace. When Tucca says, 'I'll be your intelligencer, we'll [. . .] hang upon him like so many horse-leeches, the players and all' (4.3.126–8), he further suggests the connection between metadrama and informing. When Demetrius offers to write to this purpose, Tucca offers him 'a drachma to purchase gingerbread for thy Muse' (4.3.163), encouraging Demetrius to be creative in his augmentation. Jonson's metadramatic construction of both poetasters, 'that common spawn of ignorance' (Ind. 79) and audience along these bestial lines, works to deny either group a moral competence, which Jonson is then free to appropriate with his 'well erected confidence', which, he argues, may 'fright their pride, and laugh their folly hence' (Ind. 74–5). The satirical 'mean' which Jonson insists he is pursuing between 'vanity' and 'base dejection' (Ind. 82–3) is one which he hopes 'all free souls will allow' (Ind. 86), with obvious appeal to the audience, and after such an introduction how could they not?

Continuing this concern Jonson broadens his attack on the poetasters to include a construction of the audience, aiming for the moral high ground. Seated with the exhibitionist 'gallants' on a stool upon the stage, Crispinus occupies a space between performance and reception, most obviously a metadramatic device designed to mock self-aggrandisement.[42] Additionally, however, in encroaching on the authoritative space of the stage, he represents an unwelcome aspect of potential audience-power. Initially Crispinus is scripted to represent a possibility of pure observation, albeit in comedic form, asking only 'to observe, till I turn myself to nothing but observation' (2.1.161–2). Pure observation, Jonson wants to suggest, is the precondition for pure, trouble-free representation.[43] Crispinus, however, is a poetaster, identified with Marston, so this prelapsarian innocence cannot last.[44] In his aberrant role, Crispinus forces Horace to be audience to his doggerel. Horace responds, in a metadramatic aside, that it is tyranny to 'take mine ears up by commission, / [. . .] and make them stalls / To [. . .] lewd solecisms and worded trash' (3.1.104–7). In sharing this experience of the tyranny of the author and alluding to the *Satires*, Horace draws the offstage audience into complicity with this depiction of Marston, and thus suggests the appropriate critical response.

Throughout these texts, the metadrama offers constructions of the audience as poetasters, informers, or honest critics. When Tucca causes Histrio the player to become audience to the Pyrgi's bad acting, the offstage audience is watching Crispinus the audience-poetaster, watching (or, depending on staging, watching with) Histrio, watching the Pyrgi's terrible acting, and they are able to see onstage a critical model of both audience and players, all of whom are obviously to be rejected as caricatures. This framing continues as Demetrius the author (representing Dekker) arrives and Jonson pre-empts the insults of Dekker's coming commission by referring to his own smell as that of a 'goat' or 'satyr' (3.4.366). Typical of Jonson's defensive self-deprecation, this projected bestial 'insult' resounds with poetic self-assertion – 'satyr' at this time being popularly (but erroneously) supposed the origin of 'satire'.[45] This reminds the audience of the connection between Jonson and Horace and suggests a model Horatian critical response to those whose ears may be stalls for 'lewd solecisms and worded trash'. The audience are thus afforded both positive and negative examples of interpretation which should leave them in no doubt as to what kind of discernment is required of them.

This bestial imagery backfires on Jonson, however, as his rivals play upon it to characterise him not as a 'satyr', but a 'fawn'. Though nearly synonymous, this carries derogatory connotations to do with 'fawning'.[46] One needs only to think of Nashe's informing 'curre, that flatters & fawns' to appreciate how much Jonson is hoist with his own petard here as Marston and Dekker capitalise on this connection.[47] In Marston's metadramatic *Parasitaster or The Fawne* (1606), Nymphadon, in response to the pious Jonson-figure Hercules' railing, takes this a stage further by asking, 'wil *Fawne* now turn an informer?'[48] Its prologue wishes those who 'with malice lurke', to know that ''Tis base to be too wise, in others worke.'[49] In *What You Will* (1607), Marston also addresses Jonson's perceived over-critical nature and obsession with informing, having Lampatho Doria (another Jonson figure) rail that despite 'Informer and slie intelligence, / Ile stand as confident as *Hercules*, / [and] [. . .] launce our times impieties' (3.1.197–200).[50] Lampatho, though himself 'a hypocrite who will fawn on a patron and then ridicule him', as Cain argues, plainly represents a moral crusader who feigns slight concern over informers.[51] When Lampatho demands of his audience, 'bend your listning vp, / For Ile make greatnesse quake', they promise to 'Hang on [his] toungs end'.[52] Lampatho nevertheless misunderstands and reacts with bizarrely excessive violence, expostulating,

> Ile see you hang'd first [. . .]
> This is the straine that chokes the theaters [. . .]
> Forsooth to raile [. . .]
> This some would heare, to crack the Authors neck,
> This admiration and applause persues,
> Who cannot raile, my humors chang'd 'tis cleare,
> Pardon Ile none, I prise my ioynts more deare. [53]

This change of 'humors' in relation to the prospect of such close observation shows that Jonson's preoccupation with informing was very well appreciated by his contemporaries. It is tempting, therefore, to see Jonson in Dekker's poem 'A Papist Couchant. OR The Fawner' (1616) with its reference to one whose 'Spaniell-fawning' saves his neck, and who 'would pull down Stars'.[54] Indeed, 'fawning' may already have been an issue between the poets before the outbreak of hostilities as, even when Horace first arrives in *Poetaster*, he assertively declares himself unable to 'sing unconquered Caesar's deeds' (3.5.17). In any case, it seems that the issue persisted through the temporary reconciliations of the early 1600s and is still a bone of contention in these later works.

More seriously, the connection between informing and theatre in these plays also carries implications of plotting, conspiracy and treason. When the poetasters wish to play gods at Julia's feast, *Poetaster*'s metadramatic crisis, they approach Histrio the actor for props including a crown and a sceptre, and he passes 'intelligence' (4.4.4) of this volatile symbolism to Lupus the informer. Lupus responds, metadramatically, 'Speak lower, you are not now i' your theatre, stager' (4.4.7) and describes his misinterpretation as drama in accord with the mechanisms of authority, 'A conspiracy, this! / [. . .] I'll act a tragedy i'faith. / [. . .] Player, I thank thee; the emperor shall take knowledge of thy good service' (4.4.14–15, 17–18). Lupus not only conflates the roles of informer and actor, but also deliberately takes this costume-symbolism for more than is intended: 'A crown and a sceptre! This is good. Rebellion now!' (4.4.21), in the mould of the informers of the Essex debacle, as Cain suggests.[55] In his zeal Lupus draws Horace along, exiting with 'if you love the emperor and the state, follow me' (4.4.46–7). When the betrayed revellers are discovered and Caesar is prevented from killing Julia on the spot for blasphemy, he represents an audience that has been practised upon by informers, and Horace has been drawn into the same misinterpretation. Through this metadrama, the offstage audience are thus presented with an interpretative model which they can easily reject. For his part in this, Tucca says Horace has 'turned fawn now, an informer [. . .] 'tis he has betrayed us all' (4.7.9–10).[56] Regretting his involvement, Horace identifies Lupus as the true informer, with his 'wolfish train' (4.8.11), who

> Care not whose fame they blast, whose life they endanger;
> And under a disguised and cobweb mask
> Of love unto their sovereign, vomit forth
> Their own prodigious malice; and pretending
> To be the props and columns of his safety [. . .]
> Disturb it most with their false and lapwing cries. (4.8.18–23, 24)

Here the usual imagery of depredation disrupts legitimate authority through appetite, dissimulation and malicious ambition. But there is also a lack of any contrast drawn between the malice of such manipulators of information and Jonson's own threatening Horatian poetic assertion:

> he that wrongs me, better, I proclaim,
> He never had assayed to touch my fame,
> For he shall weep, and walk with every tongue
> Throughout the city, infamously sung. (3.5.75–8)

The moral issue here seems not to be so much concerned with generating infamy as it is with its motives. The problem for Jonson is that his desperation to distinguish himself from those informer-authors he so explicitly despises in *Poetaster* is bound by the very remit of the project itself to perform the same defamatory function. His defence is based upon a fixed idea of the authority of the 'authentic' poet, which is to be distinguished from both poetaster and mere audience-member by deprecating both.[57] The metadramatic forms he chooses also serve to undermine such distinctions by their conflation of the interpretative roles of author, audience and actor. Moreover, despite itself, *Poetaster* works to suggest that all of these may be accurately accused of being informers of one kind or another. These connections are expressed through metadramatic modes whose self-referentiality is broadly bound up with the politics of dramatic production at this time. Such interchangeability of roles is also suggested in *Sejanus*, where Silius notes of the eponymous informer who would be emperor, that although 'Hell and Elysium / Are in his look' (1.207–8) as the new god of the court, 'His smile is more than e'er (yet) poets fained / Of bliss, and shades, nectar' (1.211–12). Meanwhile Arruntius laments Tiberius' insincerity as 'the space, the space / Between the breast and lips' (3.96–7) and indicates the inherent theatricality of his office in a metadramatic aside: 'Well acted, Caesar' (3.105).

In *Poetaster*, Julia and Ovid, the main victims of Lupus' information, are forced to accept a less dramatic version of reality, and audience reactions to this would obviously have depended upon their proximity to the machinations of the wider authorities (the demographic of a Blackfriars audience contrasting with that of the Globe, for instance). Either way, Horace has been an accessory to their plight. This could work as a warning to those offstage who might jump to erroneous conclusions in their interpretation of theatrical acts, but its main function is simply to suggest that such informing misapplication is ubiquitous, possibly also being a tacit admission of Jonson's own complicity in such practices. However, such equivocation over the nature of the poet does not last for long, and Caesar's apologetic paean to that most 'abstract and perfect' of faculties, 'sweet poesy', follows:

> She can so mould Rome and her monuments
> Within the liquid marble of her lines
> That they shall stand fresh and miraculous,
> Even when they mix with innovating dust. (5.1.18–24)

'Abstract' here means without 'contaminating material considerations', while 'innovating' has the sense of 'revolutionary', emphasising the potential disturbance to authority; nevertheless Maecenas declares this encomium will withstand 'dull detractions' (5.1.33).[58] When, setting a chair for Virgil, Caesar disparages Horace's poverty (as Marston had Jonson's),[59] Horace reprimands him and Jonson has Caesar thank Horace for his 'free and wholesome sharpness / Which pleaseth Caesar more than servile fawns' (5.1.94–5). Up to this point the poet occupies the celebrated ideal position of the true satirist in service to an ideal ruler, who is 'attentive to good counsellors'.[60] This is metadramatic inasmuch as the author is perceived to be a part

of the whole dramatic production. However, as Virgil is finally persuaded to read from the *Aeneid*, the narrative is again interrupted
by Lupus presenting Caesar with a 'dangerous, seditious libel', an
emblem found in Horace's study. Horace again asserts he does not
fear 'traducing tongues / [. . .] a tyrant's ear / [. . .] wrested laws /
Or the red eyes of strained authority' (5.3.58–61) but Lupus pursues
his misinterpretation regardless: 'Is not here an eagle [. . .] meant by
Caesar?' (5.3.65–6). As Horace waves him away, explaining that the
figure is of a vulture meant to represent '*the base and ravenous multitude*' (5.3.76), an oblique metadramatic mode operates, constructing
the offstage audience as another body, in this case intended to contrast ironically with the 'ravenous multitude'. As Horace explains that
the emblem represents 'A vulture and a wolf [. . .] Preying upon the
carcase of an ass' (5.3.86, 90), Lupus slowly realises that the emblem
represents not a seditious depiction of Caesar, but an apt one of himself: 'My name's Lupus, I am meant by the wolf [. . .] You mean me by
the ass' (5.3.88, 92); Maecenas advises, 'leave braying then' (5.3.93).
Jonson thus adds another figure to the bestiary of the informer: the
braying ass. He includes this in his Apologetical Dialogue (225), and
echoes it later in 'An Ode. To himself', on theatre: 'lyes Thespia wast /
[. . .] by chattering pies defac't / [. . .] Make not thyself a Page / To
that strumpet the Stage / Sing high and aloofe / Safe from the wolves
black jaw, and the dull Asses hoofe'.[61] If the ass's hoof represents one
aspect of the audience, Donaldson identifies the 'black jaw' of the
wolf here with the Elizabethan state and its informers, like Richard
Topcliffe and Sir Edward Coke.[62] This again operates as a warning to
the 'base multitude' to avoid the position of the informer-poetasters,
wresting meaning from what may be plainly seen and forcing it to
mean something else entirely. This is practised, Jonson suggests, only
at the risk of displaying corrupt and bestial motives, but it is a risk
Jonson also seems to fear that he is running himself.

    When Lupus is able to pass responsibility for this accusa-
tion onto another informer, Jonson has Caesar order Histrio the
actor whipped for calumniating a poet. In Tucca's words, he is a
'sycophant-like slave, and a politician' (5.3.104), and Histrio thus
becomes a theatrical whipping-boy as Jonson has him punished for
his interpretative offence. It is worth noting here that Jonson accuses
the informers Demetrius and Crispinus, whose provocateur is Histrio, of 'ambitiously affecting the title of the untrussers or whippers
of the age' (5.3.591–2), something he himself aspires to in the person of Horace. Lupus, for his 'fierce credulity', is to be fitted 'with
a pair of larger ears' (5.3.124–5), and meanwhile, Caesar has him

gagged, like *Every Man In*'s Carlo Buffone. Virgil, the true poet, adds his own authoritative perspective, that the body of the state is not wounded by the 'modest anger of a satiric spirit', but rather by

> the sinister application
> Of the malicious ignorant and base
> Interpreter, who will distort and strain
> The general scope and purpose of an author
> To his particular and private spleen. (5.3.132–9)

Though Virgil is not directly representative of Jonson, he is made here to ventriloquise Jonson's attack on the 'sinister application' of the 'wresting' poet-apes. The Induction's envious poetasters (and with them, potentially, the interpretative audience) are now cast not merely as moral and artistic failures, but as traitors to the state. Given the 'particular and private spleen' which Jonson is venting in these texts, however, this must be seen as ironic and inevitably self-reflexive.

As Horace is requested to arrest Crispinus and Demetrius 'on the statute of calumny' (5.3.168), he protests, with some dissimulation, 'I am the worst accuser under heaven' (5.3.170); meanwhile Caesar declares his own audience of the spectacle. Metadramatic audience now in place as a court of law, the trial hears poetry mimicking Marston and Dekker's intention to slander Horace. Jonson uses this to contrast his self-made authority with Dekker's lack of learning: Demetrius, voicing Dekker, says of Horace, 'I know the authors from whence he has stole / And could trace him too, but that I understand 'em not full and whole' (5.3.306–7). Tucca further parodies Marston in calling Demetrius and Crispinus 'a couple of chap-fallen curs' (5.3.334–5) and thus reinforces their status as informers until, like Lupus, he himself is gagged by Caesar (5.3.426).[63] As Demetrius confesses his envy of Horace, he makes explicit his connection with the Induction, and Crispinus is chemically induced by Jonson to vomit up words in excess of his true authority.[64] Virgil rounds off the case against the two 'Players [. . .] barking wits' with:

> May with their beggarly and barren trash
> Tickle base vulgar ears in their despite,
> This, like Jove's thunder shall their pride control:
> The honest satyr hath the happiest soul. (5.3.365–70)

We are reminded here that it is the poetasters who are the very barking dog-like informers Jonson later describes in *Timber* as 'enemies of my fame [. . .] Barkers',[65] and of their contrast with 'the honest satyr'. Again the metadrama constructs the offstage audience in order to set up a contrast with these 'base vulgar ears'. As co-audience with the voluntarily disempowered Caesar of this accusation, the offstage audience are offered only a passive role in the proceedings, of which Virgil and Horace are firmly in charge. It is made clear that those who respond positively to Marston or Dekker are to understand themselves as the vulgar of Virgil's description, open to the 'beggarly and barren trash' of the dogs of the state. This degraded potential audience is always hovering around at the margins of these descriptions of poetaster-informers, who thus constitute an example of bestial (mis)interpretation intended to be instructive and to inform the responses of the real offstage audience.

If *Poetaster* addresses the fraught relationship between poetic legitimacy and political authority in the murky realms of the informer, *Sejanus* elevates this discourse to the world of bloody revolution at the heart of imperial Rome. For the political authorities of the time, however, Jonson's desire to monopolise poetic legitimacy in the production of his own dramatic and social authority seems one step of self-determination too far. There is so much practical continuity between Jonson's metadramatic play-world here, representing what Barish calls 'a government tyranny establishing itself through the use of informers', and the realpolitik of early seventeenth-century England, that Northampton's accusation of Jonson's treason comes to look menacingly plausible.[66] Despite this, after 1603, as David Norbrook persuasively argues, Jonson is increasingly supportive of the state, and, possibly because of this, felt able to propose an ideal monarch who did not lend an ear to the sycophant and the informer, but rather valued the poetic corrective of an authoritative author.[67]

To some extent, during this period, metadrama is simply the most convenient field within which the connections between poetic legitimacy, audience interpretation and the control mechanisms of authority may be explored. But in many ways, Jonson's metadrama is much more overt than many of his contemporaries, and especially Shakespeare, in its staging of the interaction of these sites of authority, and its potential for application to contemporary issues and persons. The audiences of these metadramas may not have reacted well to their exploration of the structures of power, or Jonson's very personal style, but he nevertheless has more to say on this matter. In *Timber*, Jonson is quite specific about the compromised nature of authority which relies on these mechanisms of control: 'These [informers] are call'd instruments of grace, and power, with great persons; but they are indeed the Organs of their impotencie, and markes of weaknesse. For sufficient Lords are able to make these Discoveries themselves [. . .] They are base, and servile natures, that busie themselves about these disquisitions.'[68] Jonson clearly sees his own merit in contrast to such natures, as the passage suggests. In his conception, however 'great' a person may be, their authority is morally compromised if they rely on informers, and they too become 'base, and servile'. His depiction of his poetic rivals in these terms resounds therefore with a deep criticism of the authority structures of his whole society.

However, with an eye on the critical function of these plays, we might wonder to what extent Jonson recognises his own complicity in these mechanisms. His rivals certainly recognise this, and at times he even seems to play with the issue himself. Perhaps his concern to differentiate himself from the poetasters and illegitimate authorities, in these and other plays, is born from an acute awareness of his similarity to them.[69] Maybe then, as it sings forcefully out, addressing illegitimate authority and its informers, there is an element of metadramatic confession in *Poetaster*'s final lyric: 'Detraction is but baseness, varlet; / And apes are apes, though clothed in scarlet' (5.3.614–16).

Notes

1. Ben Jonson, 'An Epistle to a Friend to Persuade Him to the Wars', ed. Colin Burrow, in *The Cambridge Edition of the Works of Ben Jonson*, Vol. 7, p. 124.
2. Kaplan, pp. 66–80, 83.
3. Donaldson, p. 192.
4. Kay, p. 68.
5. Meskill, pp. 86, 95.
6. See Jonson, *Poetaster*, pp. 30–6.
7. Ibid. 'satire': (3.5.43–9, 85–9); 'merit': (5.3.351, 610).
8. Ibid. pp. 23–4.
9. David Riggs, *Ben Jonson: A Life* (Cambridge, MA: Harvard University Press, 1989), p. 76.
10. Ben Jonson, *Sejanus*, ed. Philip J. Ayres (Manchester: Manchester University Press, 1999), pp. 9, 38. Unless otherwise stated, all references to *Sejanus* are from this edition.
11. For Jonson's reading of Apuleius where he marks 'mercenary loquacity' and the 'venomous tongues of professional accusers', see Robert C. Evans, *Habits of Mind: Evidence and Effects of Ben Jonson's Reading* (Lewisburg: Bucknell University Press, 1995), p. 120.
12. See note on 'comments' here, and (5.4.74, 101).

13. Jonson, *Poetaster*, p. 14.
14. Meskill, pp. 100, 92.
15. Ibid. p. 108.
16. Jonson, *Volpone*, p. 9.
17. Donaldson, p. 191.
18. Jonson, *Sejanus*, p. 17.
19. See Donaldson, p. 188. *Sejanus* was published in 1605 with comprehensive annotations disproving Northampton's accusation. See Dutton, '*Volpone*', p. 368.
20. Thomas Carew, *Coelum Brittanicum* (Thomas Walkley, 1640), <http://gateway.proquest.com/openurl?ctx_ver=Z39.88-2003& res_id=xri:eebo&rft_id=xri:eebo:image:7793:106> (last accessed 25 September 2015).
21. Ben Jonson, 'An Epistle', p. 124.
22. 'Promoting' includes 'informing': see Jonson, *Poetaster*, p. 71, n. 26.
23. For further discussion of this practice, see Donaldson, p. xiii.
24. Ben Jonson, *Timber, or Discoveries*, in Herford et al. (eds), Vol. 8, p. 571; see also Vol. 11, pp. 220–1.
25. Jonson, *Timber*, Vol. 8, p. 572.
26. Ibid. p. 573.
27. *OED* cites *Poetaster* for its definition of 'traduce': 'To speak evil of, esp. [. . .] falsely or maliciously; to defame, malign, vilify, slander, calumniate, misrepresent; to blame, censure'.
28. Jonson, *Timber*, Vol. 8, p. 572ff.
29. Jonson, *Sejanus*, ed. Barish, p. 17, n. 8. It is tempting to conjecture a connection between the *Isle of Dogs* and the 'Nation of Barkers'.
30. Jonson, *Sejanus*, p. 11; it is interesting that Shakespeare may have played Tiberius, see p. 37.
31. Jonson, *Poetaster*, p. 41.
32. Anon., *The Informer's answer to the late character* (London: T.C., 1675), p. 2, <http://gateway.proquest.com/openurl?ctx_ver=Z39.88-2003& res_id=xri:eebo&rft_id=xri:eebo:citation:9657632> (last accessed 22 September 2015).
33. Beresford, p. 225.
34. For Jonson's Horatian *imitatio*, see *Poetaster*, p. 10.
35. Houston, p. 27.
36. Dekker, *The Guls Horne-booke*, p. 30.
37. Chambers, Vol. 3, p. 293.
38. Thomas Dekker, *Satiromastix*, in Fredson Bowers (ed.), *The Dramatic Works*, Vol. 1 (Cambridge: Cambridge University Press, 1953–61) (4.1.132–5).
39. G. K. Hunter, *English Drama 1586–1642: The Age of Shakespeare* (Oxford: Clarendon Press, 1997), p. 300.
40. In Horace's defence of satire he is keen to deny his own resemblance to 'the opportunistic informers who stalk Rome with notebooks in hand, identifying potential victims', see Keane, p. 79.

41. Jonson, *Poetaster*, p. 182, n. 115–16.
42. Ibid. p. 103.
43. For further notes on 'observation' see ibid. p. 33. Jonson identifies 'observation' as one of the 'Tryers of Arts'; see Ben Jonson, *The English Grammar*, ed. Herford et al., Vol. 8, p. 465.
44. See Jonson, *Poetaster*, p. 65
45. See Angus Fletcher, 'Jonson's Satiric-Comedy and the Unsnarling of the Satyr from the Satirist', *Ben Jonson Journal*, Vol. 7 (2000), pp. 247–69. Lupus refers to Horace as 'satyr' (5.3.32).
46. See *OED* for contemporary connections with servile flattery.
47. Nashe, *Saffron-Walden*, p. 106.
48. John Marston, *Parasitaster, or The Fawne* (London: T.P. for V.V.C, 1606), n.p., <http://gateway.proquest.com/openurl?ctx_ver=Z39.88-2003&res_id=xri:eebo&rft_id=xri:eebo:citation:99845539> (last accessed 23 August 2015).
49. Ibid. n.p.
50. John Marston, *What You Will* (London: G. Eld, 1607), n.p., <http://gateway.proquest.com/openurl?ctx_ver=Z39.88-2003&res_id=xri:eebo&rft_id=xri:eebo:citation:99845540> (last accessed 18 August 2015).
51. See *Poetaster*, p. 35.
52. Marston, *What You Will*, n.p.
53. Ibid. n.p.
54. See Thomas Dekker, *The double PP* (London: T[homas] C[reede], 1606), <http://gateway.proquest.com/openurl?ctx_ver=Z39.88-2003&res_id=xri:eebo&rft_id=xri:eebo:citation:99840977> (last accessed 2 September 2015).
55. *Poetaster*, pp. 40–2.
56. For the association of this with Jonson, see ibid. p. 201, n. 8.
57. Cain notes the hypocrisy here 'in a play which so clearly attacks two individual writers'; see ibid. p. 18.
58. See ibid. p. 212, n. 19, n. 24.
59. Ibid. p. 4.
60. Ibid. p. 17.
61. Ben Jonson, 'An Ode. To himself', *The Underwood*, XXIII, ed. Herford et al., Vol. 8, p. 175. See also *Poetaster*, p. 7.
62. Donaldson, p. 175.
63. See *Poetaster*, p. 244, n. 335.
64. For earlier emetic devices, see pp. 26, 39, 57, n. 81.
65. Jonson, *Timber*, p. 573.
66. *Sejanus*, ed. Barish, p. 16.
67. David Norbrook, *Poetry and Politics in the English Renaissance* (London: Routledge, 1984), pp. 16–17, 175–94.
68. Jonson, *Timber*, p. 613.
69. A mechanism noted by Freud; *Civilization*, p. 90.

Chapter 5

Falstaff, Hal, Coriolanus: Metadrama and the Authority of Policy

The metadrama which proliferates around Hal and the substantial figure of Falstaff offers a significant contrast with the dramatic austerity associated with the eponymous agonist of *Coriolanus*. This chapter explores how metadrama, haunted by the insidious figure of the informer, can reveal disjunctions between an ideal of authentic authority and what is termed 'policy'. The contemporary meaning of the word 'policy' involves the aggressive Machiavellian social role-play and self-counterfeiting often associated at the time with political parasites and informers, but in these plays it also takes in the performative aspect of authority, reaching right to the very top of the social hierarchy.[1]

In its staging of its austere protagonist, *Coriolanus* gives Shakespeare an opportunity to deal with these issues surrounding authority and authenticity through a character who is hostile to the theatre of political power. The excessively self-dramatising Falstaff, on the other hand, provides an affectionate parody of authority which is aided by his perceived nature as Shakespeare's *homo repudiandus*, the representation of all that is to be rejected.[2] It is a testament to the continued currency of his dramatic character that Falstaff has become one of Shakespeare's most enduring dramatic creations: as David Scott Kastan points out, there are 'more references to the fat knight up until the end of the eighteenth century than to any other literary character'.[3] Nicholas Rowe's *Life of Shakespeare* (1709) declares that '*Falstaff* is allow'd by every body to be a Master-piece' and claims that the Queen herself asked Shakespeare write a play of Falstaff in love.[4] *Coriolanus*, however, was more or less forgotten until Nahum Tate's revival of the play in 1681, and played only sporadically thereafter.[5]

The relationship of these perceptions of authority and policy to dramatic authorship and its interpretation may be seen in Chapman's letter of c.1608, which is contemporary with *Coriolanus* and addressed most probably to the Master of the Revels, protesting the censorship of his own *Byron* plays. Chapman had of course been in serious trouble, along with Jonson, for *Eastward Ho!* just three years previously, imprisoned and threatened with what Dutton calls 'judicial mutilation'.[6] His specific complaint in this vexed text is that he has been the victim of an informer in the audience.[7] It begins, however, by shifting the blame onto the actors (three of whom were gaoled)[8] for the subversion of the demands of the censor:

> Sir – I have not deserv'd what I suffer by your austeritie; if the two or three lynes you crost were spoken; my uttermost to suppresse them was enough for my discharge [. . .] I see not myne owne Plaies; nor carrie the Actors Tongues in my mouthe; The action of the mynde is performance sufficient of any dewtie, before the greatest authoritie.[9]

Chapman's plea of the purity of his authorly 'action of the mynde' is in direct contrast to how he envisages the informer's role. Whoever it was, he argues, 'that first plaied the bitter Informer before the french Ambassador', did it by taking amiss what was 'a matter so far from offence' for what Chapman calls his own 'Politique' advancement. He accuses the informer of playing his part like an actor, 'with the Gall of a Wulff'. The informer's tainted perspective is reflected upon the French Ambassador himself who is implicated as the informer's 'maister' as Chapman mentions. There is some irony in the fact that the plot of the play in question also involves informers and their accusations.[10] Chapman argues that these 'hautie and secrett vengeances taken for Crost and officious humors are more Politique than Christian; which he that hates will one day discover in the open ruyne of their Auctors'. The word *auctors* here is being used in the sense of both 'source' and 'author' and Chapman enlists God, 'he that hates [. . .] hautie and secrett vengeances',[11] as his enforcer in their eventual 'open ruyne'. Chapman insists that 'though they be trifles [God] yet laies them in Ballance (as they concern Justice, and bewray Appetites to the greatest Tyrannye) with the greatest'.[12] He thus equates the interpretative sins of the Ambassador and his informer with the very powerful discourse connecting 'honesty' with regimens of desire and consumption in which uncontrolled appetites are linked to idolatry.[13] Moreover, his implication that the Master of the Revels has failed to defend the poor playmaker and 'soften the fiercenes of those rude manners' also places him within the same category – as voracious as a 'Wulff'.[14] Chapman is suggesting that the Master of the Revels's exercise of policy is also at the mercy of his appetites and that he too is on a moral level with the insatiable informer. His description here of 'Illiterate Aucthoritie which setts up his Bristles against Poverty' portrays these courtiers as ignorant of received Christian morality and of the value of poetry. The 'bristles' mentioned are in this period typically those of the boar, and may allude to William Baldwin's *A myrrour for magistrates* (1563) in which the dismembered poet Collingbourne was persecuted by 'the eager hog' Richard III, and the 'wuluishe teeth' of his 'bloudhound', for alluding to 'his badge the Boare'.[15] This also brings to mind the Boar's Head tavern. Like Chapman, Collingbourne was victim of his own inability 'to hide the sence which they so wrongly wrest'[16] from Richard, whom Shakespeare calls 'hell's black intelligencer', a synonym for 'informer'.[17] If the subversive theatrical spirit of Richard III lurks in the iconography of the sign of the Boar's Head, this portent of a future usurper, from a past play, also brings to mind the ghost of the usurped Richard II, who certainly haunts the authenticity of Henry IV's claim to the throne. Further, the typical currency of such bestial images around authorship and policy attests to the moral instability of an authority perceived to be sustained by mercenary interpreters.

The representation of compromised authority that these texts evoke is always significant to the study of metadrama, which often links it with performance, exploring questions of authenticity, authorship, interpretation and informing.[18] In *1 Henry IV*, for instance, Falstaff simultaneously acts as both the de facto tutor to the future king and as the theatrical Vice at the Boar's Head, which is the onstage 'scene' of his play with the heir and also a real London inn serving as a minor public playhouse at the time of writing: a doubly metadramatic space.[19] While Coriolanus not only fails to play to the crowd but, further, cannot hide his deep hostility to them, ever resistant to the temptations of policy and the metadrama it generates, Falstaff performs happily to onstage and offstage audiences alike, both as a representation and a misrepresentation of authority in the worlds of riotous reality and of the theatre. Coriolanus' idealist insistence on untheatricalised authenticity also makes him unfit for rulership. Falstaff, meanwhile, is the monarch's picture in little, or rather perhaps writ large: a twisted proxy father in loco parentis to the king-in-waiting, whose ultimate rejection on the part of authority's legitimate heir is therefore inevitable. Falstaff may be a defective stand-in for Hal's father, but his play-acting at the Boar's Head nevertheless produces a metadrama which addresses the relationship between such ultimate authority and certain expectations of conduct.[20] In this respect, Berger cites the 'puritan parody' of Falstaff's act which targets the 'self-righteous rationale he predicts Harry will resort to in casting off his misleader'; moreover this may be, as he says, 'a performance perversely aimed at soliciting Harry's contempt, giving the prince further incentive to cast him off'.[21] In the play-world of the Boar's Head, Falstaff is both authority and riotous underminer of authority. Eventually, however, outside the onstage play-space, the simple comedic contradiction this sets up will be complicated by Hal's own propensity for performance, and shifted into another register. Both authorship and self-authorship are at play here. Though theirs are metadramatic performances which produce different results, they each nevertheless stand in stark contrast to Coriolanus' refusal to adopt the same self-determining, and self-interested dramatic abilities. Although there are many choric scenes in his play, allusions to a classically metadramatic model, mirroring an audience of a kind, Coriolanus always resists their interpolation. His own form of anti-dramatic self-determination ultimately produces an authority which is as pure as it is brittle. The idea of an unperformed authenticity derived from a divine authorship, the contemporary theological validation of monarchy, is nuanced by the metadrama deployed in *1 Henry IV*. That this play is haunted by the shade of a deposed Richard II undercuts this essential premise, but it is most significantly problematised by Hal's dramatic hypocrisy, his acted authenticity, which proposes the ultimately performative nature of all authority.[22]

The nature of Hal's authority is at play throughout the plays which concern him and there are hints at his consciousness of this as he discusses jobs for Falstaff when he becomes king. When Hal tells Falstaff that he shall hang thieves, the fat knight inevitably interprets this as a sign of authority: 'O, rare! By the Lord, I'll be a brave judge!'; Hal responds 'Thou judgest false already. I mean, thou shalt [. . .] become a rare hangman' (1.2.61–2, 65). Falstaff counters that this is just as good as 'waiting in the court [. . .] for obtaining of suits, whereof the hangman hath no lean wardrobe' (1.2.67–70). Through this repartee, both the expectation of future favour and the nature of authority is being established. The 'suits' mentioned, referring primarily to the victim's clothes often appropriated by the hangman, are also either legal pleas or simply requests granted within the usual processes of policy and patronage, to which Falstaff is assumed to have acceded. With their thoughts now turned towards the identity tropes and language games of court, Falstaff complains he is as melancholy as 'a lugged bear'; Hal asks in comparison, 'What sayest thou to a hare, or the melancholy of Moor-ditch?' (1.2.71, 74–5), and Falstaff replies, 'I would to God thou and I knew where a commodity of good names were to be bought' (1.2.79–80), his identity and reputation now under question. Gail Kern Paster mentions the baited bear as 'a sign of anxiety about future persecution at the hands of authority', but there is also an element of self-parody in this.[23] Falstaff's humoural imbalance, here figured as a fluidity leading down to the drainage ditch of Moorgate, is the classic melancholy of the malcontent, who is always conventionally suspected of politic plotting or informing.[24] His application of these tropes to himself and Hal together invites a critical comparison of the two by the off-stage audience. Falstaff's suggestion of Hal's equal reputation leads him to the half-joking accusation of corruption on Hal's part: 'O, thou [. . .] art indeed able to corrupt a saint. Thou hast done much harm upon me [. . .] Before I knew thee, Hal, I knew nothing, and now am I [. . .] little better than one of the wicked' (1.2.87–91). With a sense of irony, Falstaff's claim about his own education here turns around the scholar–master relationship and prefigures the inevitable reversal of their positions.

The extent to which Falstaff regards himself as a kind of actor in this fantasy of power is not made clear, whereas Hal clearly sees himself as a masquer in an artificial role-playing world, a role which he is able to cast off at any time. Indeed, after plotting to play the thieving trick on Falstaff, Hal reveals his dramatic scheme of personal reformation, confiding in the offstage audience:

> herein will I imitate the sun,
> Who doth permit the base contagious clouds
> To smother up his beauty from the world,
> That, when he please again to be himself,
> Being wanted, he may be more wondered at
> By breaking through the foul and ugly mists
> Of vapours that did seem to strangle him. (1.2.187–93)

This metadramatic gesture involves the audience in its implicit interpretation and opposes the integrity of authority to performance, the value of which is predicated upon its supposed abandonment in favour of the future role of king.

In his own performance, Falstaff recalls rather more of the simplicity of the medieval moralities than the subtlety of Renaissance drama. He is imagined by Hal as the Vice or devil of the morality play: he is called: 'white-bearded Satan' (2.4.451), 'reverend Vice' (2.4.441), 'grey iniquity' (2.4.442), and elsewhere 'feeder of [. . .] riots' (*2HIV*, 5.5.61), a lord of misrule.[25] Considering these familiar and still popular dramatic models, and the contemporary view of Satan's role in history as instigator, plotter and accuser of the righteous, this places him very much within the familiar territory of the reviled informer.[26] When Hal refuses to help him to his horse, Falstaff explicitly, if light-heartedly, threatens to turn informer: 'If I be ta'en, I'll peach for this' (2.2.44), that is 'impeach' Hal. These connections continue: in setting up the device on Falstaff, Poins asks Bardoll for news, calling him his 'setter' (2.2.49), another contemporary word for informer.[27] As the subject of their metadramatic device, Falstaff heaps insults on the travellers involved that apply mainly to Falstaff himself, including the term 'whoreson caterpillars' (2.2.82), which primarily means 'parasites', a term employed of politicking courtiers, but again more often of their informers.

Throughout, references to informing surround the metadrama; its 'devices' can be dramatic, political, or criminal stratagems, connoting authorship and a dubious authority. One is the metadramatic 'device' by which Falstaff is cosened, or 'colted' (2.2.38) as Hal says. Back at the Boar's Head, when he has revealed his own part in the plotted role-play and Falstaff's resulting cowardice, Hal maintains this pattern when he asks, 'what trick, what device [. . .] canst thou now find out to hide thee from this open and apparent shame?' (2.4.255–7). Falstaff protests that it was his instinct to protect the future king that made him run, and asks 'shall we have a play extempore?' (2.4.271), almost as a distraction from the embarrassments of the recent role-play. Not letting Falstaff off the hook, Bardoll tells the King that he 'blushed to hear his monstrous devices' (2.4.303–4) in which Falstaff had his accomplices give themselves nose-bleeds and hack their sword-edges with daggers to make it look as if they had been in a fight. All of this deceptive meta-acting on Falstaff's part, and critical interpretation on Hal's part, is followed directly by the news that political rebellion is afoot in the land, involving Hotspur, Owen Glendower and others. Thus the revelation of both minor and major plots and devices forms the backdrop to the metadrama of the tavern play which is eventually authored by the Prince, as he initiates a performance of his own relationship to authority, commanding: 'Do thou stand for my father and examine me upon the particulars of my life' (2.4.366–7).

This performed exchange prefigures Hal's later conversation with the King, but although their mock interview at first involves merely mild euphuistic ribbing by Falstaff, it turns into something rather more serious when Hal takes the King's part, ominously rejecting Falstaff and in the most insulting terms. Thus when the metadrama of their respective roles clash and authority is scrutinised, the subtleties of acting expose the political brutality of language. The requisite hierarchies are then established as the effects of linguistic domination, of a kind of authorship. But moreover, their roleplay extends beyond this mere drunken ad-libbing into something more concrete when the Watch arrives and Hal orders Falstaff, in a conventionally metadramatical gesture, 'Go hide thee behind the arras' (2.4.486), the place of the hidden watcher, the overhearer and informer. After Hal deals with the crisis with a simple exercise of authority, and Falstaff is discovered there asleep, they pick his pockets, finding '*certain papers*' (s.d. 2.4.518–19). Reading firstly an inn bill, Hal tells Peto, 'what there is else keep close; we'll read it at more advantage' (2.4.528–9); here the heir himself acts in the very mode of the informer, the dealer in information. The effect of this on the offstage audience is to suggest a dramatic community with the more powerful of these metadramatic characters, the Prince at the centre. Though he is acting as the most despised element in the networks of power here, the informer, nevertheless, as author, he soon closes the frame of the metadrama, firmly, turning his attention to matters requiring another level of authority: 'I'll to the court in the morning. We must all to the wars' (2.4.530–1).

The conversation corresponding to this mock-interview, where the King berates Hal for his 'passages of life' (3.2.8) produces an element of what Peter Hollindale calls 'comic parallelism', though I would suggest there is also something more than comedy at issue here.[28] This doubling is an oblique form of metadramatic self-reference which works by juxtaposition, or a kind of atemporal metalepsis, to produce an interpretative framework that operates once the passages' equivalence is perceived. The parodic relationship between these conversations draws attention to the artificiality of Hal's world as a whole, to the role-playing of authority in general, and to the construction of monarchy. For a live audience, the staging must guide this perception to provide the heightened sense through which the trope of performance is perceived as the key to each scene. In such a metadramatic atmosphere, it is interesting to note that the first excuse Hal offers is that the information the King has received is faulty, relating it to the 'many tales devised / (Which oft the ear of greatness needs must hear), / By smiling pickthanks and base news-mongers' (3.2.23–5). A 'newsmonger' is of course a private dealer in information: not at this time a journalist, but an informer. Hal's own recent practice is enough to establish the irony here. His father responds by outlining the extent of his own role-play in obtaining and maintaining the crown: he dressed himself, he says, 'in such humility / That I did pluck allegiance from men's hearts', likening his own presence to 'a robe pontifical, / Ne'er seen but wondered at' (3.2.51–2, 56–7), a clear admission of Machiavellian policy. Hal's penitent response is 'I shall hereafter, my thrice-gracious lord, / Be more myself' (3.4.92–3), which may, or may not, again, be unintentionally ironical; nevertheless the King still accuses Hal of siding with rebels, 'under Percy's pay, / To dog his heels and curtsy at his frowns' (3.2.126–7). Hal again invokes his father's advisors and informers, who have, as he says, 'sway'd / Your majesty's good thoughts away from me' (3.2.130–1) and responds to this accusation of rebellion and dog-like fawning to Hotspur by describing his own full determination to display himself in the acts and trappings of absolute authority:

> I will redeem all this on Percy's head
> And in the closing of some glorious day
> Be bold to tell you that I am your son,
> When I will wear a garment all of blood
> And stain my favours in a bloody mask. (3.2.132–6)

In this way, Hal aims to reproduce Henry IV's public-image role-play as a serious contender for the role of king. But there is an anomaly at the heart of this which remains unmentionable within the play: that real monarchical authority is meant to proceed from an authenticity derived from divine appointment, not merely from the effects of a public show.

Here, as always, authority depends to some extent on an idea of the authentic. Falstaff himself is flattered that he is 'authentic in [his] place and person' (2.2.205) in *The Merry Wives of Windsor* (c.1599), when being practised upon by Ford in disguise.[29] As flattery, this only makes sense in terms of the desire to distance Falstaff from the opposite: the inauthentic and the performative, in terms of both social position and identity. This plays upon the dramatic irony in Falstaff's lack of awareness of his own performativity, and

constructed selfhood, which may perhaps explain both his successive downfalls in this play and the Histories, and the great sympathy
this generates for him amongst contemporary and later audiences. In
contrast, Hal seems very much aware of his own inauthenticity. This
awareness however, never stops him from performing and directing
the roles requisite to securing and perpetuating his claim to kingship.
Performance and policy seem to go hand in hand in his world. The
burgeoning Hotspur, he tells the King, is merely his agent, gathering up deeds of glory to be submitted at Hal's feet, on pain of death
(3.2.147–52). It is not insignificant that he feels the need to call God
as his witness to this stake (3.2.153–4). Hal's subsequent confident
and efficient organising of the rascals into military order is an indication of his deliberate shift of role induced by the metadramatic
revelation of the performance of his father's authority.

Not to be confined to the theatre of the court, or the inn-yard,
metadrama and inauthenticity also persist in the heat of battle,
where other dramatic narratives are at play. Falstaff, commenting
on Hal's duel with Hotspur says, presumably to Hotspur, 'Nay, you
shall find no boy's play here, I can tell you' (5.4.74–5), punning
on sword-play; but when Falstaff tells the tale of how it was he
that killed Hotspur, Hal is prepared to gild his lie 'with the hap-
piest terms I have' (5.4.158). It seems increasingly clear that Hal's
confessional rejection of his old performance is just the prologue to
a new one, and he appears acutely aware of this himself. This suggests both the imperative of an inescapable performativity inherent in monarchy itself, and, simultaneously, simply that Hal is a
successful product of his training at the hands of his thoroughly
self-performative tutor.

It is also significant here that Hotspur's intrigue and rebellion
are figured theatrically. The connection is obvious, and the wordplay typical, when he asserts 'my Lord of York commends the plot
and the general course of the action' (2.3.19–20). Hal later parodies
Hotspur's utterly unselfconscious military roleplay (2.4.94ff.) and
metadramatically intends to play Hotspur in the Boar's Head, though
this is overtaken by Falstaff's outrage at being robbed. Hotspur himself embodies a kind of noble masculinity that is susceptible to ridicule and parody. Although, like Coriolanus, he claims he 'cannot
flatter' (4.1.6), this is questionable since he flatters Mortimer when
he is slandered by the King, ironically defending him against what
he terms 'bare and rotten policy' (1.3.108). Additionally, Hotspur
is also very much aware of the policy and role-playing of the King,
saying that he

seems to weep
Over his country's wrongs; and, by this face,
This seeming brow of justice, did he win
The hearts of all that he did angle for. (4.3.81–4)

Hotspur declares that he is 'whipped and scourged with rods, / Nettled and stung with pismires when I hear / Of this vile politician Bolingbroke / [. . .] this king of smiles' (1.3.237–9, 243); he recounts the courtesy this 'fawning greyhound' offered him, adding 'the devil take such cozeners!' (1.3.249, 252). The language of the streets and the court connects in this invective against the King's acting, his metadramatic inauthenticity and the taint of his policy. But Hotspur's own fame is also inadvertently tied to a theatricality which is finally reliant on not only his own words but those of others. When he refuses to listen to the Earl of Worcester's story, Northumberland accuses him of 'Tying thine ear to no tongue but thine own!' (1.3.236); in other words he is in danger of failing to recognise his own theatricality, and believing his own self-image. Nevertheless, and despite these contradictions, the metadrama continues to surround him and is sustained at the moment of his death; upon considering how his father's illness may weaken their cause, Worcester tells Hotspur that they must 'stop all sight-holes, every loop from whence / The eye of reason may pry in upon us', declaring that his father's absence 'draws a curtain / That shows the ignorant a kind of fear' (4.1.70–3). Their vulnerability to the watcher, the hidden overseer, is framed within a familiarly theatrical, and metadramatic, geography of curtains and prying eyes which draws the offstage audience into its paranoid world, now in the knowledge of just what a good self-performance might achieve. In these ways, through supporting characters also, the play's metadrama addresses the relationship between authority, authenticity and performance, and continues to provide an interpretative framework through which the offstage audience may perceive this connection. Hotspur, on the other hand, sees his father's absence as an opportunity.

Throughout all their play-acting, Hal and Falstaff's disguise and pretence circulate around the central issue of Hal's royalty like dancers around a maypole. Authority, as may be recognised, is largely a performance of itself, but authenticity may only be legitimately performed in so far as it attaches to authority. Hal is aware of this even at his major crisis, in *Henry V*, as before the battle of Agincourt his apologetic lament for kingship admits that 'thrice-gorgeous ceremony' (4.1.259) is all that separates his everyday life from those of his subjects. Falstaff's inadequate reply to Hal's derogatory descriptions of him also attests to this. Set against the performative throughout is the underlying discursive power of the authentic, which is the root of Hal's royalty; this emerges, for instance, in Falstaff's 'instinct' not to kill the prince (2.4.263ff.). However this also provides metadramatic matter for discussion about the nature of the counterfeit. Douglas, encountering Henry IV on the battlefield asks, 'what art thou / That counterfeit'st the person of a king?' (5.4.26–7) and says 'I fear thou art another counterfeit, / And yet, in faith, thou bearest thee like a king' (5.4.34–5). This uncertainty that cannot distinguish between a king and the likeness of a king must be seen in relation to Falstaff's description of the counterfeit as role-playing. Falstaff, rising up after feigning death on the battlefield, observes,

> 'twas time to counterfeit, or that hot termagant Scot had paid me [. . .] Counterfeit? I lie; I am no counterfeit. To die is to be a counter-feit, for he is but the counterfeit of a man who hath not the life of a man. But to counterfeit dying when a man thereby liveth is to be no counterfeit but the true and perfect image of life indeed. (5.4.112–18)

Thus his role-playing (which Falstaff himself freely equates with cow-ardice) has saved his life. But moreover, he will now use the oppor-tunity afforded by Hotspur's death to counterfeit a heroic narrative out of his false-acting on the battlefield and perform a role which he hopes will aid him politically: 'I'll swear I killed him [. . .] Noth-ing confutes me but eyes, and nobody sees me' (5.4.124–6). Again the irony sticks with a live audience, even as they perceive Falstaff's bare-faced policy. The last metadramatic line frames the whole pas-sage within a self-conscious dramatic framework, and his assertion that 'nothing confutes me' recalls his previous speech about 'honour' where he declared, 'Detraction will not suffer it. Therefore I'll none of it' (5.1.138–9).

All of this seems to suggest that the opposition of authenticity to performance is inherently false, since authenticity must be per-formed, and, like any other performed act, is always subject to inter-pretation, confutation and detraction. Hal's ironic statement, as Henry V at Agincourt, 'I think the King is but a man, as I am' (*Henry V*, 4.1.102–3), performs an authenticity which appeals to an audi-ence because it is the mildest of all possible rebukes to subversion in the ranks. Hal's earlier promise to his father, to be 'more myself' (3.2.92–3), also speaks of the performance of the authentic, though this is nuanced by his claim in *2 Henry IV*, that 'being awaked, I do despise my dream' (5.5.50). Here Falstaff is disowned by Hal, now King, in his pursuit of an unperformed authenticity which will be unattainable to him, despite his ability to control what Falstaff himself called 'detraction'. Notwithstanding his attempts throughout the play to qualify and control the figures of his own performance, this dream of the authentic is thoroughly problematised by Hal's own self-conscious acting.

This problematic is played out further in these plays in the associations between role-play, the flow of information and the general degradation of authority. In *2 Henry IV*, for instance, the metadramatic induction of Rumour plays upon contemporary paranoia over informing and the debasement of authority as it enters '*painted full of tongues*' (s.d. 1.1.1). He declaims that 'Upon my tongues continual slanders ride, / [. . .] Stuffing the ears of men with false reports' (1.1.6, 8). His audience is envisaged as a 'blunt monster with uncounted heads / The still-discordant wav'ring multitude' (1.1.18–19) and he associates them with himself when he asks, 'what need I thus / My well-known body to anatomize / Among my household?' (1.1.20–2). Both the mob and the informer are typically imaged as beasts. This monstrous correlation established, in the first scene, Northumberland dramatises the news of political stratagems, figuring contention as a wild horse who 'madly hath broke loose / And bears down all before him' (1.1.10–11); when he receives news of his son's death, however, he turns a metadramatic phrase:

Let order die,
And let this world no longer be a stage
To feed contention in a ling'ring act;
But let one spirit of the first-born Cain
Reign in all bosoms, that each heart being set
On bloody courses, the rude scene may end
And darkness be the burier of the dead! (1.1.154–60)

With the offstage audience offered complicity in these framing concepts of unruly and beastly uses of information, and murderous political drama, Bardolph delivers a letter to Hal in which Falstaff again plays the rumour-mongering informer.[30] The audience's response to the Rumour's address will establish varying amounts of sympathy, as will their perception of his own awareness of being staged, his metadramatic function. Berger argues that Falstaff here 'performs the role of prince's dog for himself as well as for Harry'.[31] Hal's perspective on Falstaff at this point is clarified when he says that he may be 'as familiar with me as my dog; and he holds his place, for look you how he writes' (2.2.100–2). Here Falstaff now stands for the bestial, fawning informer, offering 'vital' information on Poins such as that 'he misuses thy favours so much that he swears thou art to marry his sister Nell' (2.2.120–1). Continuing the theatrical parody of what is a commonplace thing, Hal questions Poins on the matter directly (2.2.130–4); his next statement, however, is a blatant metadramatic appeal for audience sympathy, in contradiction to Rumour's low opinion of them: 'thus we play the fools with the time, and the spirits of the wise sit in the clouds and mock us' (2.2.134–5). This, along with the rest of this passage, both parodies and links issues of debased authority, role-play and the flow of information, and Hal is again implicated in all of these as much as is Falstaff. It is interesting to note also that Falstaff has referred to Hal as 'he my dog' (1.2.142); theirs it seems is a reciprocal bestialisation.

This sense of the debasement of authority by informing and performance is pervasive even when the conventions of patronage are honoured; for instance when Hal asks for information on Falstaff and receives it, he is told he may be found in low company, with Doll Tearsheet; and when he suggests sneaking up on them at supper and Poins replies, 'I am your shadow, my lord; I'll follow you' (2.2.151); and also when he pays Falstaff's man, Bardolph, to keep silent about his presence (2.2.152–3). As Hal descends further into this low role-play, with these social power structures forming an appropriately dramatic background, he arranges a metadrama with Poins on familiar ground to make Falstaff again the subject of a device. Their plan to disguise themselves as 'drawers', to see Falstaff 'in his true colours, and not ourselves be seen' (2.2.162), forms a metadrama in which identity and social status are ambiguous. In the planning of this interlude, Hal notes the accompanying descent into the bestial: 'From a god to a bull? a heavy decension! It was Jove's case. From a prince to a prentice? A low transformation that shall be mine, for in everything the purpose must weigh with the folly' (2.2.165–8). The anatomy of both Rumour's debased information and of lower-rank role-play in *2 Henry IV* turns out to be the dissection of a beast.[32] But, mirroring the Boar's Head role-play of *Part 1*, here again the metadrama is interrupted as the real world once more intervenes, and it is Falstaff this time who is summoned to court (2.4.366). The call to higher things may leave the audience with the false sense that such performativity applies only to the lower ranks, and those who would play therein. The Archbishop of York's use of bestial imagery to describe the rebellious 'commonwealth' in the person of an audience, attests to this:

O thou fond many, with what loud applause
Didst thou beat heaven with blessing Bolingbroke,
Before he was what thou wouldst have him be!
And being now trimmed in thine own desires,
Thou, beastly feeder, art so full of him
That thou provok'st thyself to cast him up.
So, so, thou common dog, didst thou disgorge
Thy glutton bosom of the royal Richard. (1.3.91–8)

The metaphor of the 'common dog' which accompanies this metadramatic accusation depends upon a false dichotomy, separating the appetite of the ruler from those of the ruled.

In fact, the King, who, as Kastan points out, 'understands this new political world where power is unnervingly dependent upon popular support rather than reassuringly derived from private sanction', also understands the desires to which power is subject.[33] Thus metaphors of bestial hunger often applied to the policy of predatory informers, for instance Chapman's 'Wulff', are extended to higher ranks when the King accuses Hal of inhuman voracity in taking the crown prematurely,

Dost thou so hunger for mine empty chair
That thou wilt needs invest thee with my honours
Before thy hour be ripe?
[. . .] Thou hidest a thousand daggers in thy thoughts,
Whom thou hast whetted on thy stony heart,
To stab at half an hour of my life. (4.3.224–6, 236–8)

Furthermore, he charges Hal with dragging the commonwealth with him into a Falstaffian depravity and reducing the nation itself to canine and lupine monstrosity, in his claim that Hal, 'from curbed licence plucks / The muzzle of restraint, and the wild dog / Shall flesh his tooth on every innocent', lamenting 'O my poor kingdom, / [. . .] thou wilt be a wilderness again, / Peopled with wolves, thy old inhabitants' (4.3.260–3, 266–7).

Ever the penitent when it becomes dramatically expedient, Hal begs pardon for the premature implicit claiming of the crown, returning it with the blessing: 'He that wears the crown immortally / Long guard it yours!' (4.3.273–4). Though we are aware at this point that Hal is dealing here with an item of costume for the part he wishes to play, he still manages to gesture towards the authenticity bestowed by 'He that wears the crown immortally' and therefore claims the resulting authority for his upcoming role. Furthermore he uses this upward motion to distance himself from the accusations associated with the low animals of his and his father's imagination. This distance appears imperative, since Hal has stated that he intends,

> To mock the expectation of the world,
> To frustrate prophecies, and to raze out
> Rotten opinion, who hath writ me down
> After my seeming. (5.2.125–8)

Hal's metadramatic wish to resist the informing power of Rumour's painted tongues and play a new role thus produces what has been traditionally thought of as a kind of Judas moment, his betrayal of his teacher and mentor in rebellion:

> FALSTAFF
> My king, my Jove, I speak to thee, my heart!
>
> KING HENRY V
> I know thee not, old man. Fall to thy prayers.
> How ill white hairs becomes a fool and jester!
> I have long dreamt of such a kind of man,
> So surfeit-swelled, so old, and so profane;
> But being awaked, I do despise my dream. (5.5.45–50)

But Falstaff is right in a profound sense when he suggests that this is just a 'colour' (5.5.84) that the King is assuming to adhere to the form of the role he now must play. This view fits perfectly with Hal's conduct so far. Lancaster himself submits that the King, 'hath intent his wonted followers / Shall all be very well provided for' (5.5.96–7), though conditions are attached. Falstaff's banishment from within a ten-mile radius of the King's person until he is reformed does seem, as Berger says, 'surprisingly lenient'.[34] What Hollindale calls Hal's 'political calculation and emotional fraud', his policy, here often expressed through his metadrama, make him both a highly successful 'politician' and a dangerously cynical self-performer.[35] If Falstaff never recovers his position in Hal's company it may simply be because he fails to adapt to the particularly treacherous conditions attached to role-play at this higher level.

Such layered and interwoven metadrama points also to the vagaries of interpretation, as the frequent addresses to the audience suggest. When John betrays the rebels, whose grievances he says he allows, he adds that some of his Father's advisors have 'too lavishly / Wrested his meaning and authority' (4.1.282–3). This interpretative 'wresting' is what the rebels had been primed to hope for by the operations of rumour throughout, and their betrayal shows that any interpretation, as well as the morality which attaches to it, is potentially unstable, and therefore untrustworthy. They have relied upon their own unfortunate reading of John's words, but their last words will be heard at 'the block of death / Treason's true bed and yielder up of breath' (4.1.349–50). In contrast, Warwick tells the King that Hal 'studies his companions / Like a strange tongue, wherein, to gain the language' (4.3.68–9) and thus has indulged in immorality merely to master it, them and the nation they represent. Perhaps the crown lies uneasy on Henry IV's head significantly because he understands the inherently unstable conditions involved in being a role-player at the very highest level.

From Henry IV's initial devout intentions to make a pilgrimage in the Holy Land, through the slanders of Rumour in the second part of the narrative, to the clear metadrama of the prologue-chorus of *Henry V* (1599), there is a movement towards ever more explicit theatrical self-reference, and towards a curiously Machiavellian exploitation of the resources of language. Henry IV only gets as far as the Jerusalem room of Hampton Court Palace, which is hardly a pilgrimage. The frame-narrative of *Henry V* places Hal's role-play within a specifically metadramatic world, where the theatre of monarchy celebrates its own inauthentic policy in devices of self-conscious representation, as the Chorus suggests:

> O for a Muse of fire, that would ascend
> The brightest heaven of invention,
> A kingdom for a stage, princes to act
> And monarchs to behold the swelling scene!
> [. . .] let us, ciphers to this great accompt,
> On your imaginary forces work.
> [. . .] Piece out our imperfections with your thoughts;
> [. . .] For 'tis your thoughts that now must deck our kings.
> (Prologue 1–4, 17–18, 23, 28)

But, despite this metadramatic framing inviting the popular imagination to co-create Hal's next drama, Falstaff remains a ghost in *Henry V*. Pistol gives him an honourable mention: 'bristle thy courage up! For Falstaff he is dead'; Bardolph adds 'would I were with him, wheresome'er he is, either in / heaven or in hell!' (2.3.5–7). The consensus that he is killed by the King's rejection is apparently widely accepted. When Fluellen suggests that, as Alexander killed his friend in his cups, 'so also Harry Monmouth [. . .] turned away the fat knight with the great belly-doublet: he was full of jests, and gipes, and knaveries, and mocks; I have forgot his name', Gower replies simply, 'Sir John Falstaff' (4.7.45–50). Either Falstaff is excluded, or he excludes himself from the high drama where princes act before an audience of monarchs, and monarch-imaginers; both ways his lack of representation causes his metadramatic identity to fade, and the impression that the King's authenticity is unperformed to grow.

Falstaff appears in *The Merry Wives of Windsor* as a character who has not adapted to the new dramatic conditions offered to him, and persists there as the buffoon of the dramatic stratagem, the dupe of the device. Although he is initially plotting to practise a device of his own in this play, Falstaff is almost immediately informed upon and from this point on is continually so. Even his own servant is in the pay of others, and the arising intelligences form the basis for him being practised upon as the subject of much inner-playing and many metadramatic devices. These devices have a negative effect on Falstaff throughout: he is thrown into a river, beaten with a cudgel, placed in the stocks, and pinched and burned by people disguised as fairies. Here Falstaff's appetite and predatory policy are to a certain extent resolved through a barrage of metadramatic processes which subject him to the narratives of others until he becomes assimilable. Once he has been fully and bodily subjected to the dramatic narrative of his peers he can be forgiven, and included in the final celebration, though offstage. Both here and in the history plays he remains the failed but outrageously inventive actor, the other which defines by its opposition the performed authenticity of Hal and others dramatising their lives at the highest level of policy. This contrasts in many respects with Coriolanus, whose troubled existence is dogged by his innocence of the dramaturgy of political realities. They both struggle with the contradiction between authenticity and acting at this level, but for entirely different reasons.

In stark contrast with Hal and Falstaff, Coriolanus believes he cannot act at this or any other level: he is all authenticity, no policy. Unfortunately for him, his political authority is thereby undermined, unbalanced by a kind of blunt battlefield honesty that seems unnatural in his new social role and which is certainly unwelcome. This lack of theatrical dexterity is clearly a weakness in Coriolanus in the context of the republican Rome that makes demands upon his presentational competence. Though Coriolanus sees a pure 'nobility' as one untainted by policy, yet policy nevertheless engulfs him like a rising tide. Coriolanus is, as G. R. Hibbard says, 'a man without a mask in a world where hypocrisy and double-dealing hold sway'.[36] But this ideal opposition of political intrigue and deception on the one hand and authentic nobility on the other sets up what may be a false contradiction; as we have seen, in many contexts it is far more the case, in fact, that the latter actively depends on the former. Hibbard mentions Coriolanus' *sprezzatura*, the 'nonchalant ease of manner and studied contempt of popular opinion' of the Jacobean courtier.[37] But Coriolanus succeeds at only the second of these; moreover the performance of nonchalance that partly defines *sprezzatura* can only be achieved by rigorous preparation for the skill to be acted out at the right place and time. In terms of contemporaneous court contexts, Coriolanus is a failed courtier who simply cannot assimilate the idea of role-play, or politic practice, with that of authority with integrity.[38]

When his plain-speaking has infuriated the tribunes, and he says to his mother, 'would you have me / False to my nature? Rather say I play / The man I am' (3.2.14–16), Volumnia replies,

> You might have been enough the man you are
> With striving less to be so. Lesser had been
> The tryings of your dispositions if
> You had not showed them how ye were disposed
> Ere they lacked power to cross you. (3.2.19–23)[39]

The explicit association of acting with moral falsehood here exposes to view Coriolanus' own unwavering perspective on life, and the source of his political downfall. Volumnia develops the point, saying, 'I would dissemble with my nature where / My fortunes and my friends at stake required / I should do so in honour' (3.2.64–6). Partly persuaded, he speaks into the paradox, 'You have put me now to such a part which never / I shall discharge to th' life' (3.2.107–8). Musing on the nature of the act he must stage before the people, he declaims with reluctance, 'Away, my disposition, and possess me / Some harlot's spirit!' (3.2.113–14), continuing,

> The smiles of knaves
> Tent in my cheeks, and schoolboys' tears take up
> The glasses of my sight! A beggar's tongue
> Make motion through my lips, and my armed knees,
> Who bowed but in my stirrup, bend like his
> That hath received an alms!
> [. . .] I'll mountebank their loves,
> Cog their hearts from them, and come home beloved
> Of all the trades in Rome. (3.2.117–22, 134–6)

Here he connects the act of playing a role with low social status: that of harlots, schoolboys, beggars, knaves, mountebanks and the 'cogging' politic fawner. To some extent, his instinct struggles with the idea that true authority may include a performed authenticity, something that neither Hal nor Falstaff question, though he is unaware that his own 'nobility' is itself already a performance, and thus he loses himself in what is, in the circumstances, a fragile idealism. It is with some irony that he parts with, 'I'll return consul, / Or never trust to what my tongue can do / I'th' way of flattery further' (137–9). His performance before the people is of course is an abject failure, not for the first time ending in violence; he is, as Robin Headlam Wells notes, 'a liability to the state he serves',[40] although the state itself does not escape criticism. In terms of the structures of the text, to the extent that the application of 'policy' is resisted, so any metadramatic element is resisted as a strategy to depict these pressures; as the one fails so the other fails to appear. Despite this structural resistance, Coriolanus is the object of a kind of choric-metadramatic commentary by the other characters and his personality and political career become the focus of the play. Throughout, he actively resists the interpretation of the very many people who discuss, judge and plot around him, and they therefore continue to be subject to the force of his presence. In this way, in despite of the theatrical workings of the political world around him, and even of his personal demise, Coriolanus' ultimately unattainable ideal of nobility persists. This nevertheless, and with some irony, makes good tragic theatre.

However, he is also exposed as a very incomplete politician; for instance he despises too publicly the lower ranks of the Roman state, failing to recognise the extent to which they are a powerful audience of kinds, who might potentially respond to the theatre of his power, were he to compromise. The perception of the crowd is an issue here, and the imagery that surrounds them is familiarly bestial to those who wish to portray them so. They are depicted as vermin, as Menenius advises, 'Rome and her rats are at the point of battle' (1.1.159); they are also continually imagined as curs, dogs, geese, even the hydra (c.f. 3.1.95), not only, but often, by Coriolanus himself.[41] Both Menenius and Cominus use the word 'wolf' to describe the populace (2.1.7, 4.6.116, respectively).[42] Coriolanus meanwhile is imagined as various animals of prey: as a bear, dragon, osprey, or tiger. This reciprocal bestialisation is connected with ideas of monstrous authority from both directions: for Coriolanus this means authority reluctantly deriving from the people, whilst for them it means Coriolanus performing tyrannically, as ruler.

But moreover, and typically, such bestial authority is again connected with the concept of the power of the uncontrolled and informing tongue. In a discussion of events between citizens, one says, 'if he show us his wounds and tell us his deeds, we are to put our tongues into those wounds and speak for them; so, if he tell us his noble deeds, we must also tell him our noble acceptance of them. Ingratitude is monstrous, and for the multitude to be ingrateful, were to make a monster of the multitude' (2.3.7–11). When Sicinius and Brutus arrive at one point Coriolanus makes an astute connection between the monstrous multitude and the Roman authorities (Sicinius and Brutus) as he sees them, announcing they are, 'The tongues o'th' common mouth. I do despise them, / For they do prank them in authority / Against all noble sufferance' (3.1.23–5). Further, he calls their constituency a 'herd' (3.1.35) and implies their own complicity in the rebellion, asking, 'You being their mouths, why rule you not their teeth?', suggesting that their rebellion against the nobility 'grows by plot' (3.1.38, 40); Brutus responds, 'Call't not a plot. / The people cry you mocked them, / [. . .] called them / Time-pleasers, flatterers, foes to nobleness' (3.1.41–2, 44–5). When Coriolanus replies, 'Why, this was known before,' Brutus says 'Not to them all.' Coriolanus then asks accusingly, 'Have you inform'd them sithence?'; Brutus is outraged at the suggestion: 'How! I inform them!' and Coriolanus, despising him, says, 'You are like to do such business' (3.1.48–50). Amongst all of this posturing, accusation of informing and the failed role-playing of authority, Coriolanus still refuses to act in any way that might placate the populace in their grievances by representing to them anything other than his own adversarial version of events. His warning about the production of any representational compromise nevertheless employs a familiar imagery of predation and bestiality, though with its natural hierarchy inverted,

> Thus we debase
> The nature of our seats, and make the rabble
> Call our cares fears, which will in time
> Break ope the locks o'th' Senate and bring in
> The crows to peck the eagles. (3.1.137–41)

This trading of the imagery of mutual bestialisation, denoting the unworthy, monstrous, or predatory, suggests an extreme instability in the medium of exchange between these groups: the policy of the theatre of state. The problem with this miscommunicative theatre is that its primary audience, the republican Roman populace, is empowered by the very act of interpretation, as Aufidius notes: 'So our virtues / Lie in th'interpretation of the time' (4.7.49–50).[43] Coriolanus himself, however, both lacks the actor's control of language, as he says, 'when blows have made me stay I fled from words' (2.2.70), and, unlike Hal, is a defective interpreter. The level of his dysfunction in this regard is displayed when he accuses soldiers of flattery when they are simply congratulating and praising him. Perhaps it is because of this political dysfunction, that Coriolanus wants to deny the Roman commonality the power and influence inherent in republican representation. He is clearly worried by the dichotomy that this competition generates:

> when two authorities are up,
> Neither supreme, how soon confusion
> May enter 'twixt the gap of both and take
> The one by th'other. (3.1.111–14)

Lacking any real representational intelligence, in order to avoid the further complication of this situation, he merely advises the tribunes Sicinius and Brutus,

> at once pluck out
> The multitudinous tongue
> [. . .] Your dishonour
> Mangles true judgment and bereaves the state
> Of that integrity which should become't. (3.1.157–8, 159–61)

Sicinius responds by stating that Coriolanus has 'spoken like a traitor, and shall answer / As traitors do' (3.1.163–4); Brutus agrees that, within the context of the Roman republic, this is treason. Where the populace is empowered, authorities like these may define their own terms, and thus 'treason' means whatever they want it to mean, here an offence against the people rather than against a single figurehead. Under such a system anything perceived, rightly or wrongly, to be a critique may be subject to the accusation of defamation or sedition. This is much more the case for Coriolanus than it is for Falstaff and Hal, both of whom are able to control their own interpretation to some extent, through the performance of policy which produces metadramatic structures. Coriolanus, however, exists within a dramatic context in which his resistance to metadramatic play may be read as an idealistic opposition to the politicking which typically accompanies it. His stance also suggests that the ideal nature of authority is not merely bound up with social production, but also with self-production, which he imagines through the person of his young son:

> I'll never
> Be such a gosling to obey instinct, but stand
> As if a man were author of himself
> And knew no other kin. (5.3.34–7)

Coriolanus possesses the Machiavellian *virtu* to authorise himself, but his most metadramatic comment points to a failure to engage with the wider community that constructs him as the defender of Rome: 'Like a dull actor now, / I have forgot my part, and I am out / Even to a full disgrace' (5.3.40–2), and hardly indicates success in creating an appreciative audience.

Whether we read this self-authored self as a doomed ideal of personal authority or a simple contradiction in terms, the tragedy here lies in an acknowledgement of the fact that political success will only be possible to those who accept the inevitability of continually shifting self-performance, especially in a world where 'two authorities are up, / Neither supreme' (3.1.111–12). Recognition of this fact is the shared characteristic of the metadramatic author and the successful 'politician' of the Renaissance court. Nobility and policy, authority and acting, are thus necessarily connected, not merely in that they mirror each other, but in the fact that they possess almost identical attributes. In the authorship of metadrama, as in policy/politics, the *polites* are at the centre, the audience are at the heart of the drama, and eliciting a positive interpretative response is the aim of each, in both cases from an ever-shifting platform. In this world Coriolanus fails, falling victim to his own brittle and unattainably high representational ideal of valour as virtue, and thus, as R. B. Parker says, 'Rome's weakness is traced [. . .] to the very characteristics that made Rome great.'[44] Hal, however, eventually succeeds at making a smooth transition from one platform to another, his performance of integrity and authority finally indistinguishable from the real thing. Perhaps it says as much about British culture as about the pressures of contemporary theatre, though, that the noble loser Falstaff, author and informer whose dramatic success is limited by his own metadramatic subjection, has become over time by far the most popular figure of the three.

Notes

1. The early modern term *policy* is roughly equivalent to the modern *politics*, dirty and otherwise; i.e. variously, *statecraft, intrigue* and *expediency*.
2. Negative responses to this troublesome self-performance may be seen in the objections of the descendants of Sir John Oldcastle which occasioned the creation of the Falstaff identity in the first place; see *The Oldcastle Controversy*, ed., Peter Corbin and Douglas Sedge (Manchester: Manchester University Press, 1991), pp. 235–41; William Shakespeare, *Henry IV, Part One*, ed. Nick de Somogyi (London: Nick Hern Books, 2004), p. xxxvi, ff.; William Shakespeare, *Henry IV, Part 1*, ed. Barbara A. Mowat and Paul Werstine (New York: Washington Square Press, 1994), pp. liv-lvii; William Shakespeare, *Coriolanus*, ed. R. B. Parker (Oxford: Oxford University Press, 1998), p. 13; and William Shakespeare, *King Henry IV, Part 1*, ed. David Scott Kastan (London: Arden, 2002), pp. 51–62; unless otherwise noted, all references herein are to this last edition.
3. Shakespeare, *King Henry IV, Part 1*, p. 2.
4. Nicholas Rowe, *Some Account of the Life, &c of Mr William Shakespeare* [1709] cited in *William Shakespeare: The Critical Heritage*, ed. Brian Vickers, Vol. 2 (London: Routledge, 1995), pp. 195, 239. Falstaff's dramatic centrality may be indicated by the fact that *Henry IV, Part 1* was played on 'New-years night' 1624–5 as *The First Part of Sir John Falstaff*, see Shakespeare, *Henry IV, Part 1*, p. 15, whilst *Henry IV, Part 2* may well have been played as *Sir John Falstaff* during the nuptial revels of Elizabeth and Prince Frederick of Heidelberg as early as 1613, see Shakespeare, *Henry IV, Part One*, ed. Nick de Somogyi, pp. xxviii–xxix.
5. William Shakespeare, *Coriolanus*, ed. Philip Brockbank (London: Arden, 1976), p. 77.
6. Richard Dutton (ed.), in *The Cambridge Edition of the Works of Ben Jonson*, Vol. 3, p. 7.
7. Chapman was also a friend of Marlowe and hence was familiar with informers, the shady Nicholas Skeres being one; see Nicholl, p. 30.
8. Chapman, p. 10.
9. Clare, p. 163. See also Richard Brome, *Antipodes* last page for similar complaints about actors changing 'original' works for the worse.
10. Chapman, p. 25.
11. Bible, Romans 5: 19, 'Vengeance is mine; I will repay, saith the Lord.'
12. Bible, Daniel 5: 27, 'Thou art weighed in the balances and found wanting.'
13. For instance, 'the belly [. . .] [is] said to be the god of some people and [such] covetous men are called "idolators" ', see Jacobus Arminius, 'Disputation 23: On Idolatry', in *Writings*, trans. James Nichols, Vol. 1

(Grand Rapids: Baker Book House, 1956), p. 603, cited in David Hawkes, *Idols of the Marketplace* (New York: Palgrave, 2001), p. 57.

14. Clare, p. 163.

15.   Here Tyraunt Rychard played the eager Hog,
      His grashyng tuskes my tender grystels shore:
      His bloudhound Lovell playd the ravenyng Dog,
      His wuluishe teeth, my gylteles carkas toar
   William Baldwin, *A myrrour for magistrates* (London: Thomas Marshe, 1563), p. 143, <http://gateway.proquest.com/openurl?ctx_ver= Z39.88-2003&res_id=xri:eebo&rft_id=xri:eebo:image:656:138> (last accessed 13 November 2015).

16. Baldwin, p. 145.

17. Shakespeare, *Richard III*, ed. Honigmann (4.4.71).

18. For more in this connection, see Bill Angus, 'The Roman Actor, Metadrama, Authority, and the Audience', *Studies in English Literature 1500–1900*, Vol. 50, No. 2 (Spring 2010), pp. 445–64.

19. See Herbert Berry, *The Boar's Head Playhouse* (Washington, DC: Folger, 1986).

20. For more on this episode working as an inset play see Richard L. McGuire, 'The Play-within-the-Play in 1 Henry IV', *Shakespeare Quarterly*, Vol. 18, No. 1 (Winter 1967), pp. 47–52.

21. Berger Jr, p. 59.

22. For this haunting, see Shakespeare, *Henry IV, Part 1* , p. 25.

23. Gail Kern Paster, 'Melancholy Cats, Lugged Bears and Early Modern Cosmology: Reading Shakespeare's Psychological Materialism Across the Species Barrier', in Gail Kern Paster, Katherine Rowe, Mary Floyd-Wilson (eds), *Reading the Early Modern Passions: Essays in the Cultural History of Emotion* (Philadelphia: University of Pennsylvania Press, 2004), pp. 113–29, esp. p. 115.

24. See also ibid. p. 115.

25. William Shakespeare, *Henry IV, Part 2*, ed. Stanley Wells (Oxford: Oxford University Press, 2008); unless otherwise noted, all references herein are to this edition. See also Chapter 3 herein dealing with the internalisation and normalisation of the Vice figure.

26. For a later development of this theme, see Fox, n.p.

27. See *OED*, 'setter, n.1 [. . .] A confederate of sharpers or swindlers [. . .] one who is employed by robbers or murderers to spy upon their intended victims.'

28. William Shakespeare, *Henry IV, Part 1*, ed. Peter Hollindale (Basingstoke: Macmillan, 1983), p. 15.

29. William Shakespeare, *The Merry Wives of Windsor*, ed. T. W. Craik (Oxford: Oxford University Press, 2008), see pp. 11–13; unless otherwise noted, all references herein are to this edition.

30. Here 'Bardolph', rather than *1HIV*'s 'Bardoll'.

31. Berger Jr, p. 66.

32. Hal has referred to Doll Tearsheet previously as a 'parish heifer' (2.2.150).
33. Shakespeare, *Henry IV, Part 1*, p. 32.
34. Berger Jr, p. 42.
35. Shakespeare, *Henry IV, Part 1*, ed. Hollindale, p. 22.
36. William Shakespeare, *Coriolanus*, ed. G. R. Hibbard (London: Penguin, 1995), p. 20.
37. Shakespeare, *Coriolanus*, ed. Hibbard, p. 10.
38. For an excellent overview of other views of Coriolanus's theatrical reluctance, see Eve Rachele Sanders, 'The Body of the Actor in *Coriolanus*', *Shakespeare Quarterly*, Vol. 57, No. 4 (Winter 2006), pp. 387–412.
39. William Shakespeare, *Coriolanus*, ed. R. B. Parker (Oxford: Oxford University Press, 1998); unless otherwise noted, all references herein are to this edition.
40. Robin Headlam Wells, ' "Manhood and Chevalrie": Coriolanus, Prince Henry, and the Chivalric Revival', *The Review of English Studies*, Vol. 51, No. 203 (Aug. 2000), pp. 395–422, esp. 395.
41. For further treatment of the crowd in Shakespeare, see *2 Henry VI*; see also herein Chapter 4.
42. R. B. Parker notes connections between Coriolanus' relationship with Menenius and Hal's with Falstaff: see Shakespeare, *Coriolanus*, pp. 13–14.
43. The play's offstage audience might have seen resonances in these depictions of the populace with the troubles of their own times, such as the Diggers's petition of c.1607, and the Midlands uprising of 1607–8 against hoarding and enclosures; see Shakespeare, *Coriolanus*, p. 35.
44. Ibid. p. 12.

Chapter 6

'Three Cranes, Mitre, and Mermaid men': Metadramatic Self-Deprecation and Authority in *Bartholomew Fair*

First played in the uneasy year of 1614, it is well attested that *Bartholomew Fair* presents both a satirical allegory of London life in general, and microcosmic parodies of types of authority in particular.[1] Critical consensus has it that troubled authority is especially embodied and mocked in the play's middle-class characters, and that the play then proceeds to mock this very mockery.[2] This interesting compound duality has, however, led to dichotomous interpretations among critics: as Frances Teague has argued, the play is 'impossible to agree on', and it has led, according to John Creaser, to a 'critical impasse'.[3] Leah S. Marcus describes how the play is either a 'dark indictment of human irrationality and moral decay' or a 'celebration of the rejuvenating energies of folly and festival disorder'.[4] I suggest a middle ground which views the play as a self-conscious offering of its own theatrical folly as both a critique of the decay of moral authority and a self-deprecating admission of complicity in it. Jonson's assertion of the poet's Horatian duty to critique official corruption is well known, but in this case his satire of general social venality very much includes 'authority like his own', as Alan Fisher argues.[5] If this is Jonson's friendliest play, as Fisher claims (other critics have also noted the amiability of Jonson's approach), it is surely because of the self-directed cast of its humour and the inclusivity which arises from it.[6] This chapter explores the genial fellowship of metadramatic self-mockery that *Bartholomew Fair* offers to both commoners and King, which both allows and defuses the play's critique of authority.

Though it was first performed at the Hope theatre in Southwark, *Bartholomew Fair* was engaged for the King's personal entertainment at court, most probably before rehearsals began.[7] It is not possible to know whether Jonson rewrote parts of the play for this event, or whether the unusual step of such early commission for the court is due simply to circumstance. Somewhat troublingly for Jonson, the play's reworking of the period's fundamental question of where authority lies is energised partly by the royal 'imposition' controversies of the time, with which some of Jonson's 'Mermaid men' were legally involved.[8] Also, in a play so 'crammed with abuses of authority', as Creaser puts it, there is not only an implicit critique of the nature of authority, but also of structures, methods and specific examples in which the King himself could not escape implication.[9] In presenting a world which offered such a critique of authority, it is perhaps understandable that Jonson opted to take the force of this on himself by deploying a method of defensive self-deprecation.[10] In this, he tips a knowing wink at compromising associations between his own role, that of watching authorities, and his venal audiences, even hinting at the darker aspects of the role of judging interpreter, and exploring the similarities between satirists and the authorities' informers.[11]

To some extent, the play's carnivalesque ethos, and its ambiguous status in relation to the jurisdiction of the City, license the extremes of behaviour of those in authority in the play and their potential for venality. But more than this, the play's genial atmosphere of critical fellowship provides what Fisher calls a '*cordon sanitaire* [. . .] [which] tempers wit's hostility with the urge to trust' and creates a place 'where control is not needed [. . .] [and] laughter can be taken in good part'.[12] Although the staged Fair's metadrama portrays note-taking, tale-bearing and mercenary onstage audiences, its benign comedic resolutions also suggest a safe space for an admission of the place of theatre in this world of venal authority.[13] If 'the reports of informers' are not quite 'banished' by this friendly context, as Fisher suggests, they are at least ultimately nullified.[14] In early modern drama generally, the metadramatic management of perspective often entails the presence of the informer. Perhaps understandably also, metadramatic forms are often employed to configure the kinds of authority that influence interpretation. In the theatre, as John Gordon Sweeney III argues, 'perspective *is* authority', and he is right in saying that Jonson was 'more self-consciously aware of this fact than any other playwright of his generation'.[15] As we have already observed, characters standing aside, informer-like, comprise metadramatic audiences and these are often used to shape the responses of offstage audiences.[16] The tendency to wish to control audience reaction through metadrama is evidence of Jonson's agon, what Richard Helgerson describes as 'an unresolved struggle of the self against the very conditions of its expression'.[17] Accordingly, he positions his readers and audiences for interpretation as much in drama as in his masques and poems. In many of his plays, Jonson gives himself the place of the monarch in a masque, 'above and beyond the others as both primary actor and primary audience', as Sweeney suggests, and manages a court of his own, both of which allow him some control over potential interpretations.[18] But in the case of *Bartholomew Fair*, though not quite retiring after the Induction and letting the play 'unfold in his absence' as Helgerson claims, Jonson's involvement in the fate of the play's audiences is much less assertive of his own superiority.[19] Here, the dramatist seems to prefer the interpretative model his poetry often employs, which Stanley Fish describes as a 'community of virtue in which everyone is, by definition, the same as everyone else'.[20] So, while the Induction emphasises many of the typical concerns of the era over potentially venal, foolish, or treacherous audiences, and the puppet-play offers a highly critical inner play, they also mock their own devices, and in the process they defuse criticism.[21] Rather than treating its playhouse and court audiences with what some have seen as contempt, the Induction's hyperbole and the puppet-play's scathing parody afford the audiences self-awareness and offer them alternative models of audienceship.[22] Jonson's parodic Fair is thus not only a social space where ersatz authorities make the nature of authority itself negotiable but also a metadramatic space which manages the offstage audience's perspective with self-effacing humour to neutralise any potential accusation of excessive critique of authority. The figure of the informer is key to an understanding of this process.

In the play, the appropriately named Justice Overdo condenses these issues in himself; he is a source of authority that operates as his own informer, a composite parody of both roles, excessively searching for trivial 'enormities' perpetrated in the libertine atmosphere of the Fair.[23] As an officially interested observer of the detailed business of the Fair, Overdo engages the sympathies of the offstage audience while at the same time connecting the idea of a watching authority with that of an audience of potential informers. Although his character sits easily as a satire of the 'disguised Duke' plays of the early years of James I/VI's reign, Overdo is still finally made to feel the consequences of what is judged by the community to be an excessive exercise of authority, especially for one who represents the Fair's internal 'Courts of Piepowders' (2.1.32), a temporary court drawn up for the duration of the Fair. His is only an ersatz authority in reality, and his name of course discloses his major malfunction. Overdo nevertheless carries shades of both recent Lord Mayors: Sir Thomas Myddelton, who had 'gone himself disguised' and had 'informed himself' of 'lewd houses' and other vices, and Thomas Hayes, who also investigated the city incognito in 1614.[24] But more significantly, it was also well known that the King had himself made at least one of these secret visits, to observe merchant practices in the Exchange.[25] The portrayal of Overdo then, advertently or otherwise, involves him in activities relating to the King himself. Other critics have also remarked upon similarities between the King and the Justice; for example, Keith Sturgess proposes that the Jacobean court might have recognised Overdo as 'a burlesque portrait of James' in their shared 'pedantry [. . .] classical quotations [. . .] urge to inveigh against tobacco and [. . .] protective attitude towards young favourites', while Marcus goes so far as to identify Overdo as a 'distorted shadow of James'.[26] Any recognition of these similarities to the activities of the King could have been problematic for Jonson, except for the significant fact that, with his little 'black book' of critique, Overdo also caricatures Jonson's own authority. In particular this involves a reference to Horace, Jonson's role-model, who in his defence of satire, repudiates his own similarity to the 'the informers who stalk Rome with notebooks in hand, identifying potential victims', as Keane notes.[27] Jonson is safe in assuming that the King will understand the reference, since James's principal tutor as a child was George Buchanan, known as 'The Scottish Horace' for his translations and interpretations of the classical author.[28] Overdo's actions mock exactly the kind of acute satirical judgement of society that underpins not only this play, therefore, but also Jonson's whole project.

The play addresses the idea of a tainted authority with self-mocking metadrama from the first, with the Stage-Keeper immediately referencing the temperament of the offstage audience in his address: 'Gentlemen, have a little patience, they are e'en upon coming instantly' (Ind. 1–2) and asking them to excuse the character John Littlewit, a 'proctor', or ecclesiastical agent at the Court of Arches, because of a 'stitch new fall'n in his black silk stocking' (Ind. 3). As a proctor, Littlewit is recognisable as someone involved in the everyday surveillance of the community; his work at the moral mooting ground of the Court of Arches suggests involvement either as an informer or as a habitual user of informers, and his concern with his silk stockings connotes the vanity and tenuous wealth associated with this role. When the Stage-Keeper assures the audience that Littlewit 'has a very pretty part' (Ind. 5), he is referring in part metadramatically to his acting role and, disparagingly, to his occupation, 'pretty' here carrying the added sense of being 'significant'. Littlewit's profession as proctor, however, never really relates to his role in the play so much as it relates simply to his name. Despite his nominal professional authority he is both ruled by his own and his wife's greed and witless enough later in the play to leave her in the hands of the dangerous informers Whit and Knockem. Having made this initial metadramatic connection with lack-wit authority, the Stage-Keeper then goes on to expand it by means of criticism of both the play and the writer who, he claims 'has not hit the humours [. . .] [and] has not conversed with the Barthol'mew-birds' (Ind. 9–10), presumably thus failing to represent the authentic inside story of the Fair. As he does this, the Stage-Keeper checks around him and declares: 'I am looking lest the poet hear me, or his man, Master Brome, behind the arras' (Ind. 6–7), in a little self-deprecating exposition that constructs Jonson and his apprentice Richard Brome comically in the minds of the offstage audience as both incompetent authors and as potential informers, the stereotypical lurkers behind the arras. In this way, any perceived criticism of authority is tempered by a humorous and pre-emptive self-racking. When the Stage-Keeper is sure of having established confidentiality between himself and the audience, he goes on to detail what the author has left out of the representation of Bartholomew Fair and to make his own interpretative criticism of it, claiming that, if a certain other writer had written the play, it might have contained more sex: 'he would ha' made you such a jig-a-jog i'the booths, you should ha' thought an earthquake had been i'the Fair!' (Ind. 18–20). It is interesting to wonder where Jonson might be at this moment; the role of the Stage-Keeper would surely have been tempting to him. In any case, this profusion of metadrama serves to set up a framework of reception in which the critical authority of the author is simultaneously asserted and undercut. Inscribed within the deprecating voice of the Stage-Keeper is Jonson's own: 'these master-poets, they will ha' their own absurd courses; they will be informed of nothing!' (Ind. 20–1). Here the author alludes to his own creditable resistance to the activity of the informer through the mouth of a character who is at that moment acting like a critical informer to the audience. This is one of those moments where the metadramatic device provides simply the most natural vehicle for commentary on how the culture of informing compromises authority. But more so, it is also a self-critical parody of the way an author's typical concern to distance himself from this culture actually serves to affirm his connection with it.[29]

In a gesture which again parodies an issue of real anxiety for dramatists, the Stage-Keeper next conjectures that actors both living and dead (Tarleton and Adams) might have acted the play with such force that 'a substantial watch [would] ha' stol'n in upon 'em and taken 'em away, with mistaking words, as the fashion is in the stage practice' (Ind. 32–3). This narrative of the imaginary arrest of Tarleton and Adams, through some informing observer 'mistaking' their words, resonates not only with the Stage-Keeper's own critical character, but also with the feared 'Master Brome, behind the arras', and his authorly master, whose own arrest for 'mistaken words' and whose actual experience with informers might help to emphasise just how complex a form of self-deprecation this is. This parody of the real conditions of dramatic production of course echoes the actions of the King's censoring authorities and makes explicit the association between venal interpretation and authority; this is soon extended by the Book-Holder and Scrivener with their lengthy legal stipulations to which the audience are expected to give their consent before the play can 'begin'.

Metadramatic self-reference, and very specific foregrounding of the offstage audience, are active throughout these introductory passages, but the audience does not need to understand either the implications of this, or the legal jargon used, to feel the weight of the hyperbolic parody of this conventional apology. The author's words should offend nobody, provided the audience 'have either the wit or the honesty to think well of themselves' (Ind. 63), a characteristic Jonsonian defence, with its roots in Martial, against the malicious interpretation of informers.[30] This self-mocking agreement allows for every person to have 'his or their free-will of censure, to like or dislike at their own charge, the author having now departed with his right' (Ind. 64–6). As the author is to be supposed absent, having been paid 'his right' for delivering the manuscript of the play to the company, the audience now bears the sole, but circumscribed, democratic responsibility for the interpretation of the play. Thus the Scrivener suggests that it shall only be 'lawful for any man to judge his sixpenn'orth, his twelvepenn'orth' (Int. 66–7), with critical rights linked to spending power. This is obviously comedic playfulness, yet it also points to what is perceived to be an inappropriate empowerment of audiences, both at the Hope theatre and at court, through the medium of 'censure' linked to wealth. Of course the King has paid the most for the performance and is therefore positioned as the most privileged interpreter, but paradoxically he is simultaneously invited by the parody to share Jonson's criticism of the act of interpretation itself. However humorous and self-deprecating it is, this demarcation of the boundaries of critical analysis leads to a further commitment demanded of the 'hearers and spectators', which is rather less playful:

> that they neither in themselves conceal, nor suffer by them to be concealed, any state-decipherer or politic picklock of the scene so solemnly ridiculous as to search out who was meant by the gingerbread-woman, who by the hobby-horse-man, who by the costermonger, nay, who by their wares. Or [. . .] what 'Mirror of Magistrates' is meant by the Justice, what great lady by the pig-woman, what concealed statesman by the seller of mousetraps, and so of the rest. But that such person or persons so found, be left discovered to the mercy of the author. (Ind. 101–10)

The genuine fear which this exposes and addresses through parody is the audience's propensity to hide within it informers of various kinds: concealed offstage people looking for what onstage characters conceal. The politic informer at 'the mercy of the author', rather than the other way around, is a central fantasy of *Bartholomew Fair* and this will involve establishing common ground and community with the interpreting audience, in this case most importantly the King. Two examples of these morally deficient figures are the 'statedecipherer' of the play, Justice Overdo, whose search for 'enormities' ridicules both over-sensitive authority and its venal agents, and the puritan 'picklock of the scene' Zeal-of-the-Land Busy, whose taking the puppets to task for idolatry operates as both a *reductio ad absurdum* of antitheatrical rhetoric at the same time that it provides a mockery of the self-interested wrester of the meaning of drama, the mistaker of words. By the end, both of these incompetent audiences are made to suffer the consequences of such misused authority and 'inspired ignorance'. We might note, however, that, even as Jonson treads the fine line between satire and libel by employing these highly self-referential defensive metadramatic devices, the satiric critique of Busy's venality is still far more vicious than the softer treatment of Overdo's excessive authority.[31]

Throughout the play, this sense of tainted authority is aligned with the imagery of hunting and falconry commonly used to depict the predatory activities of informers, and the atmosphere of predation which prevails in the Fair leads to all kinds of chaos for the weaker characters. The 'Barthol'mew-birds' (4.5.11) Knockem and Whit, with whom the author was supposed not to have spoken, are clearly birds who prey; the pig-woman Ursula sets them upon Littlewit's wife Win, who, as one of the 'fowl i'the Fair' (4.5.12), is deemed fit to be hunted, until she too becomes 'a bird o'the game' (4.5.14) or a prostitute. The ballad seller Nightingale, with his 'hawk's eye' and 'beak' (2.4.37, 39), and the cutpurse Edgworth, prey on the dupe Cokes; Quarlous the gamester preys on Edgworth, Overdo and mad Trouble-All. Overdo's desirable ward Grace Wellborn is pursued throughout by Quarlous and Winwife. Busy is hunting the widow Purecraft, who, as it turns out, has been preying upon him and his kind for many years. In this atmosphere of ubiquitous predatory commerce and consumption, people are commodified in ways far more extensive than merely as prostitutes of Ursula the pig-woman, and it is within this predatory environment that Overdo arrives, in heavy disguise, metadramatically playing the part of a ranting preacher as a cover for his information-gathering. However predatory his role is, he has his justification at the ready for adopting the despised perspective of an informer as he addresses the audience, declaring, 'Well, in justice' name, and the King's, and for the commonwealth! Defy all the world, Adam Overdo, for a disguise, and all story; for thou hast fitted thyself' (2.1.1–3). With his own defensive self-deprecation, he jokes that the audience 'may have seen many a fool in the habit of a justice, but never till now a justice in the habit of a fool' (2.1.6–7). His justification for his upside down brand of surveillance is both authorised by the King's name, and was, as we have seen, based upon recent historical precedent. However, given the dubious nature of the informer's position, he also feels the need to justify himself on moral grounds: 'Thus must we do [. . .] that wake for the public good, and thus hath the wise magistrate done in all ages. There is a doing of right out of wrong, if the way be found' (2.1.7–9). This equivocal acknowledgement of both the 'wrongness' and the usefulness of gathering information in this way is reminiscent of Nashe's reluctant acceptance of the informer as 'a necessarie member in a State to bee usde to cut off unneccessarie members'.[32] Robert Pricket's 1607 report of Lord Cokes's speech on 'the abuses and corruption of officers' also sounds a reluctant acknowledgement of the need for informers, alongside a comment on their general condition, stating 'their Office, I confesse, is necessarie: And yet it seldome happeneth, that an honest man is imployed therein'.[33] And yet, despite his own role as informer, Overdo also exposes the corruption inherent in the system of informing as a means of gathering useful information:

For, alas, as we are public persons, what do we know? Nay, what can we know? We hear with other men's ears; we see with other men's eyes! A foolish constable or a sleepy watchman is all our information. He slanders a gentleman by the virtue of his place (as he calls it) and we by the vice of ours must believe him. (2.1.21–5)

He also details the potential of the system for generating random and damaging inaccuracies: 'a while agone, they made me [. . .] mistake an honest zealous pursuivant for a seminary, and a proper young bachelor of music for a bawd' (2.1.25–7). He also identifies the root of the problem: that by its very nature information gathered along these lines will be unreliable; as he says, 'all our intelligence is idle, and most of our intelligencers knaves – and, by your leave, ourselves thought little better, if not arrant fools, for believing 'em' (2.1.28–30). As a predator among predators, Overdo expresses something of the moral paradox which is felt in relation to authority and informers. His attempts at equivocation show that the potential connection of such anomalous authority to the person of the King requires very careful handling, especially where the corrupting influence of money is concerned.

In further self-defence as an apologist for such informer-authorities, Overdo goes on to describe their detailed surveillance of any area where a profit is to be made, even down to the humblest bakery. He commends 'a worthy worshipful man, sometime a capital member of this city' (2.1.10), who would disguise himself in 'the habit of a porter [. . .] a carman [. . .] the dog-killer [. . .] a seller of tinderboxes' (2.1.11–13). This cloaked authority would travel around the city in order to gather information for himself, going 'into every alehouse, and down into every cellar' (2.1.14) where he would 'measure the length of puddings [. . .] the gauge of black-pots and cans [. . .] weigh the loaves of bread on his middle finger' (2.1.15–16). The legislation surrounding informing at this time bears this out and describes a similar picture of the level of control over even seemingly trivial misdemeanours. However, this also accords with Lenton's 1631 description of the self-interested informer who 'peepes into the breaches of penall Statutes, not for loue to the Commonwealth, as his owne lucre, amongst which [. . .] th'assize of bread and beere are his greatest Reuenues'.[34] Like Overdo here, Lenton's informer 'transformes himselfe into seuerall shapes to auoyd suspicion of Inne-holders', and, though Overdo does not explicitly do this for 'his owne lucre', unlike Lenton's informer, the exchange of money is

nevertheless implicit in the action.[35] Pricket also describes a function-
ary similar to Overdo, 'the *Clarke* of the *Market*, [who] will come
downe and call before him all waights and measures, and where a
fault is found, there must a Fee be payd, which is deuided betwixt
him and the Informer'.[36] This official also, predictably, 'enricheth
himselfe, by abusing his Maiesties lawes, and wronging his Subiects'
by receiving bribes.[37] Overdo shows his awareness of these issues
when he tells us that the worthy of the city he is describing 'would
not trust his corrupt officers; he would do't himself' (2.1.19–20), but
the very admission of this financial corruption suggests the same of
the authority which underpins Overdo's own. When he makes his
metadramatic declaration to the audience about the policing of the
'yearly enormities' of the Fair (2.1.31–2), he draws together in his
own person these moral anomalies:

> I, Adam Overdo, am resolved [. . .] to spare spy-money hereafter,
> and make mine own discoveries [. . .] Here is my black book for the
> purpose, this [*Indicating his disguise*] the cloud that hides me: under
> this covert I shall see and not be seen [. . .] And as I began, so I'll
> end: in justice' name, and the King's, and for the commonwealth!'
> (2.1.30–1, 34–6)

With the royal source of his authority repeated, as an informer he
'*stands to one side*' (s.d. 2.1.37) to watch the arrival of people at the
Fair, seeing and not being seen: a hidden and potentially threatening audience. This both acknowledges the culture of informing for
'spy-money' at the same time as it critiques it, offering the offstage
audience an authoritative perspective which will also in its turn be
mocked as excessive, and that will fail with Overdo's own authority
that produces a form of justice, but one which is overdone.

Overdo not only offers a parody of the informer, therefore, but
also provides a model of a pedantic and excessively empowered
audience whose nominal freedoms to interpret the play are tainted
by the association. From the title-page's authoritative Horace quota-
tion: 'Democritus [. . .] would gaze at the audience more attentively
than at the show itself, as offering him something more than the
actor', to the Induction's semi-parodic implications, the metadramatic spectacle Jonson presents to the offstage audience in this play
is primarily one of various venal audiences which suggest their own
potential for venality.[38] When he observes, overhears and notes
down such 'crimes' as using stale ingredients to make gingerbread
(2.2.9), misreckoning bar bills, cutting tobacco with coltsfoot 'to

itch it out' (2.2.76), prostitution (2.5.36) and apparently merely
being Ursula the pig woman (2.2.59–60), he simultaneously nar-
rates them in metadramatic asides to the offstage audience: 'This
is the very womb and bed of enormity! Gross as herself! This must
all down for enormity, all, every whit on't' (2.2.87–8). Addressed in
this way, the audience are manipulated to respond to the conduct of
other characters as Overdo directs them, and the cumulative effect
of sharing his perspective is to draw them into collusive knowledge
about the secret crimes of the Fair-goers. This invites them to join
him in doing just what Jonson's Induction has good-humouredly
asked them not to do: to keep record of perceived faults in others
and to make capital of personal accusations that arise therefrom.
In this way the audience is interpellated subtly as fellow informers. This model of course may be resisted, in fact it is constructed
precisely to be resisted, and although the play's metadrama works
most obviously as a critique of methods employed by those in public
authority, it also parodies a particular kind of private subjectivity
seen most publicly in portrayals of the early modern audience: one
predicated upon a predatory use of information. The portrayal of
Overdo embraces both of these interpretative modes, in which the
King's own authority is implicated.

  If the image of Bartholomew Fair here corresponds to a London
of tainted authorities, then the puppet-play and its audience offer a
parody of the metadramatic devices which are typically employed to
represent these questions of authority. The outer play here makes the
puppet-play a frame narrative, though the constant interjections of
the audience, and the trivial medium itself, arrest any scopic pulsion
towards the inmost point of the narrative. Since the offstage audience is not drawn into the small frame, which thereby remains visible
throughout, the puppet-play works more as a literal objectification of
the dramatic medium, a kind of displaced metadrama in which representations of audiences, licensing authorities, interpreters and even
metadrama itself are at their most parodic: a meta-metadrama. Here,
any semblance of an authoritative narrative centre is as much in flux
as the observing peripheries, shifting with the interaction between
onstage viewers and the puppetry. In the puppet-play, the play's own
self-referentiality is itself ridiculed, as Marlowe's 'Hero and Leander'
and Edwards's *Damon and Pithias* are transformed into slapstick
farce, and the onstage audience is engaged in a game of total satire in
which all authorities, but especially theatrical authority, are held up
for derision. The focus throughout is again on the onstage audience,
whose exaggerated critical responses to what is merely a puppet-play

can be read as a statement about the absurdity of informing upon issues to do with the theatre when, as Jonson seems to suggest, there is far greater corruption to be found elsewhere.

Jonson's monstrous onstage audience, gathered from the appetite-driven Fair-goers and characterised by drunkenness, moral vacuity, stupidity and aggression, is an insulting parody, meant of course to encourage the opposite behaviour in the offstage audience. It posits an educated, sober, reasonable, friendly, interpretative community by the very absence of these qualities onstage. Overdo joins them, again in disguise, to gather information on their enormities and those of the puppet-play itself. Littlewit's anxiety to 'see how it passes' (5.3.19ff.) before being identified as the author of this mini-play both recognises the likelihood of this type of predatory 'concealed' audience-member in attendance and reiterates the real authorial concerns parodied in the Induction. Besides Overdo, another predator is Cokes, who, it is said, will 'interpret' (5.4.87) the play to Wasp, another failed authority figure. When Leatherhead asks Cokes to stop interrupting the play with 'peace, sir: they'll be angry if they hear you eavesdropping, now they are setting their match' (5.4.245–6), he is implicitly cast as an illicit listener: an eavesdropping informer. Whit, meanwhile, is explicitly an informer, who 'lishen[s] out noishes' and informs the watch of where to make arrests of 'gallants' in return for a share of the profits (3.1.1–4). In the context of this festival of venal and venereal desire, it is interesting that the antitheatrical Busy also expresses Jonson's typically voracious and bestial representation of the audience, as he confesses, 'I have long opened my mouth wide and gaped, I have gaped as the oyster for the tide after thy destruction' (5.5.16–17). When he declares, 'I am zealous for the Cause', Leatherhead replies 'As a dog for a bone' (5.5.62–3). More than a mere critic, Busy aims to be the destroyer of the show and Leatherhead exposes his bestial voracity in doing so. These characters are entirely in keeping with the Fair's atmosphere of hungry predation and facilitation of ersatz authority, both of which are often portrayed by means of the discourse of the parasitic informer. Jonson's self-deprecation is composite and multi-layered in these instances, encompassing his role as interpreter and satirical critic of society while clearly offering a shared critical perspective on such misused authority. This duality is found in Overdo's concern with licence which is also echoed in Busy's puritan tirade. In response to Leatherhead's protesting, 'Sir, I present nothing but what is licensed by authority' (5.5.11), Busy says 'Thou art all license, even licentiousness itself' (5.5.12). Playing on the dual meaning of 'licence', this satirises both the licenser of, and the objector to drama. Despite its *reductio ad absurdum* mockery of antitheatrical rhetoric, the puppet-play's metadrama is tempered by tacit admission that, in mocking authors and audiences, Jonson's didactic theatre sometimes places him in a painful communion with antitheatricalists.[39] Overdo also parodies the perceived immorality of the theatres, again figured in terms of consumption, when he says of the puppets, in an aside, 'the favoring of this licentious quality is the consumption of many a young gentleman – a pernicious enormity' (5.3.54–5). This is of course another comedic overdoing intended to express the opposite sentiment.

Within this violent, hyperbolic, contradictory and morally ambiguous setting it is not surprising that the puppets/actors should attack the author and puppeteer. Nor that religious debate over the propriety of playing should be reduced to a pantomime exchange between Busy and the puppet of Dionysius, which runs, 'It is profane / *It is not profane* / It is profane / *It is not profane*' (5.5.55–8). As the puppet-play holds all aspects of playing up for ridicule, including meaningful interpretation, it also exposes the conditions of its own form. When Cokes asks Leatherhead of the puppets – 'which is your Burbage now? [. . .] Your best actor: your Field?' (5.3.64–5, 67), it is significant, as Arthur F. Kinney notes, that Nathan Field may well have been one of the actors in this exchange.[40] This metadramatic device reinforces the offstage audience's sense of the fictionality of the whole. The self-referential moment makes explicit the contrast between onstage and offstage audiences and facilitates the offstage audience's ability to reflect upon their own nature in relation to their negative comedic onstage representation. Not only do the negative audience models offered here warn generally against dissipation, moral vacuity and excessive aggression, however, but they also represent specific types of informer. For example, Overdo is the authoritative, authoring informer; Busy is the predatory, moralising informer; and Cokes is the foolish, misinterpreting informer. Between them they comprehensively mock the whole business, although Overdo's royal endorsement makes his the most delicate parody. But, as we have already observed, the very staging of these issues around a puppet-play satirises not only the issues but also the very act of mockery itself. Just as the absence of a community of friendly interpretation onstage posits its desirability, so it reveals the onstage absence of an intelligent and socially useful theatre. Both the puppet-play's hyperbole of theatre and the onstage audience are held up as parodies of all the pretensions of the theatrical exchange – a joyfully self-reflective invective which aims to provoke a friendly, generous off-stage audience response.

As the writing scrutiniser of the Fair's microcosm of society, with his little black book Overdo mocks not only authorities, informers and audiences, but also parodies the Horatian and Jonsonian ideal of the author, as a scourge of the sins of society.[41] This is an exemplary case of Jonson creating a safe critical space using metadrama to put himself on the rack equally with those whom he scourges. Jonson's self-mocking reference to the 'Three Cranes, Mitre, and Mermaid men' (1.1.26) of whom he was obviously one, placed in Littlewit's mouth resounds with self-contradictory sarcasm and rebounds on the character, but again such irony offers deniability and suggests a community of understanding that irony always demands. In the person of Overdo, this general mockery of authors and poetasters encompasses the perceived general blight on an increasingly legalistic society of prying, writing observers; here, as in *Poetaster*, both poetasters and informers are exaggerating misinterpreters of the world. Overdo's own misinterpretation, his failure to play his part effectively against the real 'enormities' of the Fair, argues that the informer-in-authority's excessive surveillance is a formula for the failure of his own authority, equally as informer, audience and author. The limits of his power are defined both at the stocks where Overdo receives the penalty for hiding his true identity and at the puppet-play where he ultimately fails to reassert his authority over the playgoers. Thus Jonson carefully unravels this tainted authority figure at the same time that he expresses his own limitations in satirising the 'enormities' of the society of which he is himself the observing scourge. In both the scene of punishment and the excessive theatre, the community itself offers him resistance which he is powerless to overcome.[42]

When Overdo eventually reveals his authoritative capacity at the puppet-play, declaring that it is 'time to take enormity by the forehead, and brand it; for I have discovered enough' (5.5.100–1), the venal onstage audience begin at first to steal away: Knockem says to Whit the informer, 'Would we were away [. . .] Best fall off with our birds, for fear o'the cage' (5.6.7–8). But, despite this fearful reaction, as Leo Salingar points out, the people of the fair go 'unpunished and apparently unchanged' at the end of the play.[43] In fact, when Overdo attempts to pass his judgements on both the participants in the drama and the audience, his demands for silence in authoritative, but from the offstage audience's point of view incomprehensible, Latin (5.6.16–17, 40) are overcome by the loquacity of the mocking 'gamester' Quarlous. It is finally left to this unlikely character to reveal the extent of Overdo's errors of judgement, and remind him of his own mortality:

> remember you are but Adam, flesh and blood! [. . .] Forget your other name of Overdo, and invite us all to supper. There you and I will compare our 'discoveries', and drown the memory of all enormity in your bigg'st bowl at home. (5.6.80–3)[44]

On behalf of the community, Quarlous the mocker thus disarms Overdo's 'discoveries' with his own, aimed squarely at Overdo's compromised authority. But, rather than castigate him any further, Quarlous suggests a genial reconciliation of all the parties of the fair at a common table of fellowship, which Overdo must provide. Like the tyrant Dionysius of the puppet-play's *Damon and Pithias*, and despite not really displaying any penitence as an authority, the hapless Justice is thus persuaded to waive his projected punishments of the fair-goers and provide this conciliatory feast instead. In this way he is turned from a compromised authority figure, bearing all the negative associations this play levels at informers, into a Jonsonian festive ideal of authority: one who acknowledges his own limitations and is able and willing to be persuaded by theatre and satire. He is also a marionette of Jonson's metadramatic self-effacement. When Overdo echoes the King's recent speech to Parliament and declares that he wished merely 'to correct, not to destroy; to build, not to demolish' (n. 5.6.93–4), Jonson plays again with the risky comparison of King and Justice, suggesting that, if not his failing methods, at least the Justice's intentions are associated with the very highest authority.[45] But this also implicates Jonson's own claim to authority. It is for these reasons that Overdo's downfall is a soft one, and characterised by amiable fellowship over the 'bowl' of drink, and food, in a gathering that would be very familiar to a dedicated Mermaid man.

Having made all these connections and associations, Jonson finds it necessary to soften them further at the end of the play. He does this by addressing the offstage audience's propensity for misinterpretation, with an epilogue that deftly sets its authority in carefully constructed contrast to that of the King:

> This is your power to judge, great sir, and not
> The envy of a few. Which if we have got,
> We value less what their dislike can bring,
> If it so happy be, t'have pleased the King. (Epi. 9–12)

The projected complaints of an envious 'few' will of course bring to mind the very foolish informing interpreters of the puppet-play audience, including Overdo, and pit these against the King's own judgement. Furthermore it acknowledges the King as an author himself and therefore as fit to judge what Jonson calls 'the scope of writers, and what store / Of leave is given them, if they take not more / And turn it into licence' (Epi. 3–5). With his excessive name and his book of 'enormities', Overdo is the principal writer in this play attempting to take more 'leave' than is given him, so here again Jonson successfully extricates James's authority from any entanglement with such misinterpreters, and by extension authority corrupted by association with informers, installing the monarch as their rightful judge. But even as the Epilogue does its work in clarifying the King's interpretative position, it sketches out an authoritative position which Jonson clearly shares. Fisher describes Jonson's approach to faith between people not only as a state of mutual trust and understanding but also one requiring a 'physical and temporal locale [. . .] in the Apollo Tavern, or a dining room (on a specific night) where [. . .] [informers like] a Pooly or a Parrot may not overhear'.[46] Here, in suggesting a genial gathering capable of authoritative interpretation, one which nullifies the insidious work of misinterpreting informers, it is the very self-deprecation of this 'Three Cranes, Mitre, and Mermaid' man that paradoxically affords him fellowship with the King himself. Given the play's contemporary success, it is apparent that Jonson managed to get away with such an audacious implication, which, in troubled times, must be considered a remarkable achievement.[47]

Notes

1. See for instance Alan C. Dessen, *Jonson's Moral Comedy* (Evanston: Northwestern University Press, 1971), pp. 148–66.
2. See Robert D. Hume, 'The Socio-Politics of London Comedy from Jonson to Steele', *Huntington Library Quarterly*, Vol. 74, No. 2 (June 2011), pp. 187–217, 200–1; Ben Jonson, *Bartholomew Fair*, ed. John Creaser, in *The Cambridge Edition of the Works of Ben Jonson*, Vol. 4, p. 265. Unless otherwise noted all references are to this edition.
3. Frances Teague, *The Curious History of Bartholomew Fair* (Lewisberg, PA: Bucknell University Press, 1985), p. 14; Creaser (ed.), *Bartholomew Fair*, p. 264.
4. Leah S. Marcus, *The Politics of Mirth* (Chicago: University of Chicago Press, 1986), p. 328.

5. Alan Fisher, 'Jonson's Funnybone', *Studies in Philology*, Vol. 94, No. 1 (Winter 1997), pp. 59–84, 83. For Jonson's duty to critique society, see Kaplan, pp. 66–80, 83.

6. Fisher, p. 83. See also Thomas Cartelli, 'Bartholomew Fair as Urban Arcadia', *Renaissance Drama*, 14 (1983), pp. 151–72, 154–5; and John Enck, *Jonson and the Comic Truth* (Madison: University of Wisconsin Press, 1966), pp. 189–208.

7. Creaser, p. 255.

8. Creaser, p. 261. Men of Jonson's Mermaid tribe were involved with the failed Great Contract of 1610 which addressed impositions and posited a reduction of the King's traditional feudal rights in exchange for regular funds; see Luke Wilson, 'Ben Jonson and the Law of Contract', *Cardozo Studies in Law and Literature*, Vol. 5, No. 2 (Autumn 1993), pp. 281–306, 283; I. A. Shapiro, 'The "Mermaid Club"', *Modern Language Review*, Vol. 1 (1950), pp. 6–17.

9. Creaser, p. 263.

10. Such self-deprecation may indeed be characteristic of those who feel secure in their practice or reputation, but, if so, this self-confidence will not last for Jonson, whose later forays into metadrama are harsher in their criticism of authorities who employ informers than we find here, and less inclined to self-flagellation, however mild. See Chapter 8 herein. If the grandiose derivative speeches of his *The New Inn* (1629) are Jonson's way of 'calling his critical strictures before the bar for reexamination', as Watson suggests, this form of self-deprecation seems to have backfired; see Robert N. Watson, *Ben Jonson's Parodic Strategy: Literary Imperialism in the Comedies* (Cambridge, MA: Harvard University Press, 1987), p. 224.

11. This displays considerable confidence that, at this stage in his career, he would not be misunderstood; for Jonson's stature at this time see Creaser, p. 255. For similarities between informers and satirists in Horace, see Keane, p. 79.

12. Fisher, p. 80.

13. For the equivalence of the stage and the fair, see Leah S. Marcus, 'Pastimes and the Purging of Theater: *Bartholomew Fair* (1614)', in Harold Bloom (ed.), *Elizabethan Drama* (New York: Chelsea House, 2004), p. 328ff.

14. Fisher, p. 80.

15. John Gordon Sweeney III, *Jonson and the Psychology of Public Theater* (Princeton: Princeton University Press, 1985), p. 226.

16. The term 'offstage' is borrowed from theatrical terminology to denote the house audience in its relation to those onstage.

17. Richard Helgerson, *Self-Crowned Laureates* (Berkeley: University of California Press, 1983), p. 184.

18. Sweeney III, p. 227. Fish says that, in his poetry, Jonson declares himself 'the center of a court and society more powerful and more durable than any that may seem to contain him', see Stanley Fish, 'Jonson's

Community of the Same', *Representations*, No. 7 (Summer 1984), pp. 26–58, 56–7.

19. Helgerson, p. 164.

20. Fish, p. 38.

21. *The Staple of News* holds perhaps Jonson's most explicit example of such audience-modelling, and concerns over authority and the ownership of 'information'.

22. Fisher, p. 83.

23. Overdo embodies the Fair's 'commingling of categories usually [. . .] opposed', see Peter Stallybrass and Allon White, *The Politics and Poetics of Transgression* (Ithaca: Cornell University Press, 1986), p. 27.

24. Creaser, p. 274; Kinney, *Renaissance Drama*, p. 505, ns 16–23.

25. Creaser, p. 424.

26. Keith Sturgess, *Jacobean Private Theatre* (New York: Routledge and Kegan Paul, 1987), p. 171; Marcus, *The Politics of Mirth*, pp. 55, 40.

27. Keane, p. 79.

28. L. B. T. Houghton and Gesine Manuwald (eds), *Neo-Latin Poetry in the British Isles* (London: Bloomsbury Academic, 2012), p. 155.

29. Freud's 'narcissism of small differences' describes this same mechanism; Freud, p. 90.

30. See Creaser, p. 271, n. 10.

31. The puppet-play may be partly Jonson's response to criticism of himself and his audience from such puritan detractors as Robert Milles, whose sermon at Paul's Cross damned those who preferred 'the idle and scurrilous invention of an illiterate bricklayer to the holy, pure, and powerful word of God'. See Kinney, *Renaissance Drama*, p. 487. His puritan onstage audience here are certainly dangerous, inasmuch as they are duplicitous and playing the part of informers, though this is very much mitigated by their explicit stupidity, with Overdo again acting as the equivocal anomaly.

32. Breight, p. 49.

33. Robert Pricket, *The Lord Coke his speech and charge VVith a discouerie of the abuses and corruption of officers* (1607), <http://gateway.proquest.com/openurl?ctx_ver=Z39.88-2003&res_id=xri:eebo&rft_id=xri:eebo:citation:99840729> (last accessed 16 December 2015).

34. Lenton, n.p.

35. Ibid. n.p.

36. Pricket, n.p.

37. Ibid. n.p.

38. See Creaser, p. 270.

39. Melinda Gough argues that a number of the play's elements in fact 'support the antitheatricalists' disparaging descriptions of the playhouses and the audiences who frequented them'; see 'Jonson's Siren Stage', *Studies in Philology*, Vol. 96, No. 1 (Winter 1999), pp. 68–95, 84.

40. See Kinney, *Renaissance Drama*, p. 546, n. 100.

41. Thomas Heywood describes this ideal as inspired by the muse Melpomene, who 'whipt Vice with a scourge of steele, Unmaskt sterne Murther [. . .] [and] sham'd lasciuious Lust'; see *An Apology for Actors* (London: Nicholas Okes, 1612), <http://gateway.proquest.com/openurl?ctx_ver=Z39.88 2003&res_id=xri:eebo&rft_id=xri:eebo:citation:99841 838> (last accessed 1 March 2016).

42. G. M. Pinciss notes: 'that all three authority figures – Overdo, Busy, and Wasp are placed simultaneously in the stocks [. . .] reduces them all to a common footing'; see '*Bartholomew Fair* and Jonsonian Tolerance', *Studies in English Literature, 1500–1900*, Vol. 35, No. 2 (Spring 1995), pp. 345–59, 350.

43. Leo Salingar, *Dramatic Form in Shakespeare and the Jacobeans* (Cambridge: Cambridge University Press, 1986), p. 193.

44. See Creaser, p. 273, n. 7.

45. The speech of 21 March 1610: see Gillian Manning, 'An Echo of King James in Jonson's *Bartholomew Fair*', *Notes and Queries*, Vol. 36, No. 3 (September 1989) pp. 342–4; also Kinney, *Renaissance Drama*, p. 555, n. 140–1.

46. Fisher, p. 81.

47. See Frances Teague, 'The Mythical Failures of Ben Jonson', in James E. Hirsh (ed.), *New Perspectives on Ben Jonson* (Cranbury, NJ: Associated University Presses, 1997), p. 169.

Chapter 7

'Ministers of Fate': Politic Oversight and Ideal Authorities

Although the fantastical metadrama of *The Tempest* and *A Midsummer Night's Dream* displays some ambivalence over the extent to which authority is compromised by the use of informers, it still registers some of the typical pressures of dramatic production relating to unstable oversight, mistaking agents and confused audiences. Indeed the plays' magical settings may serve to license a more revealing picture of authorities' reliance on these figures than either Jonsonian realism or tragic form generally achieves.

In proposing that *The Tempest* 'challenges the boundaries between illusion and reality', Vaughan and Vaughan's 2011 Arden introduction echoes much of the critical consideration of the metadramatic aspect of the play.[1] In his edition of 1968 Stanley Wells argued that Shakespeare played with these boundaries 'in the consciousness that reality must triumph in the end'; until *Pericles* (1608–9), he says, the distinction between 'levels of reality' had remained as clear as those between 'the illusory world and real world, the actor and the ordinary man'.[2] Wells's account relies on a narrower definition of metadrama than I use here.[3] If we think for instance of the continually metadramatic nature of an earlier play like *Hamlet*, doubts concerning the division between the illusory world and the real world are certainly not limited to the clearly demarcated play within the play. Nevertheless, since both *The Tempest* and *A Midsummer Night's Dream* displace the functionalities of authority into landscapes of magic, dream and fantasy, here a discourse of 'illusion and reality' must be considered. Although its socio-political roots may to some extent be obscured by these structures of 'illusion', their metadrama, and the imagery of informing which surrounds it, are no less politicised than that set in 'real-world' scenarios. In any case we need to be careful with word 'illusion' since it occurs only once in *MND* (3.2.98) and never in *The Tempest*. It may also be useful to remember that a sizeable proportion of people at this time took magic, evil spirits and the mischievous actions of fairies very seriously, as many contemporary accounts of witchcraft trials attest.[4] But if we accept that both *MND*'s forest and *The Tempest*'s island correspond in some ways to the theatre then we are dealing with the idea that the dramatic author's transformative authority is in the realm of 'imagination', a word which does occur in both, most significantly in Theseus's description of the poet, whose 'imagination bodies forth / The forms of things unknown [. . .] / and gives to airy nothing / A local habitation and a name' (5.1.14–17).[5] As we may see here, the Elizabethan concept of imagination was not divorced from a conception of the real world, but rather bridged the two. Imagination was considered to be 'a reporter [. . .] creator or inventor', as R. W. Dent has noted, and is thus linked with authorship; however, as he continues, if dominated by unreason or passion, it became a 'false reporter and/or inventor' and to this extent it also mirrored the popular perception of the informer.[6] Furthermore, as we have seen, the word may also harbour revolutionary connotations.[7]

In *A Midsummer Night's Dream* (c.1595) Shakespeare suffuses metadrama with elements of a magical realm where relatively beneficent authorities oversee agents acting in playful mischief, rather than with insidious and malign intent. With its frame of magical and courtly intrigue, the plot of Oberon and Titania describes a fantastical meta-authority which is as much theatrical as it is of the real world, and, in as much as they create the inner drama, these characters also act as dramatic authors. This might seem to imply an ideal exercise of power in a world magically free from the kind of hierarchical dysfunction we have witnessed in other plays. But this is also a world where confusion, discord and misprision are administered and withdrawn at leisure by these authoritative overseers. Oberon's employment of drugs echoes with Machiavellian manipulation, especially with its use of the minion as agent-provocateur.[8] Meanwhile, Puck's erroneous administration of 'love-in-idleness' juice of Oberon's prescription to the male lovers' eyes is the cause of scenes of dramatic bewilderment and misprision which are mirrored both in the engineered delusion of Titania, and in the rude mechanicals' metadramatic interlude itself and their fear of misinterpretation by what they assume will be a naive audience. Even in their intent of benign playfulness then, these structures of authority are inherently flawed in their operation.

The Tempest's (c.1610) metadramatic form also displays a relatively benign authority and again the geography and magical setting facilitate such a fantasy. For the most part Prospero plays the role of a retiring manipulator here, a puppet-master who relies almost entirely on his agents to perform his will and make his thoughts concrete, although he has often been seen as a mirror for various publicly authoritative figures: Rudolph II of Bohemia, Robert Dudley, James I/VI, John Dee who was, in his youth, also a 'producer of stage spectacles', and obviously Shakespeare himself.[9] Although he is cast in an overseer's role that is authorial and ultimately benevolent, his manipulation of the desires of the other characters seems insidiously Machiavellian.[10] A contrast may be drawn here, however, with Dollimore's reading of surveillance in *Measure for Measure* where, despite the overt authorities' moral opposition to desire, 'the play discloses corruption to be an effect less of desire than authority itself'.[11] For Prospero neither desire nor authority is in itself corrupt, rather both are in need of theatrical management. And despite the habitually opaque nature of his purposes, he does open himself up to the off-stage audience with occasional metadramatic asides, allowing access to an inwardness which has the effect of creating audience sympathy for his cause.[12] It is Prospero's reliance on indentured minions for all of this magical and theatrical manipulation that undermines his ostensible narrative of benign oversight.

But these depictions of flawed systems of authority are simply inherent to the forms of metadrama, rather than calculatedly subversive in any way. In the same way that corruption and other forms of anti-social behaviour are resolved theatrically on *The Tempest*'s magical island, but with a view to a future in the 'real' world of Milan, the dangerous licence of *MND*'s fantasy forest world only works to the benefit of its human subjects because the wild theatre to which it subjects them is balanced by the relatively solid civic authority of Athens.[13] And in both cases any perceived apology for theatre offered is thus bound up with its final acquiescence to external legitimising authorities.

Both plays register key issues relating to informing and authority, including the potential menace of those whose authority is exercised through informing minions, the obvious emphasis on scenes of oversight, and the theatricality of that process. Oberon rules the fairy kingdom, and attempts to exercise power over it; his difficulty is that he cannot fully control his queen who refuses to give up the 'Indian boy' that he covets. Prospero appears to be an entirely Shakespearean creation whose capacity for oversight is, perhaps, suggested by the etymology of his name; this might include classical Latin 'prō' (preposition) before (of place), in front of, for, on behalf of, instead of, 'prospect' looking forward [. . .] seeing to a distance [. . .] outlook, aspect, exposure, or 'prospicient', having or exercising foresight.[14] Though these possible allusions to observation and oversight may not fully reflect Prospero's opacity as a character, they are entirely consistent with him as both author and occulted observer, and with a focus on surveillance.[15] The nearest we get to the meaning of Miranda's name is 'wonderful',[16] though her wide-eyed and naive wonder may have some affinity with the Spanish, *mirar* 'to look', and *mirando*, 'looking'. If Miranda is associated with 'looking' then it is with a gaze that is circumscribed by the patriarchal power of her father, suggesting that in this play the perspectives of oversight are carefully managed. Ariel provides an ideal of pure agency: a combination of intelligent perspective, information and, for the most part, obedience. Being a spirit of the air, he is able, as Burton's *Anatomy of Melancholy* (1621) claims, to 'cause tempests, thunder, and lightenings' and Prospero utilises such manipulative power in order to construct a theurgy of his island state.[17] Although he is a spirit among spirits, Puck, in *A Midsummer Night's Dream* offers a less reliable purveyor of perspective, though he is still an agent of power with possibly devilish connections to Harlequin of the *commedia del'arte*.[18]

In contrast, Bottom and Caliban are both subjected to oversight, although they articulate their positions in different ways. Bottom's drug-induced dream produces a plethora of confused images, incoherence and failed representation; though bestialised he is neither informer nor intriguer, but simply a temporarily monstrous pawn in the drama between Oberon and Titania, an Ovidian metamorph part of whose purpose is to demonstrate the hidden, watching power of the fairy world over a no less fraught mortal one. His sub-human monstrosity can be conferred and withdrawn arbitrarily by a high authority who embodies certain recognisable human traits. But he is also a metadramatic character: he aims to turn his 'dream' into a ballad and he says, 'I will sing it in the latter end of a play, before the Duke' (4.1.215–16). In a rather more sinister way, Caliban's monstrosity is ambiguously related to Prospero's power of surveillance, to the extent that his revolutionary urges are always contained by Prospero's own directorial authority. As subjects of metadramatic oversight, and the machinations of its minions, both survive to live beyond the imaginary worlds of the plays. If not quite an ideal this perhaps contains a seed of hope for anyone caught up in such processes.

The metadrama in *MND* is, for the most part, related to the operation of a superhuman authority whose motives are significantly benevolent, rather than tainted by a web of Machiavellian intrigue and venal observation. This resounds with a Jonsonian ideal of benign oversight, one which Jonson himself never depicts in his plays except by implication of its absence. Moreover, the present harmony of Theseus and Hippolyta here provides a more or less stable centre against which we might gauge the more turbulent operations of the forest's metadramatic authorities.

Theseus has attempted to define his earthly audience when he orders Philostrate to 'Stir up the Athenian youth to merriments; / [and] [. . .] Turn melancholy forth to funerals; / The pale companion is not for our pomp' (1.1.12, 14–15). There is to be no place for the malcontent in Theseus' dramatic self-production. Initially, however, when sketching out the territory for the drama as a prologue to their 'nuptial hour' (1.1.1), Theseus and Hippolyta produce an overall frame narrative in which the moon acts a dilatory overseer who shall, when renewed, 'behold the night / Of our solemnities' (1.1.10–11). To this extent, however, their own legitimate benevolence is subject to a classically capricious and inconstant audience-authority, the lingering, distant 'step-dame or [. . .] dowager' who is pictured venally 'withering out' the poor 'young man's revenue' (1.1.5–6). This sexualised moon hints at the inner drama of the play: an attempt at the management of sexual desire requiring the most intense form of surveillance. So Theseus and Hippolyta's world is not as stable as it may seem, and even in this Athenian idyll there is some discontent.

Here, Egeus, Hermia, Lysander, Demetrius and Helena are all unhappy in one way or another, and Lysander and Hermia's attempt to put this situation right by taking Helena into their confidence about their elopement seems to echo in Helena's statement of love for Demetrius: 'Things base and vile, holding no quantity, / Love can transpose to form and dignity' (1.1.232–3). But, moreover, this is the inverse of the widespread anxiety about dramatic interpretation, and the usual concern of metadrama: that wresting self-interest may translate things possessing 'form and dignity' into things 'base and vile'. Given its obvious application to Titania's later love for Bottom, this might be thought to be a central theme of the play. However, Lysander and Hermia's confidence, it turns out, is misplaced, backfiring when poor Helena, her interest scorned, treacherously decides to ingratiate herself with Demetrius by turning informer:

I will go tell him of fair Hermia's flight:
Then to the wood will he, tomorrow night,
Pursue her; and for this intelligence
If I have thanks, it is a dear expense. (1.1.246-9)

Thus, even here in a theatrical setting supposedly free of Machiavellian scheming, the cross-wooing plot echoes the structures of political intrigue, of the passing of 'intelligence' and reward.

The second scene, in which the mechanicals meet to plan rehearsals for their inner-play, is one of the play's most overtly metadramatic and it self-consciously parodies the confusion of the lovers in the outer dramatic action. The mechanicals' near-unanimous certainty that they would be hanged if any of the courtiers was frightened by Bottom's lion impressions is meant to establish their naivety about theatre generally, and specifically about things that might encourage negative interpretation. This farcical parody is plainly aimed at an offstage audience that would be very much aware of these issues of misinterpretation, and openly mocks any such propensity. But equally, Bottom's remedy, that he will 'roar you as gently as any sucking dove; I will roar you and 'twere any nightingale' (1.2.76-8), also ridicules the very idea of dramatic control over an audience's misprision. The mechanicals are, of course, also bound for the wood, with its Elizabethan associations of 'madness' to add to their metadramatic misapprehensions. It is here that Bottom becomes entangled with Oberon and Titania's intrigue, that is with the politics of real authority.

As the authors of the 'distemperature' (2.1.106) of the natural world, Oberon and Titania are the overseers of the world's affairs, as their previous involvement with Theseus and Hippolyta makes plain. Indeed it is such involvement with the real world that has been the grounds for the 'forgeries of jealousy' (2.1.81), which have been thought to lack relevance to the plot, but on the contrary form the basis for the play's significant metadramatic framework. Oberon's jealousy and annoyance at Titania, moreover, are the motives for his sending Puck for the potent flower which will produce Titania's 'fantasy' and cause so much other drama to occur. Having dispatched Puck on his mission and revealed his plans for drugging Titania to the offstage audience, Oberon encounters Demetrius and Helena and retires to be the lovers' hidden audience. He colludes in this informer-like perspective with the offstage audience: 'I am invisible; / And I will overhear their conference' (2.1.186-7).[19] Bertrand Evans notes that in *MND*, 'we hold advantage over some person or persons during seven of the nine scenes',[20] what Harold F. Brooks calls the 'position of vantage from which we understand aright what the characters do not'.[21] Within this metadramatic structure, it is entirely appropriate that Helena, recognisably in the guise of the informer, should identify herself with a familiar canine imagery, albeit somewhat masochistically:

> I am your spaniel [. . .]
> The more you beat me, I will fawn on you.
> [. . .] What worser place can I beg in your love –
> [. . .] Than to be used as you use your dog? (2.1.203–4, 208, 210)

Given the many connections between drama and the informer's venal audience, it also seems appropriate that it should be Helena who voices the sense of what is lurking in the wood, and that she too is being watched, as should be made obvious in any performance. Albeit unconscious of the full metadramatic significance of her words, it is she who says, 'Nor doth this wood lack worlds of company, / [. . .] how can it be said I am alone / When all the world is here to look on me?' (2.1.223, 225–6). In this regard, of course, Oberon is a very perceptibly empowered audience, working both as the hidden overseer and the manipulator of events, but in this case his responses go comedically amiss, despite his narrative promises (2.1.245–6). The offstage audience are at this point drawn through scopic pulsion into Oberon's view, which is both that of an empowered author of the scene, and also playfully dubious in its informer-like structure.

In these ways the wood's 'theatre' (as *OED* notes, simply 'a place for viewing') produces its own metadramatic frame. Within this framework Oberon and Titania's powers of oversight are exotic; though centred on the compelling power of nature, their influence comes from an occult theatre of their own, whose hidden nature makes their interpretations arcane, and therefore problematic. The portrayal of Oberon and Titania represents a potentially chaotic force, which both mirrors and is set apart from the everyday experience of the lovers in the theatre of the wood. Theirs is a metadramatic frame which establishes a continuous drama of the 'real' inner world that remains even as they disappear, leaving the lovers at the whim of the agent of its author, and the offstage audience disorientated by the shifting diegetic gravity of the metadramatic narrative.

Just as the forest is a dislocated theatre, so the state of dislocation is exacerbated by the administration of an authorial narcotic, Puck's juice applied to the lovers' eyes, suggesting a treacherous manipulation of perspective. This does not produce 'levels' of illusion and reality, rather, illusion and reality are themselves conflated in this process, producing conditions favourable to misprision. Here, the inner-drama as a whole is founded on the principle of author-generated misrecognition, and thus it plays with one of the very anxieties that dogs theatrical production at this time. Moreover, the fact that Oberon administers the drug to Titania himself, while Puck is delegated as proxy to do so for the others (for example to Lysander at 2.2.77), suggests that this form of manipulation is a top-down affair, the prerogative, in more general terms, of authority over the subject.[22] The fact that Puck gets his part wrong and causes further chaos is an additional testament to the instability of these seemingly benign authorities. Since in a sense Oberon is an author of this inner-drama, there is an element of this which operates as a defensive self-critique on Shakespeare's part.

It is significant in this regard that the mechanicals' inner play *Pyramus and Thisbe* mirrors this fear of misrecognition by what they assume will be a similarly confused audience.[23] At the outset of their rehearsal, Peter Quince's demarcation of dramatic space: 'This green plot shall be our stage, / this hawthorn-brake our tiring-house' (3.1.3–4), is itself consciously metadramatic and its conventions are reinforced as the actors begin to second-guess their hypothetical audience's responses to the dramatic action. Snout admits 'a parlous fear' (3.1.12) but Bottom, however, has a solution to their anxiety, as he says, 'I have a device to make all well' (3.1.15). His explanation of this 'device' parodies the very idea of dramatic trickery and sleight of hand: 'let the prologue seem to say we will do no harm with our swords, and that Pyramus is not killed in deed; and for the more better assurance, tell them that I, Pyramus, am not Pyramus, but Bottom the weaver' (3.1.16–20). This tactic of informing the audience of exactly who and what is meant by whom is of course anything but a 'device' in the conventional sense, though its deployment as metadrama, in drawing the offstage audience's attention to what would be an act of misinterpretation, makes it one. Nevertheless, Puck's assertion that these swaggerers in the province of the Fairy Queen are mere 'hempen homespuns' (3.1.73) makes very clear to the offstage audience the lack of sophistication that such paranoia would involve.[24]

A little later, when Demetrius and Hermia enter, Oberon's order to Puck, 'Stand close' (3.2.41), indicates that they intend to form another hidden audience to the central action of the confusion they have authored between the Athenian lovers. Again, when Puck reports that Helena and Lysander are near, suggesting, 'Shall we their fond pageant see? / Lord, what fools these mortals be!', Oberon responds, 'Stand aside' (3.2.114–16), and they model an unseen oversight of a drama of their own making. Puck's 'misprision' (3.2.90) in these cases prevails, until Oberon gives him a new herb for Lysander's eye that will 'take from thence all error' (3.2.368), the drugs standing for simple devices determining what can be perceived, and who does the perceiving. Here Oberon is cast as a relatively benign observer: when Puck describes an overworld of 'Damned spirits' who 'For fear lest day should look their shames upon: / [. . .] wilfully themselves exil'd from light' (3.2.382, 385–6), Oberon adds by way of contrast with such shady types, 'But we are spirits of another sort' (3.2.389); importantly the audience offstage have been set up by the metadramatic form to share his perspective. This works as a fantasy of authority in which the potentially vicious mechanisms of observation and interpretation to which an author may typically be subject are inverted in favour of the author. It is revealing that this apparent ideal is compromised by the fact that, in order to engender this authority, the author must stand in the typical place of the hidden, plotting informer.

A less complex model of interpretative oversight is offered as Bottom is preparing to play the inner-play before the earthly authorities. Although he is concerned over the interpretation of their drama and feels bound to instruct his actors to 'eat no onions nor garlic, for we are to utter sweet breath' (4.2.39–41), Theseus is a benign observer who tells Hippolyta, 'never anything can be amiss / When simpleness and duty tender it' (5.1.82–3) adding that, 'Love, therefore, and tongue-tied simplicity / In least speak most, to my capacity' (5.1.104–5). Set against the authorities of the forest's propensity to produce disordered perception, Theseus's audience model works most apparently as an appeal to offstage observers for a straightforward interpretative charity.

In Quince's apologetic prologue, his words are disordered (5.1.108), something that continues as Bottom plays Pyramus: '*I see a voice; now will I to the chink, / To spy and I can hear my Thisbe's face*' (5.1.189–90) and where he asks his onstage audience whether they would prefer to 'see' an epilogue, or 'hear' a dance (5.1.339–40). This synaesthesia contains a confusion of both senses and sense in which drama is parodied in a metadramatic exchange which embodies a kind of misprision. In such a context of high potential for misunderstanding it is significant that Demetrius alludes to informing practice, as he reminds the audience, both onstage and off, that 'walls are [. . .] wilful to hear without warning' (5.1.205–6). This allusion is to some extent defused, however, by Hippolyta's comment, 'This is the silliest stuff that ever I heard' (5.1.207). Theseus nevertheless picks up on its relation to the problematic interpretation of theatre: 'The best in this kind are but shadows; and the worst are no worse, if imagination amend them' (5.1.208–9), which of course his own 'imagination' does by beneficently bridging illusion and reality. In this, he is the exact inverse of Jonson's hated 'wresting' interpreter, and his statement that 'if we imagine no worse of them than they of themselves, they may pass for excellent men' (5.1.211–12) is a nuanced version of Ben Jonson's usual injunction to his audiences, that they think well enough of themselves to resist seeing themselves in any negative onstage representation.[25]

On one level, this is of course a powerful metadramatic appeal to the good sense of the offstage audience and Theseus thus models a very generous interpreter for them to emulate. However, the very dismissive nature of this onstage audience's responses to the 'silly stuff' of the inner play serves to mock the concerns of the actors as an exaggeration resulting from their uneducated status. Shakespeare's device here thus allows the expression of a real fear in the voice of an easily contained and ridiculed group which 'comically undercuts any sense of real threat', as James Kavanagh says.[26] Since, as we have seen, these fears are by no means restricted to an artisanal class, but pervade dramatic production at all levels, it is interesting, especially at this stage in his career, that Shakespeare uses the uneducated player both to express and defensively undercut these concerns over interpretation.

The clearly demarcated inner performance of *Pyramus and Thisbe* may also be useful for Shakespeare because he recognised, as Dent suggests, quoting *Love's Labours Lost*'s Biron, ' "'tis some policy / To have one show worse than" his own offering'.[27] A burlesque of lesser sources, it may, as Brooks contends, be intended to 'contrast with the lyrical beauty of Shakespeare's poetry'.[28] This is a far subtler form of demarcation of the author's authority over poetasters than that of Jonson in the same mode; perhaps this is aided by the fact that its derogatory depiction of theatre contains a more convincing element of disarming self-deprecation.

In the end all theatrical discord and misprision is brought to a concord which reconciles the realm of the imagination with the real world, and even with the often negative metaphors associated with interpretation. When Theseus is musing on how imagination bridges illusion and reality he links the forest-madness of the lovers with the physical pen of the poet:

> The lunatic, the lover, and the poet
> Are of imagination all compact:
> [. . .] The poet's eye, in a fine frenzy rolling,
> Doth glance from heaven to earth, from earth to heaven;
> And as imagination bodies forth
> The forms of things unknown, the poet's pen
> Turns them to shapes, and gives to airy nothing
> A local habitation and a name. (5.1.7–8, 12–17)

If this is being presented as a problem, it is immediately ameliorated by Hippolyta's statement that something firm and valuable has transpired in the imaginative realm of the night past, which ultimately transcends it: 'all the story of the night told over, / [. . .] More witnesseth than fancy's images, / And grows to something of great constancy' (5.1.23, 25–6). The narrative of 'all the story of the night told over' is the central metadramatic element that cements the production of unity from discord here, the 'gentle concord in the world' (4.1.142) that Theseus marvels at when he discovers the lovers in the wood. Moreover, the royal couple's dogs provide a further figure of this generative theatrical device. As explored throughout this book, the imagery of the predatory hound is often employed to represent flattering informers, their tongues being the operative medium for the production of instability, uncertainty, paranoia and physical threat. Here, however, their voices are joined in harmony, 'match'd in mouth like bells, / Each under each', and thus, 'a cry more tuneable / Was never holla'd to, not cheer'd with horn' (4.1.122–4), their concord echoing throughout this ideal dramatic land so that Hippolyta declares that 'every region near / Seem'd all one mutual cry; I never heard / So musical a discord, such sweet thunder' (4.1.115–17).

The somewhat enforced nature of this concord might be seen as an indication of Shakespeare's complicity in ideological containment; I would argue rather that *MND* speaks for an ideal of dramatic authority within a functional community, where the metadramatic dream-world of theatre might have the licence to produce something of transcendent value, something 'of great constancy', unhindered by fear of venal misinterpretation. At the end of the play, Puck offers the offstage audience an ideal interpretative position, inviting them to imagine a world where authorities can acknowledge and easily assimilate the power of the imagination without assuming representational malintention. Although, as a kind of ideal interpreter, Theseus does not require an epilogue from the actors of the inner-play, Puck nevertheless delivers one to the offstage audience, in which he expresses the hope that the play 'will scape the serpent's tongue' (5.1.419). Given the exemplary authorities and onstage audiences of the play, there is every reason to expect that it should.

The Tempest's dislocated and helpless aristocrats and courtiers also exist in a metadramatic environment, but one where all authority and information are more specifically subject to the informing minions and manipulative magical plot devices of Prospero as both author and onstage audience. It begins with them on the foundering ship, occupying a social space in which their authority counts for nothing, and ends with its restoration upon occult theatrical foundations. Although this transformative play produces its own ideal of dramatic empowerment, it is one which resonates with structures that replicate the very authority it challenges. Finally, however radical the nature of the Ovidian fantasy,[29] Prospero's manipulative magical and metadramatic devices are exercised as recognisable structures of surveillance and control and it is these that must be abjured for his own transformation to be complete, and for him to resume his ducal privileges.[30] Prospero's authority is therefore limited by the boundaries of his own magical metadrama. As he surrenders it, he surrenders not only authorship but also the empowered position of informer-wielding authority. The fact that his legitimacy is predicated on his renunciation of these structures suggests its own ideal of authority. Whatever Elizabeth I might have thought of Titania, as Fairy Queen (it is possible she was present at MND's first performance, at least), Prospero is clearly oppositional in terms of James I/VI's comprehensively negative attitude to magic.[31] This is regardless of Prospero's magic being contrasted with that of Sycorax, since James opposed theurgy and goetry to the same extent.[32] Magic, of course, proffers its own authority, and if so James's concern may really be over encroaching illegitimate authorities. In this case it is interesting that The Tempest seems to combine the eventual rejection of magic, as Prospero drowns his books and releases his agents, with the rejection of the very structures of authority with which the state polices its legitimacy.

At the play's outset, on board the ship caught in the storm, the only applicable sign-system fails to recognise the courtiers' authority and rejects their claims to precedence. Gonzalo asks the hard-pressed crew to 'remember whom thou hast aboard'; the stark response is, 'if you can command these elements to silence and work the peace of the present, we will not hand a rope more. Use your authority! If you cannot [. . .] Out of our way, I say!' (1.1.19, 21–3, 26). And obviously, they cannot. Since 'the tempest' is an alchemical term for the boiling of the alembic to encourage the transformative process, the raging elements here are both a metaphor for, and the means of, disordering the courtiers' stable conditions.[33] Moreover, this is a storm which in any case has been 'safely ordered', under Prospero's irresistibly authoritative metadramatic direction. Indeed the entire dramatic trauma of the wreck is wrought and underwritten by his 'provision in mine art', as he reassures Miranda (1.2.28). *OED* notes that current meanings active for the term 'provision' include, 'supply of necessities [. . .] foresight, divine providence [and] purveyance'.[34] Prospero's 'provision' seems to comprehend all of these manifestations of authority; in such metadramatic territory, it seems entirely fitting that all authority is subject to the magic of the author.

Prospero's metadramatic status is established by the fact that he is both an intra- and hypo-diegetic author who stands in various places of audience within the narrative of his own making. He is another figure who sets a drama in motion, then stands aside to observe its outcome, a more obviously empowered version of *Measure for Measure*'s Duke Vincentio. Although Prospero is often a visible plotter, his precise means are occulted, and thus here too the menace of what is hidden is felt, informed by secret knowledge. Dramatically self-empowered, he can afford to employ others to do his watching and manipulation for him, though his only constant companion in his occult plotting is Ariel, who is privy to all. Although Ariel is clearly Prospero's informer, he has a god-like quality, later mirrored by the figure of Iris in Prospero's masque.[35] Robert R. Reed Jr noted the similarities between Ariel and Antony Munday's aerial spirit character Shrimp, from his *John a Kent and John a Cumber* (c.1595), whom John a Kent commands,

> Sirra, get thee to the back gate of the Castell
> And through the keyhole quickly wring thee in,
> Mark well, and bring me word what strategem
> This cunning John meanes next to enterprise.[36]

Munday's key-hole-intruding spirit has more specifically informer-like instructions than Ariel, but both perform more or less the same functions. In Munday's case this is unsurprising given his own reputation as both plotter and informer.[37] Reed also notes Shakespeare's possible debt to Munday for the precision of the musical 'device' that

Ariel uses to guide and charm the characters who are drawn ineluctably into Prospero's drama as participatory audience-members.[38]

Caliban, however, is a recalcitrant participant in Prospero's narrative and can be controlled only by force. In the nature of the perception of indigenous peoples either as 'savage' or 'Edenic Man', Caliban is either a bestial audience-gone-wrong, serving as an example of the image of a subject who resists the system of dramatic control, or he represents an implicitly ideal opposition to what Vaughan and Vaughan call Antonio's courtly 'European corruption',[39] citing his comparative lack of dissimulation and detraction, the ideal figure proposed in Montaigne's popular vision 'Of the Caniballes'.[40] Of course, he may variously function as either. As an unwilling and often unwitting actor in Prospero's narrative, he plays opposite various malcontents and draws out of them their own lack of civilisation and their hunger for authority.

Through his agents, Prospero's dramatic authority is all-pervading, his authorial influence framing every instance with the observation that pertains to subjection, and his informers directing his pre-determined plot. It is the case, as Wells suggests, that *The Tempest* tends to blur the boundaries between metadramatic levels, and this is because these are simply subsumed into the topography of everyday life on the stage of the island, its very air suffused with theatricality, just as theatre inevitably registers the pressures and structures of everyday life. So it is that Ariel subjects himself to the script and submits, 'To thy strong bidding, task / Ariel and all his quality' (1.2.192–3), the term 'the quality' at this time referring specifically to the acting fraternity.[41] As Egan notes, Prospero subjects Antonio, Alonso and Sebastian to 'an ordeal of self-knowledge and purgation through the performance of his spirits'.[42] But it is clear that Ariel combines his acting with a conventional overhearing-informing work, as Caliban states, 'His spirits hear me [. . .] / But they'll nor pinch, / Fright me with urchin-shows, pitch me i'th' mire, / [. . .] unless he bid 'em (2.2.3–5, 7).

Although they are firmly in Prospero's metadramatic world now, and subject to his agents, the nobles' awareness of their own lack of agency takes time to sink in; indeed it may be a denial fantasy in their present situation to think of themselves as having any volition at all outside of Prospero's direction and authorship. Nevertheless, Antonio's usurping threat to Sebastian, 'to perform an act / Whereof what's past is prologue, what to come / In yours and my discharge!' (2.1.252–4), and kill the sleeping King Alonso is an attempt to claim some personal dramatic and political agency. This is a small moment of metadrama which connects their discourse with both political machination and with theatre; it relates also to Antonio's previous author-like statement, 'My strong imagination sees a crown / Dropping upon thy head' (2.1.208–9). In this connection, it may be that he deploys a familiar bird imagery relating to the loquacity of the informer when he alludes ambitiously to the tongue of the counsellor Gonzalo, claiming, 'I myself could make / A chough of as deep chat' (2.1.266–7). Meanwhile, Ariel has clearly informed Prospero of their plot and returns with his orders to wake the sleepers and prevent the bloody act, as the informer tells us, 'For else his project dies' (2.1.300).

Prospero is this plotting 'projector' throughout the play, as much as he is also an onstage audience.[43] As Miranda enters to watch Ferdinand work at the task set him, Prospero also enters '*at a distance, unseen*' (s.d. 3.1.15). Ferdinand attempts to establish his position in some kind of moral hierarchy when he claims he is a king, 'and would no more endure / This wooden slavery than to suffer / The flesh-fly blow my mouth' (3.1.61–3).[44] It seems that Prospero here is a benevolent audience, merely wishing the blossoming romance well; yet if this is entirely the case we might question why he is hidden, voyeur-like, whispering in complicity with the offstage audience. Prospero's audienceship may function primarily to establish his benevolent patriarchal supervision of Miranda, but it also establishes a connection between himself and the offstage audience, modelling an oversight not merely delegated to threateningly invisible minions, but also capable of being direct, personal and dangerously manipulative. Immediately following the resolution of Sebastian and Antonio, the 'ambitious Machiavel' of the act, to use the distractions of the island to usurp the throne of Naples, Prospero directs the metadrama of the fairy banquet scene, through the agency of Ariel.[45] Here he is again acting as a hidden audience to the inner-play, the 'living drollery' (3.3.21), as stage directions tell us, '*on the top (invisible)*' (s.d. 3.3.18), although he is visible to the offstage audience and again interacts with them through asides commenting on the responses of the nobles to the inner drama. Theatre again offers an appropriate response here to political machination, firstly by providing a contrasting 'harmony' (3.3.18) in the music and the metadramatic dumbshow of the banquet, and secondly by administering a corrective.

Ariel, playing the part of the harpy, tells the men what he knows of them: 'You are three men of sin, whom destiny / [. . .] Hath caused [the sea] to belch up' (3.3.53, 56) and although at this Alonso, Sebastian and the others draw their swords, their resistance to Ariel's performance is useless, and he continues, 'You fools!

I and my fellows / Are ministers of fate [. . .] / The powers [. . .] / [. . .] do pronounce by me / Ling'ring perdition, worse than any death (3.3.60–1, 76–7). Gonzalo may eventually ascribe authorship of their personal drama to the gods, who, he says, 'chalked forth the way / Which brought us hither' (5.1.203–4), but the offstage audience knows better: it is the hidden agency of Ariel, acting for Prospero, that has marked out their path and his metadramatic revelation makes this clear for them. As throughout, Ariel's bluster here about he and his fellows being 'ministers of fate' has been entirely authored by Prospero, who reviews Ariel's metadramatic performance, 'Bravely the figure of this harpy hast thou / Performed, my Ariel [. . .] / Of my instruction hast thou nothing bated / In what thou hadst to say' (3.3.83–6). He also comments on the success of his own authorial plans, which have been both theatrical in nature and fundamentally political in intention, and this works as an unstated aside to the offstage audience, whether or not it is directly addressed to them by the actor, tending to create sympathy with the metadramatic process and an affinity with Prospero's newly re-empowered perspective:

> So, with good life
> And observation strange, my meaner ministers
> Their several kinds have done. My high charms work,
> And these, mine enemies, are all knit up
> In their distractions. They now are in my power;
> And in these fits I leave them. (3.3.86–91)

Prospero then sets up another more elaborate device in honour of Ferdinand and Miranda's betrothal, telling Ariel, 'Thou and thy meaner fellows your last service / Did worthily perform; and I must use you / In such another trick' (4.1.35–7). He orders their performance of the characters of Iris, Juno and Ceres in a production which recalls *Hymenaei*, Jonson's 1606 wedding masque, and other 'island'-based courtly entertainments.[46] But this is no simple celebratory interlude, rather it is an inner drama with an Ovidian backstory which suggests conceptual connections again between the theatrical, of which this is a representation, and the workings of power and information. E. M. W. Tillyard notes here that 'on the actual stage, the masque is executed by players pretending to be spirits, pretending to be real actors, pretending to be supposed goddesses and rustics', calling these 'planes of reality'.[47] But these planes do not in fact present easily demarcated or ideally individuated social roles; rather, there is something more complex involved. First to appear is Iris, Juno's 'messenger' (4.1.71, 76), a role which classically includes that of informer.[48] Ceres, whose presence and blessing is also invoked, has her own experience of an injurious informer. In Ovid, a long-recognised source of Shakespeare's, she is the mother of Proserpine, whose abduction by Pluto caused Ceres to search the world over for her.[49] Upon finding her, Ceres appealed to Jupiter for Proserpine's release, which he granted provided only that she had not eaten the food of the underworld. Unfortunately she had eaten seven pomegranate seeds and, more to the point, had been overseen doing so by one informing Ascalaphus, who, as Ovid says, 'by telling what he had seen, cruelly prevented her return'.[50] At this Proserpine visited his bestiality upon him, and, with familiar imagery, 'changed the informer into a bird of evil omen [. . .] clad in tawny wings [. . .] he developed long hooked talons [. . .] He became a sluggish screech owl, a loathsome bird, which heralds impending disaster'.[51] Back in the metadrama of the play, Ceres is therefore extremely wary of plotters such as Venus and Cupid who 'did plot / The means that dusky Dis my daughter got' (4.1.88–9) and fears they are trying to ruin the happiness and vows of the relative innocents Ferdinand and Miranda. Iris reassures her, and Juno and Ceres offer the couple a blessing. Ferdinand terms this 'a most majestic vision, and / Harmonious charmingly', adding, 'May I be bold / To think these spirits?' (4.1.118–20). Prospero replies that they are 'Spirits, which by mine art / I have from their confines called to enact / My present fancies' (4.1.120–2), and requests the passive complicity of Ferdinand as audience,

> Sweet now, silence!
> Juno and Ceres whisper seriously.
> There's something else to do. Hush and be mute,
> Or else our spell is marred. (4.1.124–7)

This is a curious passage in which Prospero's art seems to be dependent on the receptive silence of the audience, as the stage directions tell us that '*Juno and Ceres whisper, and send Iris on employment*' (s.d. 4.1.124) to summon the Naiades and country reapers; yet the next stage directions specify that they '*join with the Nymphs in a graceful dance, towards the end whereof Prospero starts suddenly and speaks; after which* [. . .] *they heavily vanish*' (s.d. 4.1.139). Here, the dizzyingly shifting 'planes' of drama, intrinsically tied to the mental state of the author and director, distract him from the machinations of the 'real' world he is meant to be directing, as he states to the offstage audience in an aside,

> I had forgot that foul conspiracy
> Of the beast Caliban and his confederates
> Against my life. The minute of their plot
> Is almost come. (4.1.139–42)

So Prospero arrests the inner performance, and interprets Ferdinand's audience-reaction in a metadramatic apology which establishes his identity firmly as the director of theatre and the source of meaning, both within the play and beyond it to the time when not even the Globe will exist,

> Our revels now are ended. These our actors,
> As I foretold you, were all spirits and
> Are melted into air, into thin air;
> And – like the baseless fabric of this vision –
> The cloud-capped towers, the gorgeous palaces,
> The solemn temples, the great globe itself,
> Yea, all which it inherit, shall dissolve,
> And like this insubstantial pageant faded,
> Leave not a rack behind. (4.1.148–56)

The metadramatic force of this *theatrum mundi*, centred on the defining power of the author over all other 'plots', flows into the lines: 'We are such stuff / As dreams are made on, and our little life / Is rounded with a sleep' (4.1.156–8). Ferdinand and Miranda's forgiving response to this as they exit is simply, 'We wish your peace' (4.1.163). Prospero's dreams are the dreams of dramatic ideals, and the peace of Ferdinand and Miranda's wishes is the sleep of acquiescence in the will of the god-like author whose authority acts as a proxy here for all authority.

Next Prospero turns his attentions to Caliban's crew and summons Ariel to 'come with a thought' (4.1.164); Ariel enters with, 'Thy thoughts I cleave to. What's thy pleasure?' (4.1.165). From this agent, who it seems is interchangeable with Prospero's own thoughts, he requests information about the plotters; Ariel reports that they were,

> So full of valour that they smote the air
> For breathing in their faces, beat the ground
> For kissing of their feet, yet always bending
> Towards their project. (4.1.172–5)

The loaded word 'project' here reminds us of Prospero's own 'project', complicating the suggestion that these plotters are treacherously ambitious subjects of a legitimate authority. Ariel continues his account of the means employed to lead them astray: as he beat his tabor they

> lifted up their noses
> As they smelt music; so I charmed their ears
> That calf-like they my lowing followed, through
> Toothed briers, sharp furzes, pricking gorse and thorns. (4.1.177–80)

Not only are they bestialised in their pursuit of Ariel, but, like *MND*'s rude mechanicals, they too suffer from synaesthesia in the world of theatrical devices that they have entered, in this case they 'smelt music'. This seems to imply that a heightened sensitivity to theatre, accompanied by the intention to perform illegitimate acts of one's own, results in a diminished resistance to its devices. Thus Ariel leads them, and leaves them 'I'th' filthy-mantled pool beyond your cell, / There dancing up to th' chins, that the foul lake / O'erstunk their feet' (4.1.182–4). Prospero's response, 'This was well done, my bird', alludes to familiar informer-imagery, and, following the same train of thinking, he orders Ariel to collect material for a further metadramatic device, a 'stale to catch these thieves' (4.1.184, 187). Here metadramatic structures fit simply and naturally with the general atmosphere of misprision and plotting, and with the exercise and policing of various kinds of authority.

He and Ariel again remain invisible, again a dangerously hidden audience, as Caliban, Stephano and Trinculo enter in search of Prospero, to murder him in his sleep. The offstage audience share their perspective over these usurpers, which is that of both author and informer. Caliban performs a parody of the Machiavellian plotter with the help of Stephano and Trinculo as *zannis*,[52] directing them,

> This is the mouth o'th' cell. No noise, and enter.
> Do that good mischief which may make this island
> Thine own for ever, and I, thy Caliban,
> For aye thy foot-licker. (4.1.216–19)

As they argue over the clothes left out for them as bait, the stage directions tell that a *'noise of hunters'* is heard. Immediately enter *'diverse Spirits in shape of dogs and hounds, hunting them about'* (s.d. 4.1.255), with Prospero ordering Ariel, to 'Let them be hunted soundly' (4.1.263–7). This typical hunting metaphor is apt to the coney-catching nature of this kind of metadramatic device, one which offers a kind of dramaturgical banana-skin and is self-consciously contrived to open its dupes to ridicule. Thus the pile of noblemen's clothes which Prospero ordered Ariel to array is the enticement here, offering the illusion of authority, but, as the hounds indicate, this form of ambition merely opens the takers to other forms of predation. The metadramatic device critiques similar political desire in reality.

Again using the term indicative of a political plot, at the beginning of Act 5 Prospero tells Ariel, 'Now does my project gather to a head. / My charms crack not; my spirits obey; and time / Goes upright with his carriage' (5.1.1–3), and asks again for more information: 'Say, my spirit, / How fares the King and's followers?' (5.1.6–7). When Ariel informs him of their state, Prospero decides his theatre of controlled transformation has had the desired effect, and, persuaded by Ariel, decides to end their dramatic subjection to his narrative: 'My charms I'll break; their senses I'll restore; / And they shall be themselves' (5.1.31–2). In all of this Prospero has employed authorly theatrical devices resembling those of the Machiavel, the informer and the agent, to manipulate his way through a narrative of his own devising, and towards his own political re-empowerment. Despite all of these shows of theatrical and authorly authority, however, both Antonio's and Stephano's 'resistance' depends on a vision of authority, both generic and ontological, that is somehow firmer than the play eventually posits, through which the characters' rebellion is robbed of its sting. As Simon Palfrey says 'their worldview [. . .] appears redundant', their blunt vision finally inadequate to the political and metadramatic complexities that will overtake them.[53]

Prospero's next speech has often been taken as Shakespeare's own metadramatic valediction:

> this rough magic
> I here abjure; and when I have required
> Some heavenly music (which even now I do)
> To work mine end upon their senses that
> This airy charm is for, I'll break my staff,
> Bury it certain fathoms in the earth,
> And deeper than did ever plummet sound
> I'll drown my book. (5.1.50–7)

Nevertheless, for the moment at least, the theatre continues to the sound of solemn music as Prospero commands his onstage audience, forgives and reconciles himself to them by name as the charm dissolves and decides to dress in a way they will recognise, putting off the costume of his current role, again sending Ariel as his agent in preparation for this. When Alonso and Gonzalo express doubts about the reality of their current situation, Prospero reassures them with an authorial authority, 'You do yet taste / Some subtleties o' th'isle, that will not let you / Believe things certain. Welcome, my friends all' (5.1.123–5). Aside to Sebastian and Antonio, however, he threatens to play the informer,

> But you, my brace of lords, were I so minded,
> I here could pluck his highness' frown upon you
> And justify you traitors! At this time
> I will tell no tales. (5.1.126–9)

Here Prospero plays upon the dual meaning of being a tale-teller to intimidate Sebastian into easy compliance with the unfolding scene as Prospero has arranged it; Sebastian's response to this is undirected, but he adds in an accusatory aside to the offstage audience, simply, 'The devil speaks in him' (5.1.129). Prospero is quick to deny this, and to offer forgiveness for past sins against his political person, restoring the lost Ferdinand to Alonso, the beginning of his surrender of informer-wielding authority.

Following this, there is not much further restoration in the play itself, which ends with incomplete information, a lack of resolution and a sense of withheld communication. When Alonso asks for an oracle to 'rectify our knowledge' (5.1.245), Prospero precludes external interpretation, promising merely, 'I'll resolve you / [. . .] of every / These happened accidents. Till when, be cheerful / And think of each thing well' (5.1.248–51). As with *Hamlet* and *Othello*, this promises further tale-telling beyond the end of the production, and here again Prospero promises to 'deliver all' (5.1.314) and tell Alonso the rest of his story after the play has ended (5.1.305–7). Wells argues convincingly that the effect of this 'is to suggest that the play goes on beyond the formal limits of its fifth Act, that it runs into and shares the reality of its audience'.[54] In these terms, Prospero is empowered as the metadramatic author and authority not merely of the theatrical isle but in worldly terms also, projecting his island theatre into his own, and his author's, political futures. In many ways *The Tempest*'s devices do casually blur the boundaries between metadramatic levels, but the metadrama here differs mainly from that of other of Shakespeare's plays in the intensity of its self-assurance about the position of the author within his creation. As the Epilogue weaves its conventional apology, however, this sense of empowerment is counter-balanced by Prospero's further surrendering of his informer-wielding authority in the act of handing over responsibility to the audience, and more specifically to their 'breath', for the completion of his plotting: 'Gentle breath of yours my sails / Must fill, or else my project fails' (Epi. 11–12). The effect of this is to implicate the audience directly in the political mechanisms into which they have been drawn throughout by conventional metadramatic devices, hidden audience observations and collusive asides. Therefore the effect of the appeal in the Epilogue is not so much what Egan calls a 'celebration of their shared humanity' as it is a recognition of their shared responsibility.[55] As Shakespeare combines the rejection of magic with the rejection of the mechanisms of state authority, the self-assured metadrama works to subsume the offstage audience's perspective into this magical ideal of political rehabilitation.

The imagery and geography of *MND* extends many of its associations with the theatre, taking authority into the realm of the lawless and fantastical, while *The Tempest*'s island is a theatre in itself, abolishing those boundaries. *MND* sets plays within plays; *The Tempest* sets a world within a world, and suggests that these are the same kinds of entity, or at least that they share a transformational possibility. Thus 'dramatic levels' and 'planes of reality' are continually transgressed; that this may be a force for good and not evil is suggested by the play's outcomes of forgiveness, romantic union and the dissolution of structures of manipulative oversight. But despite the relative lightness of tone here, the configuration of these metadramatic structures of 'illusion and reality', and the dominant imagery of authority, mirror the early modern political reality of informing that we have been describing. Even in these illusory worlds, real authority requires the considerable skills of authorship, and the close observation of unseen overseers empowered by the 'magic' of device and artifice, to transcend the limitations of their own political reality.

Notes

1. William Shakespeare, *The Tempest*, ed. Virginia Mason Vaughan and Alden T. Vaughan (London: Arden, 2011). Unless otherwise noted, this is the primary text for all references to this play.
2. William Shakespeare, *The Tempest*, ed. Stanley Wells (Harmondsworth: Penguin, 1968), pp. 44–5.

3. Vaughan and Vaughan plough this furrow to some extent, noting the four levels of illusion in Yukio Ninagawa's metatheatrical *Tempest* of the 1980s; see Shakespeare, *The Tempest*, pp. 151–3.

4. See for instance Alaric Hall, 'Getting Shot of Elves: Healing, Witchcraft and Fairies in the Scottish Witchcraft Trials', *Folklore*, Vol. 116, No. 1 (Apr. 2005), pp. 19–36.

5. William Shakespeare, *A Midsummer Night's Dream*, ed. Harold F. Brooks (London: Routledge, 1989). Unless otherwise stated, all references are to this edition.

6. R. W. Dent, 'Imagination in *A Midsummer Night's Dream*', Shakespeare Quarterly, Vol. 15, No. 2 (Spring 1964), pp. 115–29, at 123, 115–16.

7. See Chapter 1 herein, n. 55.

8. For Machiavellian influences, Vaughan and Vaughan identify John Marston's *The Malcontent* and Beaumont and Fletcher's *Philaster*, see Shakespeare, *The Tempest*, pp. 142–7.

9. See Shakespeare, *The Tempest*, pp. 38–9, 67 and William Shakespeare, *The Tempest*, ed. Stephen Orgel (Oxford: Oxford University Press, 1998), p. 10. For connections of interest between Prospero and *Bartholomew Fair*'s puppet show, see Kenneth Gross, 'Puppets Dallying: Thoughts on Shakespearean Theatricality', *Comparative Drama* Vol. 41, No. 3 (2007), pp. 273–96, esp. 289–92.

10. For potential problems with previous accounts of Prospero's authority, based on Strachey and other possible source narratives, see Arthur F. Kinney, 'Revisiting *The Tempest*', *Modern Philology*, Vol. 93, No. 2 (Nov. 1995), pp. 161–77.

11. Jonathan Dollimore, 'Surveillance and Transgression in *Measure for Measure*', in *Political Shakespeare: Essays in Cultural Materialism* (Manchester: Manchester University Press, 1994), p. 74.

12. See William Shakespeare, *A Midsummer Night's Dream*, ed. Stanley Wells (London: Penguin, 1967), 1.2.495, 3.1.31, 3.1.74–6.

13. This line of thinking tends towards a possible Shakespearean worldview, and in this regard *MND* may be taken as a defence of poetry, see Dent, p. 129.

14. *OED*: 'pro', 'prospect' and 'prospicient'. Or possibly it is simply a combination of 'prosper' plus 'espero', Spanish for 'I hope', making the composite 'I hope to prosper'.

15. In this regard Prospero relates to the Italian for Faustus, see Robert Egan, 'This Rough Magic: Perspectives of Art and Morality in *The Tempest*', *Shakespeare Quarterly*, Vol. 23, No. 2 (Spring 1972), pp. 171–82, at 175. For connections between *The Tempest* and metadrama in Marlowe's *Dr Faustus*, see John S. Mebane, 'Metadrama and the Visionary Imagination in *Dr. Faustus* and the *Tempest*', *South Atlantic Review*, Vol. 53, No. 2 (May 1988), pp. 25–45, esp. 29–30. See also Hutson, p. 17.

16. *OED*: 'wonderful', from the classical Latin.

17. Burton, p. 166.
18. Winifried Schleiner, 'Imaginative Sources for Shakespeare's Puck', *Shakespeare Quarterly*, Vol. 36, No. 1 (Spring 1985), pp. 65–8, at 68.
19. For Puck and Oberon as eavesdroppers, see Shakespeare, *A Midsummer Night's Dream*, p. xc; Bertrand Evans, *Shakespeare's Comedies* (Oxford: Oxford University Press, 1960), pp. 34, 38, 40.
20. Evans, p. 34.
21. Shakespeare, *A Midsummer Night's Dream*, p. cxxxv.
22. See editor's stage direction at (2.2.25).
23. For connections between *Pyramus and Thisbe* and *Love's Labours Lost*'s show of the Nine Worthies, see Shakespeare, *A Midsummer Night's Dream*, pp. lxxvi–lxxvii.
24. See J. W. Robinson, 'Palpable Hot Ice: Dramatic Burlesque in *A Midsummer-Night's Dream*', *Studies in Philology*, Vol. 61, No. 2, Part 1 (Apr. 1964), pp. 192–204.
25. See for instance the Induction to *Bartholomew Fair*.
26. James H. Kavanagh, 'Shakespeare in Ideology', in John Drakakis (ed.), *Alternative Shakespeares* (London and New York: Methuen, 1985), pp. 144–65, 155.
27. Dent, p. 123.
28. See Shakespeare, *A Midsummer Night's Dream*, pp. lxxxvii, lxxxviii, cxix.
29. For the metamorphic nature of Shakespeare's characters see Jonathan Bate, *Shakespeare and Ovid* (Oxford: Clarendon Press, 1993), p. 4ff.
30. See Shakespeare, *The Tempest*, pp. 62–6.
31. Shakespeare, *A Midsummer Night's Dream*, p. lv.
32. Mebane, 'Metadrama and the Visionary Imagination', p. 33.
33. John S. Mebane, *Renaissance Magic and the Return of the Golden Age: The Occult Tradition and Marlowe, Jonson, and Shakespeare* (Lincoln: University of Nebraska Press, 1989), p. 181.
34. *OED*, 2nd edn.
35. For connections with Jonson's masque *Hymenaei* (1606) see Shakespeare, *The Tempest*, pp. 68–70.
36. Robert R. Reed, Jr, 'The Probable Origin of Ariel', *Shakespeare Quarterly*, Vol. 11, No. 1 (Winter 1960), pp. 61–65, at 61.
37. See Celeste Turner Wright, 'Young Anthony Mundy Again', *Studies in Philology*, Vol. 56, No. 2 (Apr. 1959), pp. 150–68, at 168, where she calls him an 'informer and grubby hack'.
38. Reed, p. 63. For further connections with Munday's *John a Kent*, see Shakespeare, *A Midsummer Night's Dream*, pp. lxv–lxvi.
39. See Shakespeare, *The Tempest*, pp. 61–2.
40. Michel de Montaigne, *The Essayes, or Morall, Politicke and Militarie Discourses*, trans. John Florio (London: 1603), p. 102.
41. See Heywood, cited in Jonson, *Poetaster*, p. 38.
42. Egan, pp. 174–5.

43. 'Projection' at the time is often the actions of informer or agent provocateur; see Nicholl, p. 294.

44. 'Blow' here means 'contaminate', and it is of interest that Ferdinand associates his subjection with the corruption of the mouth, recalling imagery surrounding *Volpone*'s 'flesh-fly' Mosca.

45. Shakespeare, *The Tempest*, p. 35.

46. McDonald, *Shakespeare and Jonson*, p. 143. Also Geoffrey Bullough, *Narrative and Dramatic Sources*, Vol. 8 (London: Routledge and Kegan Paul, 1963), pp. 261–4.

47. E. M. W. Tillyard, *Shakespeare's Last Plays* (London: Chatto and Windus, 1951), p. 80.

48. See Ovid, *Metamorphoses* (London: Penguin, 1955), p. 36.

49. For elaboration of connections with this source, see Bate, p. 2.

50. Ovid, p. 130.

51. Ibid.

52. See Shakespeare, *The Tempest*, p. 12, for more information on Shakespeare's indebtedness to the *commedia dell'arte*.

53. Simon Palfrey, *Late Shakespeare: A New World of Words* (Oxford: Oxford University Press, 1997), p. 144.

54. Shakespeare, *The Tempest*, ed. Wells, p. 51.

55. Egan, p. 182.

Chapter 8

Onstage Overviews: Metadrama and the Information Market

Jonson's first work for theatre since his *Workes* of 1616, *The Staple of News* (1625) presents a dystopic fantasy of control over information-gathering in which the news produced, though authorised by the eponymous Staple's monopoly, is only as reliable as street gossip. With its concealed observers, its predatory imagery and the augmentative nature of its gathered information, this play describes the familiar conditions of both early modern informing practice and contemporary dramatic production. Throughout the play a strict contrast is also drawn between the absurdity of the agency's monopoly on information and the 'legitimate' authority of the poet, whose immanence the play's metadrama continually reinforces. And, as ever, the deficiency of an audience's interpretation is of prevailing concern. The Staple's sources are not 'journalists' in the modern sense; rather they are cast here as common informers, though entirely lacking the ambivalence of Shakespeare's magical agents, delivering information to privileged patrons. In this case, their information is publicly marketable, and thus, moving beyond its critique of nascent journalism and the universalisation of commercial informing, the play's metadrama explores how Jonsonian self-fashioning negotiates the price of information, and artistic legitimacy, and also, ultimately, authority itself. This is especially sensitive at this time, on the cusp of Charles I's accession to the throne.

The play's loose plot concerns the foolish heir Pennyboy Junior, who is determined to spend his inheritance on information while being hounded by observing tormentors who want it for themselves, one of whom turns out to be his supposedly-dead father. Meskill sees this obsession with oversight as representing a 'narcissistic desire' on Jonson's part 'to overtake his own issue' and surpass his previous work.[1] His turn towards allegory in this play, along with tendencies towards citation and bricolage, allows him to transcend the rigours of comparison to his monumental *Workes* and also to develop a critique of what that project represents.[2] In this way the later plays can be seen not so much as 'dotages' as Dryden would have it, or examples of Jonson's 'declension into the didactic'[3] but rather as a time of renewed experimentation.[4] The play was likely performed at court for Charles I's coronation in February 1626, and Donaldson sees its inter-generational conflict, more practically perhaps, as representing the new King's fraught succession to his father's throne.[5] David Riggs argues that, for the benefit of the King-in-the-audience, Jonson casts himself as this returned father whose role is to compete with 'the new journalists – the poetasters of the 1620s – for the soul of the Prince' as an influential advisor.[6] What these various interpretations share is the sense that Jonson is responding in this play to anxieties reflecting the precarious nature of authority, whether it is that of the King himself, or to the author in relation to his past work, in the form of the *Workes*, or to his past role of some influence as principal masque-maker to James I. More specifically, *Staple* outlines how all of these forms of authority are potentially tainted by a culture of slander, informing and misinforming, on both cultural and political levels, and driven by carelessness and financial greed. This critique of course reflects not only upon the way society configures authority, but also on the kind of author Jonson still aspires to be.

The main conceptual focus of the play involves the eponymous dysfunctional information agency, over whose activities Jonson positions an equally dysfunctional choric audience of gossips. This gives the play as a whole the cast of an inner-play, and any inner-playing with small set-pieces involving hidden audiences act as plays within that. In common with Jonson's other onstage audiences, these gossips are denied any significant narrative control beyond their own responses, which are frequently absurd, and their derisory interpretations provide a negative parody with which the author attempts to shape the reaction of the offstage audience. Their disappearance prior to the conclusion of the play may also have been intended to mirror the interpretative agency of the offstage audience, but, in one performance at least, their overt ineptitude nevertheless provoked a negative reaction which was of sufficient strength and significance for Jonson to feel constrained to respond later with an appended disclaimer. Though his efforts to guide offstage responses in this case appear to have failed, the imperative to do so emphasises concerns with the menacing implications of being observed and interpreted by those with negative motives or malicious intent. This is familiar territory, but, unusually in this case, both the dramatic plot and the metadrama are focused explicitly on the collection and dissemination of information. Thus, though the metadramatic power-dynamics between author and audience may have malfunctioned as a mechanism of defence, they are still very much operative here as a reflection of contemporary social structures, and even more so as evidence of Jonson's use of drama as a mechanism of raw self-fashioning.

The Staple itself, as the eager prospective customer Pennyboy Junior is told, is 'a brave young office set up [. . .] / To enter all the news, sir, o'the time – / And vent it as occasion serves. A place / Of huge commerce it will be!' (1.2.24, 26–8).[7] Here, reports will be 'issued under the seal of the Office, / As Staple News, no other news be current' (1.2.35–6).[8] D. F. McKenzie's identification of the Staple as 'the image of the theatre' is of immediate relevance here;[9] I suggest, further, that the Staple conflates the theatre, nascent contemporary news media and the informing trade, and in ways that would have been familiar to contemporaries.[10] The only difference between 'news' and material elicited by informers is that news is specifically intended for 'venting' publicly. There is a multiple pun here: to 'vent' in its primary early modern sense is to expel wind, but venting at this time also refers significantly to selling (as in 'to vend') for financial gain. Jonson uses the word in this sense in *Volpone*, referring to 'fellows that live by venting oils and drugs' (2.2.6). Intriguingly also, playing into the imagery often associated with informers, to 'vent' is also a hunting term used at this time to describe a hound on the scent.[11] Thus 'news' and 'information' are comparable in their mutual saleability, implying that the reliable authority of their authorship is always potentially compromised. In the Staple however, authorship also arrogates the authority of censorship to itself and thus circumvents multiple dangers inherent in the business of the purveyance of information. The Staple's hidden watchers, bird-of-prey imagery and augmentative practices, will by now be familiar as the material images of both informing and metadramatic production. The emphasis in this case is on an interpretative lack at all levels except that of the author, and this is implicit in one customer's exemplary request of the Staple: 'I would have, sir, / A groatsworth of any news – I care not what – / To carry down this Saturday to our Vicar' (1.4.10–12). Whether this customer is running an errand or intends the information as a gift, the casual relationship between the information's truth-value and its financial value, its debasing commodification, is what is at stake.

In keeping with conventions of representation of informers, the predatory characters of the play are often figured as birds, though this text uses the imagery more loosely than elsewhere in Jonson. The pursuivant Piedmantle says of the Lady Pecunia, 'I have a hope, sir, that I may by chance / Light on her grace as she's taking the air'; Broker replies, 'That air of hope has blasted many an aerie / Of kastrils like yourself, good Master Piedmantle' (2.2.60–3). When the lawyer Picklock threatens to sue the Pennyboys, Pennyboy Canter, recalling the bestiary of *Volpone*, responds, 'Do, do, my gowned vulture' (5.2.124–5). Most interestingly perhaps is Pennyboy Junior's light-hearted accusation against the Fashioner, the type of the author in this play, of 'leaving me to stalk here in my trouses / Like a tame hernshaw' (1.2.2–3), casting the Fashioner as the 'hawk'-like predator to the victim Pennyboy's 'handsaw'.[12]

Correspondingly, the narrative yields the usual collection of metadramatic overhearers. Pennyboy Senior, the usurious uncle, openly admits acting as a hidden audience to Broker's dismissal of the predatory 'kastril' (2.2.63) Piedmantle in his aims to 'light on' (2.2.61) Pecunia: 'Well said, Master Secretary, I stood behind / And heard thee all' (2.2.64–5). The stage directions here make this almost seem a parody of the hidden onstage audience, as it says, *Old Pennyboy leaps [out]* (s.d.2.2.63) the moment Piedmantle leaves. Again, when Picklock tries to cozen Pennyboy Junior of his inheritance, Pennyboy summons forth Thomas, his hidden listener, who had concealed himself in the previous act, to assist his legal cause: 'Come forth, Tom. / Speak what thou heardst [. . .] / What said this varlet?'; Picklock's response, 'A rat behind the hangings!' (5.2.67–70) shows us to what extent this idea has become proverbial. These occurrences, though almost incidental to the plot, are nevertheless revealing of a structure which is both highly metadramatic and characteristic of depictions of contemporary informing culture, surveillance and scenes of interpretation.

The Staple is run by a Mr Cymbal, whom the Fashioner assures us is 'a wit' (1.2.46), possibly a parodic representation of newsbook publisher Nathaniel Butter. Contemporaries might also have associated the name with the 'tinkling cymbal' of the 1611 Bible, signifying speech without charity, or love.[13] Cymbal employs four 'emissaries' who are 'men employed outward, that are sent abroad / To fetch in the commodity. / From all regions / Where the best news are made – / Or vented forth – / By way of exchange, or trade' (1.2.50–3) and as Parr notes, Jonson has linked the word 'emissaries' to odious informing and entrapment elsewhere.[14] These 'news' are to be procured at a price from 'special friends – / And men of correspondence i'the country – / [. . .] of all ranks and all religions – / Factors and agents – / Liegers, that lie out / Through all the shires o'the kingdom' (1.5.17–21). As model intelligencers, these emissaries hunt out information from the gossip picked up by their own ubiquitous informers. The inquisitive Pennyboy Junior, wanting to know how this affects contemporary news-selling, asks, 'but what says Mercurius Britannicus to this?' (1.5.22–3). The reply is revealing of the state of information-gathering:

> O sir, he gains by't half in half [. . .]
> For, where he was wont to get
> In hungry captains, obscure statesmen – Fellows
> To drink with him in a dark room in a tavern
> [. . .] As fain
> To keep so many politic pens
> Going to feed the press –
> And dish out news,
> Were't true or false –
> Now all that charge is saved.
> The public chronicler [. . .]
> No more shall be abused, nor country parsons
> O' the inquisition, nor busy justices
> Trouble the peace, and both torment themselves
> And their poor ign'rant neighbours with enquiries. (1.5.24–32, 36–9)

As we have noted previously, gaining 'by't half' is the common financial benefit of the authorities and their informers, and this description of purported news-gathering gives an insight into the opportunistic nature of informing at this time. The fact that this information-gatherer expects to be put to some charge, in a dark room in a tavern, in order to keep his 'politic pens' going, shows him operating according to the prevailing model of informing; that there is little concern for distinctions between truth or falsehood in the news he is producing provides yet another clue to this connection. Also, with 'parsons of the inquisition' and 'busy justices' no longer needing to trouble their neighbours for information, informing is placed within both a local and quasi-national judicial context. Most significantly, the fact that the Staple will provide all of these familiar services gives its ostensibly ingenuous 'news' the invidious cast of 'information' and all its employees are tainted with the opprobrium of the venal informer.

In this respect, the informing newshounds of Jonson's play are also described as authors, augmenters and purveyors of the information they receive. When Pennyboy Junior asks about the news-clerk's qualifications, he is told he, 'knows news well [. . .] / And for a need can make 'em' (1.5.121–2); Pennyboy replies that Thomas has a 'quick vain in forging news, too' (1.5.133). All of this is in keeping with the empty soundings of a 'Cymbal', but is not limited to characters in the main play, which as mentioned has the character of an inner-play, however. On the part of Jonson's onstage audience, Tattle also admits to using and augmenting information, asking, 'how should we [. . .] find ourselves in fashionable discourse for all companies, if we do not credit all and make more of it in the reporting?' (Int. 3.38–41). Thus the offstage audience are offered many examples of the connection between venality and interpretation, not only by characters involved in the plot but also by an onstage audience who are clearly implicated in the whole corrupt practice from the outset, in the hope that they might find it a corrective to their own behaviour.

This concern over interpretation may also be perceived in the level of defensive self-deprecation that Jonson introduces elsewhere in his metadramatic self-reference; for example, in *Bartholomew Fair*, and in *Epicene* and *The Magnetic Lady*, where he even goes so far as to have a character mention him by name.[15] As *Staple*'s onstage audience, the gossips, Mirth, Expectation, Tattle and Censure, sit in open judgement upon the plot, the actors, and the relative merits of the author. Accompanied by the Prologue, they proceed to draw attention metadramatically to the title of the play – 'come, gossip [. . .] The play is *The Staple of News*' (Ind. 2–3); the writing: 'you come to see [. . .] whose clothes are best penned' (Ind. 40–1); and the actors, who might 'overact prodigiously in beaten satin' (Ind. 46). When the Prologue tells them, 'there are a set of gamesters within in travail of a thing called a play' (Ind. 55–6), Tattle asserts, 'the poet has abused himself, like an ass, as he is' (Ind. 60); while, after the first act, the gossips refer intertextually to Jonson's other plays in a self-deprecating manner: '*The Devil is an Ass*. He is an arrant learn'd man that made it [. . .] he can read too' (Intermean 1.40–1). This most probably refers to Jonson's escape from capital punishment as a consequence of his ability to read Latin, after killing a fellow actor in a duel.[16] Given this self-deprecating and self-conscious tone, it is easy to see how one might draw George Rowe's conclusion, that Jonson wishes to construct a reader who is 'receptive yet critical, willing to unravel the author's threadlike argument from the correct end, but unwilling to cede complete authority to that author'.[17] However, an effect of this self-deprecation is the apotropaic pre-emption of criticism, and further, in characterising these respondents with the names 'Mirth', 'Tattle', 'Expectation' and 'Censure',

Jonson also trivialises the parameters of their responses and restricts them to manageable types.

As a metadramatic device, an onstage audience often betrays a circumstantial desire on the part of the author either to control the response of the offstage audience by simply scripting it for them, or by implying that the correct response is the opposite of that offered onstage. Functioning thus as objects of ridicule necessitates overt display. For example, when Mirth asks the Prologue, 'helpe us to some stools', he replies, 'Where? o' the Stage, Ladies?', and Mirth responds, 'Yes, o' the stage. We are persons of quality, I assure you, and women of fashion and come to see and to be seen' (Ind. 8–10). Though very visible, these gossips, however, serve to modulate the vision and attention of the offstage audience even when this has little or no scopic or diegetic bearing on the narrative of the play itself. Thus demarcated, Jonson has members of his onstage audience artic- ulate a manageable level of criticism, by which he aims to minimise the menacing censoriousness of his offstage audience. In response to Censure's over-reaction to the representation of the Infanta of the Mines, Mirth gives her a lesson in the limits of interpretation:

> Take heed it lie not in the vice of your interpretation. What
> have Aurelia, Clara, Pecunia to do with any person? Do they any more,
> but express the property of money, which is the daughter of earth, and
> drawn out of the mines? Is there nothing to be called Infanta but what is
> subiect to exception? (Int. 2.26–31)

The metadramatic mode here allows the author to offer his offstage audience models of representation and reaction. Here, for instance, Mirth's sensitivity to the motif of money which is woven throughout the play forms an element in the recommended interpretation. This kind of attempt to define an authorised interpretative position may or may not be effective, and its success is often dependent on the desirability of the perspective being offered.

In this case, by the Third Intermean, the gossips' poor interpreta- tion itself gets tangled up in the dramatic structure. As Catherine Rookwood notes, when Censure complains that London's youth should not be taught 'to speak plays and act fables of false news in this manner' (Int. 3.54–5), she 'equat[es] Jonson's work with the vice it aims to reveal and condemn'.[18] These unreliable audience members have confused the scourge with the crime, and in the process have themselves become implicated in the problem itself. The very obvi- ous nature of the onstage audience in this type of metadrama may however work against the authorial desire to control, and the off-stage audience can choose whether to react positively or negatively to their vicarious depiction in this way. In this instance, there has clearly been some resistance to Jonson's metadramatic machinations, despite his attempt at producing a self-critical audience. He is thus constrained to make explicit his concerns over interpretations that this play appears to have elicited, wherein:

> the allegory and purpose of the author hath hitherto been wholly mistaken, and so sinister an interpretation been made, as if the souls of most of the spectators had lived in the eyes and ears of these ridiculous gossips that tattle betweene the Acts. But he prays you thus to mend it. To consider the news here vented to be none of his news [. . .] but news made like the time's news [. . .] than which there cannot be a greater disease in nature, or a fouler scorn put upon the times. And so apprehending it, you shall doe the author, and your own judgement a courtesy, and perceive the trick of alluring money to the Office and there cozening the people. (2–10, 13–18)

Perhaps the laboured style of much of this response is due to Jonson, still, at this late stage in his career, having to emphasise in his own defence that his frame of reference is 'the times' rather than the activities of particular individuals. The assertion that the 'news here vented', is not the author's but rather news that is in a very general sense 'made like the time's news', runs into interpretative difficulties. Here the old argument that this is a play 'wherein the age may see her own folly' (11) is bound to reflect upon the primary interpreters of the play, the onstage audience, who, as representatives of members of the offstage audience, contribute to the impression that the whole play is itself an inner-play. The danger of this type of metadrama is that the depiction of such 'ridiculous gossips that tattle betweene the Acts' will inevitably be perceived as representing the 'souls of most of the spectators', and that the 'purpose of the Author' will thus necessarily be vulnerable to negative and potentially 'sinister' interpretation as an anticipatory, and therefore defensive, response. This is what seems to have happened here. The gossips' lack of meaningful intervention exacerbates this tendency, but even more so their eventual disappearance before the end of the play creates an open-ended frame narrative, a structure which typically affords the offstage audience the interpretative space which the onstage audience has vacated and now positions them as primary interpreters. Indeed, they are interpreters who are now in receipt of personal insult in their capacity to interpret, and the resultant paradox is enough to produce a negative and potentially menacing outcome for Jonson.

Early modern audiences, of course, harbour a perennially sinister potential because of the very material dangers for an author of being perceived as personally critical or subversive. These dangers also register in the inner action of the play itself, for instance in Lickfinger's threat to Pennyboy Senior after his obscure financial complaint: 'beware those worshipful ears, sir, be not shortened, / And you play crop i'the Fleet, if you use this licence' (2.3.50–1). Pennyboy Senior is understandably alarmed at this risk of mutilation and imprisonment, responding with a question and accusation of his own: 'What licence, knave? [*threatening him*] Informer?' (2.3.52). The authorial preoccupation with informers is evident in the expression of the substantial risk of physical retribution for texts that can be interpreted with mendacious or simply vindictive intention. As Parr and others have suggested, Jonson may have been threatened with this specific punishment himself for perceived misdemeanours in *Eastward Ho!*, and he, himself, certainly felt this physical menace.[19] This threat, clearly somewhat traumatic, recurs in Pennyboy Canter's exchange with Picklock: 'Your ears are in my pocket, knave; go shake 'em / The little while you have them' (5.2.83–4) where the interpreter is perceived to be a (dis)functional mechanism of authority. Thus, when Pennyboy Canter ruins his son's wastrel plans by revealing himself as Pennyboy Junior's father, the onstage audience's gossips sign a document to censure the poet who has deprived them of the plot they were expecting, saying, 'let a protest go out against him [. . .] in all our names' (Int. 4.76–7, 79). This is obviously a parody but in this threatening atmosphere it is perhaps not surprising that this is the last we hear of this disturbingly empowered but broadly incompetent audience.

In the place of the reaction of the gossips is the Epilogue, who is given the apologetic last word on the issue of audience reaction, asserting on behalf of the 'Maker',

> though the clout we do not always hit,
> It will not be imputed to his wit –
> [. . .] the weather of your looks may change,
> Or some high wind of misconceit arise,
> To cause an alteration in our skies.
> If so, we're sorry that have so misspent
> Our time and tackle. (Epilogue 1–4, 8–12)

This attempt to deflect serious criticism and to excuse any offence given by the author is lightheartedly dismissed as missing 'the clout' and is not to be 'imputed to his wit'. These archery metaphors serve to reinforce the thrust of the message of the General Prologue (not the Prologue for the Court), that such a miss must be caused by the 'some high wind of misconceit' or by the changeable 'weather of your looks', rather than by the author's intention. This potential for sinister change reflects a preoccupation with what Jonson perceives to be an audience over-empowered by their potential to use nefariously the 'information' they have received as playgoers. His implied reader is one who is compliant with the material limitations of the printed text with its hierarchical relationship between producer and consumer, and he wishes to maintain this for his own protection in the more volatile contemporary interpretative atmosphere of the theatre.

This desire to establish the parameters of interpretation for spectators and readers is, as we have seen, widely reflected in Jonson's writing. In his message 'To the Reader' at the beginning of *The Alchemist*, Jonson sets himself against, variously, 'antics', 'deriders of [. . .] diligence', ignorance', 'the many', the 'ill' of other writers, 'the unskillful' and 'rude things' (8–26).[20] He thus defines himself in opposition to these as sane, diligent, knowledgeable, one of the few, a good writer, skilful and polished, and hails the reader as an 'understander', provided he or she agrees. The Prologue to *Staple* refers to the audience as 'great noble wits' (Prol. 19), but this can only be interpreted as ironic, when seen in relation to his equal declaration: '[i]f that not like you that he sends tonight / 'Tis you have left to judge, not he to write' (Prol. 29–30). Such an assertion of unassailable authorship is echoed in Jonson's prefatory verses to Nicholas Breton's contemporary *Works*:

> Looke here on Bretons Worke, the master print:
> Where, such perfections to the life doe rise;
> If they seeme wry, to such as looke asquint,
> The fault's not in the object, but their eyes.[21]

For Jonson, drawing attention metadramatically to the writtenness of his work is also a way of distinguishing himself from the 'lesser' poets, which is also his abiding concern; *Staple*'s Prologue makes it clear he wishes to,

> Make a difference 'twixt poetic elves
> And poets: and all that dabble in the ink
> And defile quills are not those few can think,
> Conceive, express, and steer the souls of men
> [. . .] with their pen. (Prol. 20–4)

Such soul-steering ambitions of the authorial 'few' are notably absent, however, from the version of the play to be performed at court, which is brought instead,

> To scholars, that can judge and fair report
> The sense they hear, above the vulgar sort
> Of nutcrackers, that only come for sight.
> Wherein, although our title, sir, be News,
> We yet adventure here to tell you none,
> But shew you common follies, and so known,
> That though they are not truths, th'innocent Muse
> Hath made so like, as fant'sy could them state
> Or poetry, without scandal, imitate. (Prol. Ct. 6–14)

Here the safely abstract 'poetry' aspires merely 'without scandal [to] imitate' the 'common follies' of the world for the benefit of 'scholars' such as the King.

More than any other audience, the King carries potentially hazardous complications with regard to his own empowered authorship and authority. Julie Sanders, Kate Chedgzoy and Susan Wiseman argue that the figure of the King crucially informs Jonson's 'ideal image of the author: fixed, unmoved, unperturbed'.[22] In consideration of the contemporaneous senses of the *author* as both 'one who has authority over others; a director, ruler, commander [. . .] one who sets forth written statements' and 'an informant', it is possible to perceive in Jonson's authorship a combination of an almost monarchical level of self-determination with a consciousness of his own dependence upon the possession and venting/vending of information.[23] Both these elements are in play within Jonson's dramatic and metadramatic universe. On the one hand, Jonson regards the King as the discursive centre, fit to sit in judgement upon his subjects: in *Discoveries* he notes, 'After God, nothing is to be loved of man like the prince [. . .] He is the arbiter of life and death.'[24] On the other, bearing in mind the potential for republicanism that Sanders rightly attributes to him, I would argue that Jonson nevertheless aspires to a lofty place of judgement over his 'theatrical republic'.[25] His audience is an authorial creation, and when he muses, 'Good men [. . .] illustrate the times [. . .] placed high on the top of all virtue, looked down on the stage of all the world and contemned the play of fortune', we can detect an ideal of sorts behind the topical reference.[26] Illustrating the times can of course also be a paid occupation, and this is essentially what happens in different ways within the narrative of *The Staple of News*, in the Office itself, and in Jonson's intentions

for his play. Unfortunately for him these elements appear to have
been confused in the process of interpretation.

Throughout his career, Jonson responded to these issues of potential interpretative and authorly malpractice by instituting for himself a paternalistic version of authorship which is both assertive and
protective. This tendency may be energised by an aspiration to the
kind of essential legitimation denied him by his humble origins, his
non-aristocratic blood and his possible lack of knowledge about his
real father:

> the cotes
> Painted, or car'ud vpon our great-mens tombs,
> Or in their windowes; doe but proue the wombs,
> That bred them, graues: when they were borne, they di'd,
> That had no Muse to make their fame abide.[27]

This self-aggrandisement applies, however, even in relation to the idea
of the King: 'For in the *Genius* of a *Poëts* Verse, / The Kings fame
lives',[28] declares Jonson, and, using the same imagery, positions his
authorial control over posterity above that which is afforded by blood:

> doubt not, what posteritie,
> Now I haue sung thee thus, shall iudge of thee.
> Thy deedes, vnto thy name, will proue new wombes,
> Whil'st others toyle for titles to their tombes.[29]

Jonson here fashions for himself a legitimising role which reciprocates
the royal patronage of which he would like to think he was the beneficiary. Such risky cultural self-assertion at this time could only be
perceived as potentially subversive were it not that although he thinks
of himself as self-authored, Jonson also seems reluctant to extend this
facility to members of his public audiences. Rather, he actively denies
his audiences access to authorial levels of self-fashioning, and thus
stages an authority in which the role of author is legitimated and
fixed, while at the same time performing his own claim to primacy
in the role. When 'Johnson' removes the 'h' from his name for the
title page of his 1616 *Works* he is doing more than distancing himself
from the memory of his stepfather; he is claiming for himself a legitimate origin, as originator, in an act of self-authorship. The 'h', however, does not entirely disappear into the functionality of the name
but continues to haunt it with the spectre of patriarchal authority, the
trace of parenthood. Like the 'a' in Derrida's concept of *différance*,
Jonson's purged 'h' serves to indicate a 'movement of signification

[which] retains the mark of a past element [here the father] and [. . .] lets itself be hollowed out by the mark of its relation to a future element', here Ben Jonson the Author, who is self-fathered.[30] His impulse to prescribe audience reactions through metadramatic structures for protective means forms part of this same self-assertion.

The growing awareness of the power of the information market, however, in all its forms, stems from a cultural shift in conceptions of authority that implies the same kind of 'movement of signification' which Jonson employs in the subtle change in the orthography of his name as it appears in print: the possibility that one may differ from oneself; that seemingly prescribed roles may be adjusted to suit the individual subject. That such roles may not be solely dictated by their relation to 'a past element', but may also be 'hollowed out by the mark of [their] relation to a future element'. This acknowledgement of the radical performativity of subjecthood is not something which Jonson approaches explicitly in these works, but it is nevertheless implicated in the very nature of his self-conscious and self-referential brand of authorship, that which pushes him to produce metadrama. It is a paradox that this allows Jonson to assert his poetic supremacy; as a producer, his self-authorship is far more politically profound than what he produces, and it actively depends upon the denial of judgement or individual authority to either competitors or consumers. The author's critical acumen and the satirist's censorious judgement are attributes which Jonson must reserve for himself as authoritative overseer. His missing 'h' is the invisible disappearing point from which the author asserts his fixed and all-encompassing perspective. Nonetheless it carries the trace of step-fatherhood; it offers an authorship once removed, an authorship-as-persona which draws attention to itself as 'authentic' primarily in order to disguise its fabricated nature. There is something uncomfortable about a form of authorship founded on such a defensive imperative, but nevertheless it might encourage the perceptive spectator/reader to recognise, in both the model of the informer and metadramatic perspective, that true authority resides in the control of the narrative.

The effect of Jonson's metadrama is that each work wears the label of its provenance on the outside; this is a kind of hard sell and the inadvertently constructed commodity is Ben Jonson, Author. In this way Jonson creates for himself a meritocratic celebrity that Sanders notes is 'marked by the knowledge of the commercial relations of the public theatre',[31] and which stands in curious opposition to his centred, monarchical model of authorial control, and his own criticism of the process of commodification. The resulting tensions may go some way to explaining the necessity Jonson feels to distance himself from others who, not having the same imperative to build a new edifice of authorship, may be freer to exploit the vagaries of the emergent marketplace. Jonson declares 'It is a ryming Age, and Verses swarme / At every stall'[32] but it is this very empowering universal access to culture, and the possibility of self-transformation that accompanies it, which will arguably undermine Jonson's goal of 'elite aesthetic primacy'.[33] But the alternative way of self-making, as an informer within the widening marketplace of information, is never far from Jonson's mind as he manipulates the meaning of his characters' roles and interactions with audiences through metadrama. Jonson may not have liked the fact, but, as Dutton has argued, 'it is not monarchs, writers or texts which generate or sanction meaning: but readers in all their perplexing variety', and he has had to come to terms with that.[34] The idea of what might constitute 'sanction' for these potential generators of meaning is very heavily mediated by the culture that surrounds and informs it; and in a culture of widespread paid informing it would be naïve to suggest that the process of generation and sanction of meanings is not significantly influenced by financial imperatives and self-interest. This is the necessary concomitant to Jonson's personal project and is generated by the same kinds of social and market forces within whose orbit his own success was facilitated. Here, as the play's metadramatic gossips fade, so does the news agency, and the plot resolves into a more conventional inheritance morality; perhaps, despite his own protestations, Jonson's self-fashioning style of authorship works best, or only really works at all, in a world complicated by a market in which the price of information, artistic freedom and ultimately the legitimacy of authority itself, are negotiable.

Notes

1. Meskill, p. 132.
2. Ibid. pp. 187, 188, n. 8.
3. Rosalind Miles, *Ben Jonson, His Craft and Art* (London: Barnes and Noble, 1990), p. 232.
4. See Martin Butler, 'Late Jonson', in Gordon McMullan and Jonathan Hope (eds), *The Politics of Tragicomedy: Shakespeare and After* (London: Routledge, 1992), pp. 168–88.
5. Donaldson, p. 394.
6. Riggs, *Ben Jonson: A Life*, p. 297.

7. Ben Jonson, *The Staple of News*, ed. Anthony Parr (Manchester: Manchester University Press, 2000). Unless otherwise noted, this is the primary text for all references to this play.

8. With allusion to the dubious contemporary news sheets known as *corantos*; see Jonson, *The Staple of News*, pp. 1–60, esp. 22–31.

9. D. F. McKenzie, 'The Staple of News and the Late Plays', in William Blisset (ed.), *A Celebration of Ben Jonson* (Toronto: University of Toronto Press, 1973), p. 97.

10. Neale notes the Bacons' plan to set up a 'combined news and secret service system in other countries'; see J. E. Neale, *Queen Elizabeth I* (London: Jonathan Cape, 1958), p. 332.

11. 'My liege, I went this morning on my quest, My hound did sticke, and seem'd to vent some beast.' See George Gascoigne, *The noble art of venerie* (London: Printed by Thomas Purfoot, 1611) p. 96, <http://gateway. proquest.com/openurl?ctx_ver=Z39.88-2003&res_id=xri:eebo&rft_ id=xri:eebo:citation:99854029> (last accessed 9 March 2016).

12. For connections of interest, see Bill Angus, '"A hawk from a hand-saw"'.

13. See, respectively, Roger Chartier, *Inscription and Erasure: Literature and Written Culture from the Eleventh to the Eighteenth Century* (Philadelphia: University of Pennsylvania Press, 2007), p. 49; Bible (1611), 1 Cor. 13: 1.

14. Notably in Ben Jonson, *The Devil Is an Ass*, ed. Anthony Parr, in *The Cambridge Edition of the Works of Ben Jonson*, Vol. 4 (5.5.47); see Jonson, *The Staple of News*, p. 79, n. 47.

15. Ben Jonson, *Epicene*, ed. David Bevington, in *The Cambridge Edition of the Works of Ben Jonson*, Vol. 3 (2.2.87); and Jonson, *The Magnetic Lady*, ed. Ostovich, in *The Cambridge Edition of the Works of Ben Jonson*, Vol. 6 (3.6.92–3).

16. Jonson, *The Staple of News*, p. 110, n. 42.

17. George E. Rowe, *Distinguishing Jonson: Imitation, Rivalry and the Direction of a Dramatic Career* (Lincoln and London: University of Nebraska Press, 1988), pp. 66–7.

18. Catherine Rockwood, '"Know thy side": Propaganda and Parody in Jonson's Staple of News', *English Literary History*, Vol. 75, No. 1 (2008), pp. 135–49, esp. 137. See Rockwood also for *Staple*'s relation to Thomas Middleton's *A Game at Chess* (1624) and the politics of the Thirty Years' War.

19. Jonson, *The Staple of News*, p. 124, n. 51.

20. Ben Jonson, *The Alchemist*, ed. Peter Holland and William Sherman, in *The Cambridge Edition of the Works of Ben Jonson*, Vol. 3. This is another self-consciously theatrical play which Andrew Gurr reads as 'a mirror of playing, a metadrama', see Cave et al. p. 14.

21. Ben Jonson, 'In Authorem', in Nicholas Breton, *The Works: Melancholike Humours, In Verses of Diverse Natures* [1600], ed. Alexander B. Grosart (1879).

22. Julie Sanders, Kate Chedgzoy and Susan Wiseman (eds), *Refashioning Ben Jonson* (Houndmills: Macmillan, 1998), p. 6.
23. See *OED*, 2nd edn.
24. Ben Jonson, *Discoveries*, ed. Lorna Hutson, in *The Cambridge Edition of the Works of Ben Jonson*, Vol. 7 (704, 711).
25. See Julie Sanders, *Ben Jonson's Theatrical Republics* (Houndmills: Macmillan, 1998), p. 1.
26. Jonson, *Discoveries*, ed. Hutson (789–90, 793–4).
27. Ben Jonson, 'To Countesse Elizabeth of Rutland', *The Forrest*, in Herford et al. (eds), Vol. 8, p. 114.
28. Ben Jonson, 'An Epigram to the Household', *The Underwood*, in Herford et al. (eds), Vol. 8, p. 241.
29. Ben Jonson, 'To Sir Henry Nevil', *Epigrams*, in Herford et al. (eds), Vol. 8, p. 70, my emphasis.
30. Jacques Derrida, 'Différance', trans. Alan Bass, *Margins of Philosophy* (Chicago: University of Chicago Press, 1982), pp. 3–27.
31. Sanders et al., p. 6.
32. Ben Jonson, 'An Elegie', *The Underwood*, in Herford et al. (eds), p. 200.
33. Sanders et al., pp. 6, 7.
34. Richard Dutton, 'The Lone Wolf: Jonson's Epistle to *Volpone*', in Sanders et al., p. 127.

Conclusion

Throughout this book I have tracked a history of the perception of a social phenomenon inscribed in a significant cultural form of the age. My purpose here has not been to offer comprehensive readings of these plays, but rather to open up an aspect of their dramaturgy which has been previously obscured. To some extent theatrical representation works as a space for resistance, and for both writers the theatrical exposure of the link between informing and metadrama sets up an interpretative space between extra-theatrical authority and that which is exhibited in representation. The subject of this book has been the ways in which both manage that space. One of the most significant issues to arise from this study has been the extent to which the roles of author and informer intersect in negotiating its parameters. In one form or another this connection animates the very different kinds of metadrama present in Shakespeare's and Jonson's writing, either as something to be exploited or firmly refuted. In both ways it exposes the forms and pressures of the times on the process of writing for the theatre.

Shakespeare's metadrama often seems to emerge almost extempore within the frame of a narrative, from a spontaneous dramatic moment, natural inner performance or dramatic inset. Where this happens, as it does in the cases of Hamlet, Falstaff and to some extent even Prospero, it tends towards a blurring of the boundaries between author and audience, thereby occluding to some extent the dramatist's own role in the process of authorship. This may have been troubling for contemporary audiences, and Hamlet's hyperbolic example displays an interpreter wavering between an uncertain relationship with the potentially homicidal nature of the structure of authority and the questionable demands of a supernatural imperative. However, in the potentially murderous world of early modern politics, the suggestion that the production of meaning is, in fact, a collective practice can work to the benefit of the author. Compared to Jonson's form in the matter, Shakespeare's apparent avoidance of the threat of prosecution may be one reason for his more subtly nuanced metadramatic representation of the potential presence of the informer in the audience. While still adept at generating narrative action from the manipulation of illicit information, Shakespeare is also able to present ideal forms and structures of power. Where he is more explicit in his representations of these processes, say in *The Tempest*, he creates a community where the impact of perverse interpretation is finally controlled: one where confusion, discord and misprision may be safely negotiated and superseded by the empowerment of onstage authors. It is a self-assured author that is able to set the political intrigue and deception endemic in metadramatic structures within a fantasy world that ultimately resolves the contradictions that they generate.

Jonson's metadramatic method is more overt than Shakespeare's, and more explicit in its staging of the interaction of sites of early modern authority. He is inclined to impose the constructedness of his art as a vehicle for the establishment of his Horatian authorship upon offstage and onstage audiences, whom he often characterises as venal or incompetent. His metadramatic audiences foreground the reciprocal nature of observation and enable him to try to shape offstage responses, often by parodying an interpretative ineptitude which articulates various kinds of failed authority. His desire to control the authoritative viewpoint of his audiences derives its power from an attempt at producing his own poetical and social authority. As Richard Burt argues, Jonson's Horatian ambitions actually align him with the court censor, whose 'interpretive categories and practices' he internalises.[1] Meskill echoes this view, suggesting even that Jonson '*defaces* his own poetic creation in his own too anxious solicitude to respond to the curious or envious gaze' thereby becoming the primary censor of his own text.[2] But, more acutely, the identification here is with the censor's proxy, the ubiquitous informer, and it is he who 'is in the writer himself [. . .] watching himself in the act of writing'.[3] So, like Justice Overdo, Jonson becomes his own informer. His assimilation of that malicious predatory critical gaze, even as he seeks simultaneously to distance himself from it,[4] is the cause of an authorial tension that emerges in the self-conscious form of metadrama.

Shakespeare's approach to these issues is more challenging than Jonson's, because more surreptitious, and therefore in a study such as the present one it becomes tempting to detect in Shakespearean metadrama the negative imprint of Jonson's overt technique. But this would be an evasion of the complexity and subtlety of the structures Shakespeare offers us. Rather than claiming that Shakespeare is intentionally anti-Jonsonian, I resist the temptation to reduce this study to a monolithic contrast between the two techniques. I have deliberately tried to avoid dealing with these differences in terms of tenuous 'levels of illusion' and it would therefore seem inappropriate to attempt to construct an objective from ghostlike traces in the plays. Shakespearean metadrama tends to obscure the author's motives where Jonson's tends to expose them publicly, and this distinction should serve as the determining contrast; the resultant aporia may therefore stimulate our own perceptions and expressions of authorship, authority and interpretation. If authority is found in the control of narrative, then there is both a threat and an interpretative ideal, ambition and menace, in the metadramatic statement that 'what's past is prologue, what to come / In yours and my discharge!'[5]

The theatre itself is portrayed by its early modern apologists as an agent for moral correction, and by its detractors as the debauched exemplar of illicit pleasure, whoredom, pestilence and degeneracy. This debate reflects the broad post-Reformation crisis over authority itself. In fact both parties are correct: theatre simultaneously acts as a corrective to the society it represents and at the same time purveys potentially subversive ideas. In the broadest terms, theatre itself also performs simultaneously the role of the Horatian author and the scurrilous informer. There are however far more intimate associations between these two seemingly opposed positions, as the previous arguments have attempted to demonstrate. Though early modern metadramatic texts contain interpreters empowered in such a way as to disturb notions of social authority, they lack the kind of celebration of dispersed authority that is often expressed through metafictional and metadramatic modernist and postmodern narratives (I am thinking here of Brecht's *The Caucasian Chalk Circle*, Pirandello's *Six Characters in Search of an Author*, Calvino's *If on a Winter's Night a Traveller*, or McEwan's *Atonement*) where narratorial self-limitation and the empowerment of the interpreter are positively celebrated as part of the art-form itself. Indeed, the kind of political democracy that this celebration would imply is generally regarded as dangerous, if not anathema, in the early modern period. There seems little to celebrate in the felt anxieties over contemporary authority-structures that emerged in the plays we have considered here, which perhaps go even deeper than the fear of the punishment that could be inflicted upon the author. What is so remarkable in such a political climate is that Shakespeare and Jonson, and some of their contemporaries, were able to reflect such oppressive social pressures critically at all.

Margreta de Grazia writes of the idea of early modernity that 'once it is put at the beginning of the modern trajectory [. . .] it is committed to anticipating the modern'.[6] This might cause us to ask in what sense early modern narratives might anticipate their post-modern equivalents. If, as Derrida suggests, postmodernism 'comes back in advance from the past'[7] then elements of its theatrical and literary expression may be seen as the ghost of metadrama past: the reapparition, and foretelling, of authority deconstructed by its reliance on the distorting materialities of agents with feet of clay, and compromised by its association with economic forces.

Early modernity is an era in which augmentative interpretation is a saleable commodity and, as we have seen, it is as much the activity of the informer as it is of the author. The emerging capitalism of which this augmentation is an integral mechanism also shaped the social forces of a nation emerging onto a world stage, where 'Shakespeare' would become a national icon. Much more so than Jonson, Shakespeare emerges as the champion of a myth of cultural origin, and of nationhood, but this tale would require a teller committed to a brand of authority that is only barely perceptible within the structures of early modern drama. In fact, at the heart of embryonic capitalism, early modern metadrama cradles a sense of the disturbing implications of an authority distorted by its own venal economics. Within the ideological battles of late capitalism, the devices of both author and informer, with their small differences, persist in containing the potential for unusual assertions of personal empowerment. In our own context of political paranoia and the fear of extremism, these are still devices which may be manifested either in complicity with, or resistance to, the dominant narrative. Now, as then, it is the character of that authority which is in question.

Notes

1. Richard Burt, *Licensed by Authority: Ben Jonson and the Discourses of Censorship* (Ithaca: Cornell University Press, 1993), p. 4.
2. Meskill, pp. 82–3.
3. Ibid. p. 29.
4. As Meskill points out in relation to his prefatory poem to the Shakespeare First Folio. Ibid. pp. 36–9ff.

5. Shakespeare, *The Tempest* (2.1.253–4).
6. Margreta de Grazia, 'World Pictures, Modern Periods and the Early Stage', in Cox and Kastan (eds), *A New History of Early English Drama*, p. 13.
7. Jacques Derrida, *Specters of Marx*, quoted in de Grazia, p. 14.

Index